THE WRITER WITHIN YOU

A STEP-BY-STEP GUIDE TO WRITING
AND PUBLISHING IN YOUR RETIREMENT YEARS

CHARLES JACOBS

ENDORSEMENTS

THE WRITER WITHIN YOU

A STEP-BY-STEP GUIDE TO WRITING AND PUBLISHING
IN YOUR RETIREMENT YEARS

"The Writer Within You offers outstanding support for a class of hopeful writers, retired seniors, who deserve far more attention than they have received. This book simplifies the process of writing by carefully explaining the basics of the craft, and then guides the reader through the process of selecting the ideal method of publishing the book. Charles Jacobs, the author, stresses the importance of marketing and promotion in print media, on the Web and on the air. It is a book chock full of excellent resources that should prove extremely helpful to writers of all ages."

— DAN POYNTER, AUTHOR, COACH & PUBLISHING GURU

"The Writer Within You is a perfect tool for every 'budding' author. The format is easy to follow and queries are quickly answered. The author leads you through your topic, researching articles and other published material available on the subject. The book is a comprehensive step-by-step guide to writing, publishing and promotion with extensive written examples. Great for all libraries, school and public. For colleges, it's a must!"

— DONA SINGER, PROFESSOR OF LIBRARY SCIENCE, RETIRED DIRECTOR
BERGEN COUNTY COLLEGE LIBRARY & LEARNING RESOURCE CENTER

"No matter your writing/publishing dreams, *The Writer Within You* has everything—I mean everything—you need to know in order to succeed in this highly competitive field."

— PATRICIA L. FRY, PRESIDENT, SPAWN (SMALL PUBLISHERS, ARTISTS AND
WRITERS NETWORK AUTHOR OF 25 BOOKS, INCLUDING *The Write Way to
Write, Publish and Sell Your Book*

"Charles Jacobs' *The Writer Within You* tells you everything you could ever possibly want to know about how to write and publish your own book in your retirement years. A recent survey of seniors and baby boomers has shown that this is no far-fetched need. 'Writing a book' was the second most popular life dream articulated by the 7000 survey participants. (The first was the equally hard to achieve life dream of "losing weight.") *The Writer Within You* is crisp, clear, and comprehensive; designed to satisfy every need of the growing breed of active seniors whose ambition is to write fiction, nonfiction, memoir or anything else."

— LAWRENCE K. GROSSMAN, FORMER PRESIDENT OF NBC NEWS AND PBS, AUTHOR OF THE ELECTRONIC REPUBLIC, *Reshaping Democracy in the Information Age*

"Charles Jacobs' book *The Writer Within You* tells one how to write a book of life in a refreshing, informative manner. This is a very valuable book."

— ROBERT N. BUTLER, MD, PRESIDENT & CEO, INTERNATIONAL LONGEVITY CENTER-USA, PROFESSOR OF GERIATRICS, MOUNT SINAI SCHOOL OF MEDICINE

"Charles Jacobs covers all the basics of writing, publishing and promoting in *The Writer Within You*. With the compassion of a beloved grandson, he takes seniors step by step through their second careers as writers."

— FRANCINE SILVERMAN, RADIO TALK SHOW HOST AND AUTHOR OF *Book Marketing, from A-Z* (2005) AND *Talk Radio for Authors* (2007)

Charles Jacobs is a can-do guy with a can-do attitude that he is willing to share to inspire other writers. His book is a great starting place for anyone with a desire to write and publish, a comprehensive map that lays out the options and alternatives to this crazy business. He takes you by the hand, from research and organizing and writing to getting published to the biggest challenge of all—promoting your books or articles. Read the book, take notes, send Charles e-mails, and get him to come and talk in your community.

— TIMOTHY HARPER, WWW.TIMHARPER.COM, AUTHOR, JOURNALIST, EDITORIAL AND PUBLISHING CONSULTANT, FOUNDER OF LONG DASH BOOKS

THE WRITER WITHIN YOU

A Step-by-Step Guide to Writing and Publishing in Your Retirement Years

CAROS BOOKS
16 Pinecrest Drive
Woodcliff Lake, NJ 07677

ISBN 978-0-9793636-0-3

Publisher's Cataloging-In-Publication Data
(Prepared by The Donohue Group, Inc.)

Jacobs, Charles.
The writer within you : a step-by-step guide to writing and publishing
p. ; cm.
Includes bibliographical references and index.
ISBN: 978-0-9793636-0-3
1. Authorship. 2. Authors and publishers. I. Title.
PN151 .J33 2007
808/.02

DISCLAIMER

The Writer Within You does not purport to cover everything there is to know about writing and publishing. That would take volumes. As the subtitle clearly states, it will provide you with all you need to know to launch your writing career successfully. But just reading the book is not a guarantee of success. That depends solely on you and the effort you put in. It must be understood that the publishing industry and the Web are constantly changing and improving, so I cannot guarantee that every reference will always remain current. The chapters on financial and legal matters are not offered as a substitute for the advice of qualified professionals. The persons selected for inclusion in the WORDS OF WISDOM are all widely recognized for their expertise in the specialty they write about.

ACKNOWLEDGEMENT

Publication of this book would not have been possible without the help and support of several members of my family. The book cover was designed by my daughter Jodee who is a wonderfully talented professional graphic artist. She also created the template and chose the type fonts for the interior text of the book.

My wife Rosalind, a psychologist and prize-winning columnist, served as my alter ego as I forged through the long months of research and writing. She used her psychological skills to encourage and keep me on track and her editorial skills to evaluate my output. When I completed the first draft, I turned to Ros to edit and proof the book. Her sage comments led to my rewriting portions of many chapters. She chose the title as well. Without her input, *The Writer Within You* could never have been completed.

My thanks also go to Book Designer Suzanne Guelli who typeset the text, to Lesley Peters who developed the Index and to Regina Hamner of Bookmasters who carefully led me through the printing and distribution processes.

TABLE OF CONTENTS

PUBLISHING & MARKETING YOUR BOOK

THE NITTY-GRITTY

ABOUT THE AUTHOR

Charles Jacobs is uniquely qualified to help you find your retirement niche in the complex and confusing world of publishing. A retiree himself, he brings a wealth of experience in writing and publishing to his newest book THE WRITER WITHIN YOU.

He began his writing career more than 50 years ago, working as a stringer and reporter for the *New York Journal American* to help put himself through Columbia College and earn a Master's Degree at Columbia's famed Pulitzer Graduate School of Journalism.

Capping his journalistic career, he was named Publisher/President of the Alameda Newspaper Group in the San Francisco region. He served as CEO of the Garden State Newspaper Group, Publisher of the North Jersey Herald & News and Editor-in-Chief of *Focus*, a million circulation magazine. He has consulted for a variety of magazines and newspapers.

More than 750 of Charles' articles have appeared in magazines and newspapers throughout the country from the *Los Angeles Times* on the West Coast to the *New York Times* in the East, as well as in Canada. He has ghost written several books and published a novel *Blood Bond*. His writing has been honored with numerous awards from the Society of Professional Journalists, Working Press Association, New Jersey Press Club and the North American Travel Journalists Association.

Travel publications throughout the United States and in Canada have carried Charles' articles. He has written for Grand Circle Travel and Overseas Adventure Travel, and served as Editor-in-Chief of *Travel World International*. He has taught classes in magazine writing and has served as guest speaker for a variety of organizations and at writer's conferences sponsored by the National Writers Association.

Charles invites you to subscribe to his web site **www.retirement-writing.com** and the **retirement-writing blog** to keep you updated on new developments that supplement the contents of THE WRITER WITHIN YOU.

INTRODUCTION

Retirement has changed dramatically in the past several years. Indeed a more descriptive term might be *retreadment*, for that has become the new pattern for baby boomers and the new active breed of seniors. Once they leave their career jobs, which most plan to do at age 64, they seek new challenges. A recent Merrill Lynch New Retirement Study reports that 71 percent of adults surveyed are determined to work in some capacity, either at a paying job, as a self-employed entrepreneur or volunteer. Some prefer part-time, others anticipate a full-time schedule.

With the U.S. Department of Labor estimate that 78 million baby boomers are reaching the age of 60 at a rate of one every seven seconds the "retreadment" ranks will almost double by 2020. A study of 14,000 subscribers to *Eons.com*, a leading web site for seniors and baby boomers, found that "writing a book" was the second most popular life dream of survey participants. (For the curious, you'll chuckle to learn that the number one dream was "losing weight.")

That confirmed a conclusion I had drawn from my many speaking engagements before various organizations. Again and again, I heard members of the audiences state enthusiastically, "I've been dying to write this book. It's a fabulous story...a real winner." A long pause inevitably followed that statement and a few moments later this forlorn admission: "But I don't know how to go about it. I need help."

Hearing this plaintive exchange so frequently, it soon became obvious to me that there was a great need for a guidebook that made the confusing world of publishing accessible to the many who have the urge to write after retirement. A book that also provided basic instruction in the six categories preferred by most wanna-be retiree-authors: crafting a novel, memoir or nonfiction book; writing magazine articles or travel stories; capitalizing on their career experience to try their hand at commercial (business) writing. That's why I decided to write THE WRITER WITHIN YOU.

Since you have chosen to read this book, you too undoubtedly long to write, but like so many of your fellow retirees, you haven't fulfilled that cherished dream yet. You too are looking for guidance as you face the challenges of turning your dream into reality, whether you write a single memoir for your friends and family or decide to create a freelance business and become an entrepreneur. With help, you can accomplish your goal and become a published author as so many others have.

Marilyn, a striking 62-year-old whose tailored attire and tall, slender build belied her age, wanted desperately to write a novel based upon her years of bureaucratic frustrations while working as a Civil Servant . "I don't know where or how to begin," she told me. "The writing is tough enough, then I hear all about profit minded publishers who won't give beginners a chance and how impossible it is to find a literary agent."

Scott, a retired sales executive, had looked forward to retirement and the freedom it would afford for golf, reading and pursuing all of the activities full-time work denied him. But after ten months or so, those anticipated golden years seemed more like tarnished brass. Scott felt isolated and unproductive; longed for his former career. He was frustrated because he felt he had so much to offer others starting out in the field, but his age precluded any possibility of finding a new job.

Richard accepted early retirement when the bio-tech company he worked for was forced to tighten its belt. He has no regrets. He has enjoyed every day since leaving his job. Richard convinced the local community hospital to allow him to use the pathology lab part-time to continue the experiments he believes have the greatest potential to benefit mankind. An avid reader, he spends the remainder of his time consuming books and discussing them at book clubs. He yearned to write a memoir to leave to his children and future generations in the hope it would help them lead a life as happy and as fulfilling as his has been. "I know what I want to say, and I probably can write it well enough to please the kids, but I don't have any idea how to publish it."

With just a bit of professional guidance, all three have been able to realize their dreams. Marilyn discovered that Publishing on Demand met her needs perfectly. Her novel is now in print, and she is a very proud author. Scott launched a small consulting firm, and has publicized it by writing articles for trade magazines in his field. Richard turned to self-publishing, and was completing the final editing of his memoir when THE WRITER WITHIN YOU went to press.

It is no secret that a considerable number of retirees harbor a desire to write. But far too few ever follow through. In a very informal survey conducted before embarking on the task of crafting this book, I found to my surprise that most were intimidated more by the complexities of the publishing industry than by the challenge of actually transferring their thoughts to print. Their responses were identical to those that Marilyn, Scott and Richard voiced, and may well reflect your concerns too. "I don't know how to begin." "It's much too difficult for me to tackle." "It just seems so hard, and I'm probably not smart enough."

Hogwash! Those are just excuses, as artificial and as meaningless as those of the professional who complains of "writer's block." They are all self-imposed obstacles that can readily be overcome once you learn how to negotiate the maze of publishing and become comfortable with basic guidelines for the type of writing you choose to do. THE WRITER WITHIN YOU was developed to help you do exactly that.

The book is targeted specifically to today's vibrant retirees—seniors and the baby boomers who are rapidly joining their ranks. I use those terms without remorse or hesitation because that's what all of us are despite the current concern with political correctness. The fundamentals of writing and publishing are the same for someone who is 55-or-80-years-young as they are for a 16-year-old teenager sitting in front of his or her computer. The difference is that we "oldsters" bring a wealth of life and career experiences to the challenge of writing. As you proceed through the chapters of this book, you will realize how great an advantage that difference is, and how to capitalize on it.

THE WRITER WITHIN YOU has been carefully designed to provide you with the know-how to develop not just the skill, but also the confidence to turn your dream into reality. A careful reading will make manageable what seem to be the incomprehensible complexities of publishing. Should you seek a traditional publisher or turn to a POD (Publishing on Demand) company or perhaps choose self-publishing? Do you need a literary agent? Will writing a book or magazine articles better fulfill your desires? What is the digital writing world all about?

The responses to the survey I conducted made me realize that although hundreds of excellent books have been published on specific aspects of writing, few, if any, respond to the real concerns of retired wanna-be writers. Some concentrate on crafting a novel, a memoir or a how-to book. Others zero in on specific techniques like writing sparkling dialogue or creating crisp description. A number of fine books are devoted to finding the right agent, to writing magazine articles or to self-publishing your book. Nowhere could I find one easy-to-digest book that simplifies the labyrinthine publishing world and within the same volume introduces readers to the basics of crafting each of those six categories of writing that retirees most often tell me they hope to write.

THE WRITER WITHIN YOU certainly is not a complete course in writing and publishing. It is the kind of practical overview that so many retirees have stated they need to get them started. The book concentrates on the basic writing requirements of each selected genre, presenting more than enough guidance to begin, and then offers selected sources to fine tune that beginning. The down-to-earth introductions to various aspects of the publishing industry guide the reader through the task of selecting the most effective way to create his/her work in print.

Most important of all, my reason for writing THE WRITER WITHIN YOU is as much inspirational as it is instructional. It is designed to be an activist book that propels you to make the leap from thinking to actually doing. The fear, the hesitancy, the mystique of writing…all of those barriers that have held you back…are easily bypassed when you use the knowledge you gain from digesting each chapter.

I feel particularly qualified to tackle this task since I, like you, harbored a burning desire to write during years when my duties as a businessman, a newspaper publisher and a magazine editor left little time to enjoy the writing side. Since retiring, I have published more than 750 articles in periodicals from coast to coast and in Canada. I have published a novel, ghost-written several nonfiction books, taught writing classes and earned part of my income from commercial writing. I say this not to boast, but to demonstrate why I have been able to design the type of book that will propel you forward on the exciting path you have chosen.

Sprinkled throughout every chapter you will find excerpts from books, newsletters and web sites devoted to writing, as well as pertinent quotations from leading authors and academics. I have included WORDS OF WISDOM—advice and encouragement from outstanding writers, agents and publishers—to clarify and reinforce the concepts you are reading about. In the extensive Appendix, there are also references to web sites, newsletters, books and other tested resources carefully selected to supplement what you learn here and to help you make the leap from dream to print gracefully and easily.

The book shows you how to organize yourself to make writing pleasant, not a time-consuming chore that interferes with your pursuit of other favorite activities. If you have chosen to write a full-length book, a disciplined routine of no more than two to three hours of work a day is all it takes to accomplish that goal and still leave lots of time for the other pursuits you enjoy. For articles, poetry and essays, the demands can be still lighter. BUT the routine you select must be disciplined, not hit or miss. Like any other creative endeavor, writing demands that you honor the schedule if you want to reach your final goal.

With that commitment on your part, THE WRITER WITHIN YOU will help you find your way through the morass of the publishing world and ensure that your thoughts actually see print, whether your interest lies in writing shorter pieces or the next great American novel. Good luck!

CHARLES JACOBS

CHAPTER 1

CAN I REALLY BECOME A WRITER?

Yogi Berra, as famous for his quips as he was for his expertise on the baseball diamond, counseled, "If you don't know which road you're on, you'll likely end up somewhere else."

When you opted to read this book, you apparently chose the WRITE road, and that certainly is the right road for anyone who has a yen to memorialize his/her thoughts in print. Only by traveling the write road will you discover the thrill of seeing your name on the cover of a book or above an article in a favorite magazine. You'll discover how significant your pen can be as more and more readers, many of them total strangers, respond to your thoughts or how your loved ones react when you pass on treasured memories.

You ask, "Can I really become a writer?" Of course you can. At this stage of your life, you at last have the opportunity to realize your dream. Thanks to retirement plans and social security payments, you are probably assured of a basic income. Your schedule is flexible and free. You no longer must rush off to spend the day at the office or the plant. You have the time to write. Most important of all, you have the unique ability to call upon years of rich experiences and a great deal of acquired knowledge to jump start this exciting, new venture. That places you far in front of the starting gate where less experienced, younger would-be writers must begin. Once you start, you will be amazed at the ease with which you can place your thoughts on paper. When you discover how favorably readers respond, your confidence will expand exponentially, as will your pride in yourself and in your accomplishment.

But—and it's a very big but—there is a quid pro quo. To be successful or at the very least to see your project through to completion, you must be willing to seal yourself off from the world for at least two or three hours a day while you place those brilliant thoughts and clever phrases on paper. That's really not a pact with the devil, nor is it terribly demanding of your time. It leaves lots of hours for golf, reading, socializing and all of the other privileges of retirement. But it is vital that your writing is done on a regular, structured schedule. Continuity is the key to success in our field.

BUILDING YOUR CONFIDENCE

Having picked your path, your next task is to erase any doubt about your ability to write. No, you'll probably never be as renowned as Hemingway. But remember, he started much earlier in life, and still required endless revisions to his copy before he produced the books that have made him a household name worldwide. Seventy years ago, Dorothea Brande, one of the all-time great writing instructors, agreed that "Genius cannot be taught." But, this highly respected figure added, "I think there is a magic (to writing), and that it is teachable." I would go a step further and add, as Lawrence Block indicated in his WORDS OF WISDOM, your writing skills will flourish with practice and steady effort. If you take the time to look at much of what is being published today, I think you'll be reassured that you too will soon be able to write as effectively as many of the authors who are fortunate enough to be in print.

WORDS OF WISDOM

In his book *Writing the Novel*, Lawrence Block, author of more than 25 books, states: "Writing has this in common with most other skills; we develop it best by practicing it. Whatever writing we do helps us to become better writers."

When you actually sit down to write, shake off those inhibitions. Let the words flow. In the first days of becoming comfortable with this new endeavor, don't worry at all about the quality of what you're producing. If the thoughts make sense, but the words need massaging, you are experiencing what even the best writers frequently find. That's why revision and rewriting are so much a part of our craft. They do take effort, but it is effort well rewarded. The pride of a project completed. The gratification of having others read and enjoy your thoughts and your words. The thrill of seeing your byline in a periodical or on the cover of a book.

I choose to think Ms. Parker, known for her satirical wit, was having a bit of fun when she wrote these WORDS OF WISDOM.

WORDS OF WISDOM

Dorothy Parker, one of the wittiest and most famous writers of her day, once stated: "I hate writing, but I love having written."

Perhaps, as some have indicated, writers and writing do at times endure a love/hate relationship, but one in which love always wins out for the dedicated author. I am certain Ms.Parker believed that writers succeed best when they love what they are doing. You too can succeed and enjoy just as she did with proper guidance and a bit of determination. The chapters ahead are designed to provide you with that guidance, with an overview of the at-times confusing world of publishing you are now about to enter and a variety of tips to help you master the specific category of writing you have chosen to pursue.

DECISIONS, DECISIONS

Once you have the confidence to believe that you too can become a published author, it is important to start thinking about what it is you really want to write. In *Book Marketing from A – Z*, author and marketing expert Robin Fisher Roffer (*www.bigfishmarketing.com*) offers this advice to writers: "Find a point-of-view and then extend from there." Ms. Roffer uses Gore Vidal's concentration on history as an example of what she means. You must decide which category of writing best suits your interests and abilities. Is it fiction or nonfiction? Short stories or a novel? An article or a full-length book? History or true crime? How-to or some other nonfiction category? Perhaps the warmth that you, like so many others who have passed the mid-century mark, feel when you recall the past—those "silver" years and even earlier—impels you to write a lasting memoir for family members and those still to arrive.

Most of you are familiar with the word *genre*, as it is used to depict distinct types of literature. Although the fundamentals of creation are essentially the same for every category, you will learn in succeeding chapters the approach does vary somewhat. So it is up to you to determine what it is you want to say, the genre in which you want to present it and how best to frame your work. Should you tackle a full length nonfiction book or begin with an article on the subject? Can the message you want to deliver be more effectively presented as a parable or a longer fictional story? Would you be better served by writing an essay? These questions aren't difficult to answer once you have carefully thought through your project. Often the choice is inherent in the subject matter you choose to write about. Be sure it is something with which you are completely comfortable, for you and your project will be intimately wedded for a substantial period of time.

> ### WORDS OF WISDOM
>
> **Robin Fisher Roffer in Book** *Marketing from A-Z*: "Being known for something is what builds buzz and a following. The trick is not to pigeonhole yourself! So choose wisely the subject matter or genre that you'll work in. Make sure it resounds with your soul."

CHOOSING YOUR NICHE

You may decide to change the genre you select as you proceed through this book. Therefore it is important to understand fully the many avenues you can pursue. To my surprise, I have met students in my writing classes who did not understand the distinction between fiction and nonfiction. So let me begin at the very beginning, even at the risk of offending you, by presenting such rudimentary information. Novels, short stories and most plays and movie scripts are fictional. They are imaginary with characters and circumstances born in the writer's mind. They do not represent true reality, although they may have been inspired by a real person, event or circumstance. Fictional genres include romance, historical, adventure, risqué and science fiction books, as well as mysteries and books for children and teens.

Nonfiction categories are very different. They are all reality-oriented. Some are event-based, such as true crime or history. Others deal with subjects such as current events, economics or politics. The nonfiction grouping also includes books on how-to, scientific and technical subjects, business, travel and even memoirs. In later chapters, we will look at each of these areas more closely.

Opportunities are almost limitless for nonfiction writers. The majority of articles published in magazines and newspapers are nonfiction. Trade journals that serve a wide variety of occupations and specialties represent a very hungry market always looking for solidly based articles in their field. They offer an excellent outlet for retirees whose years of service in a particular field gives them great insight and expertise. In addition to articles on business written for trades and for general magazines, the corporate world offers opportunities to write for house organs, magazines or newsletters published by a company to pass information to its own staff or to use as promotional tools. Companies often seek part-time freelance writers to assist in writing copy for their public relations or advertising departments. As a highly experienced veteran, you may find this a rewarding way to stay in touch with the line of work to which you devoted so many years.

It is imperative that you heed Connie Emerson's advice if you decide to build your writing career on your past vocational experience. Make certain that you are current, fully updated in your thinking on the subject. Has technology or progress of some other sort passed you by? If so, there is research to do, most of which should be relatively easy based on your familiarity with the subject and the contacts you left behind when you retired.

WORDS OF WISDOM

In *The Writer's Guide to Conquering the Magazine Market,* author Connie Emerson counsels: "You don't have to be a Harvard biz school grad to write business pieces. But you must be accurate and willing to do your research thoroughly....The successful writer is one who keeps abreast of articles and subject matter currently in demand."

If you have kept up with advances and changes in your field, you may qualify to *ghost write* (although you write the piece, the person who paid you to write it is listed as the author) a book or article for an executive who will give you the general guidelines of the piece he/she seeks, but cannot take the time or doesn't have the writing skills to turn it out. In addition to accepting articles and op-ed essays from the public, newspapers often seek regional *stringers* (part-time reporters) for either their news or sports departments. These part-timers work on a regular basis covering a specific town's council meetings or the competitive sports played by a local high school.

So you see, opportunities for success in the world of words are endless. *Writer's Market*, the 1178-page bible for freelance nonfiction writers, lists 50 different categories of general magazines for the consumer and 60 categories of trade journals. The 392 pages cataloguing consumer publications range across the alphabet from magazines serving Animal lovers to Women's periodicals. The 138 pages of alphabetical trade listings begin with Advertising, marketing and public relations and end with Veterinary medicine. The directory is updated annually to maintain currency. This description of the book is based on the 2007 edition.

Writer's Market contains an enormous amount of additional information, including directories of book publishers, small presses, literary agents and articles on various aspects of writing. It is a valuable tool for anyone who chooses to write with any degree of frequency. While I strongly recommend purchasing your own copy, *Writer's Market* can be found in most library reference rooms.

CAN I REALLY MAKE A BUCK?

While pursuing a steady routine in front of your computer may never make you wealthy (although first timers have been known to reach best seller lists and the resulting big bucks), supplementing your fixed income is a welcome addition to the joy of seeing your name and ideas in print, especially in these days of economic uncertainty.

It is exciting to read of huge— sometimes seven-figure—advances for both fiction and nonfiction books. Forget them. In today's bottom line-driven publishing industry, only celebrities, well established authors and politicians ever see checks that large. The average *advance* (monies a publisher advances to you against your future royalties to help defray some expenses while you are still completing or fine-tuning your book) is limited to the four or at most five-figure bracket, and for unknowns it is usually at the bottom of that scale.

WORDS OF WISDOM

In their book *Give 'Em What They Want*, authors Blythe Camenson and Marshall Cook, counsel: "What about that $17 million Stephen King got just for signing his contract? Your advance will have considerably fewer zeroes to the left of the decimal point… (But) if you fulfill the terms of your contract and submit an acceptable manuscript, the advance is yours to keep, even if your book goes directly to remainder-table oblivion."

In the periodicals universe, compensation for articles varies widely. Much like the cost of advertising, pay scales are generally based upon circulation. The high-paying majors (from $500 to $2,500) are generally off limits to beginners. Start-up authors can anticipate receiving anywhere from $50 from a small publication to perhaps $100 to $200 if their article is accepted by a larger newspaper or a mid-sized magazine. However, that's not as glum as it sounds. Most freelancers are clever enough to multiply the earnings of a single article by selling it to several publications, as long as they are sure the areas of circulation don't overlap. This is especially true of newspapers, where articles can be sold to prestigious regional papers from coast to coast, and in many cases even multiple papers in the same state where the circulation boundaries don't clash. It takes very little additional effort to send out these multiple submissions, and the return can aggregate to a figure that is comparable to what a single major pays or even more.

EVEN DISCIPLINE CAN BE FUN

If the challenge of what it means to become a writer has excited you and reinforced your resolve to join this glorious fraternity, it's now time to get down to specifics. But before we move on to the next chapter, I want to return to a theme I stressed at the beginning of this chapter: discipline. It is the downfall of many a would-be writer. Like any other artistic creation, a work of literature will never come to life unless the author is willing to stay the course.

WORDS OF WISDOM

University of Mississippi Professor David Galef states in *Poets & Writers Magazine*: "I once took an informal poll at an artists colony and found that most of the people there believed persistence to be almost as important as talent. Writers need a daily regimen— waiting for the thunderbolt is too uncertain."

In that issue of *Poets & Writers* magazine, Professor Galef who also serves as administrator of graduate level creative writing programs at the University, wrote, "A work of art is 10 percent inspiration, 90 percent perspiration." Years before, Thomas Edison went even further. He declared that "Genius is one percent inspiration and 99 percent perspiration." But don't allow yourself to think of discipline as a negative. Just as you probably wouldn't dream of going to sleep without first brushing your teeth, any function performed regularly becomes an intricate part of your lifestyle. As author Charlie Shed promises in his book *If I Can Write, You Can Write*, discipline actually can be fun. It becomes part of your regular writing routine. For many, like "yours truly," those hours spent at the computer are a welcome escape from the hubbub of daily life. Most of us who have graduated from full-time work to full days of freedom now find more than enough hours to meet our responsibilities and enjoy the relaxation, hobbies and recreation we looked forward to for so many years. Yet we still religiously devote two, three or more hours a day to writing. Take advantage. *Carpe diem! Carpe Retirement!* Do it all.

Join me now as we get into the nuts and bolts of writing. The next chapter will show you how to trawl for ideas, determine the track you want to follow and move you from thinking to actually doing.

CHAPTER 2

DIGGING IN

It makes little difference whether you intend to write a book, an article, an essay or a poem, all writing begins with an idea. "But where does it come from?" you ask. The likelihood is the idea will sprout from your wealth of experience on the job, happenings at home with family, an interesting character you have come to know or your favorite hobbies and pastimes. It can develop from something you read or heard or possibly from a unique event or a fascinating acquaintance. You've lived a full life, and now with the luxury of time and the ability to devote undivided energy to the project, you are able to share with others the thoughts and experiences that have been so meaningful to you.

You may already have a very definite idea of what you want to write and feel that reading about idea generation is unnecessary. Read on, for there is still much in this chapter that will be helpful to you as you ferret out and compile new information to expand the research file of the piece you've already decided to write.

Or just imagine! It's possible that you will become so intrigued by your first attempt at crafting a book or an article that you decide the writer's life, at least on a part-time schedule, offers the ideal opportunity to make retirement more fun and more fulfilling. If you are one of those enthusiasts, you'll want to begin now to collect and file ideas for future articles and books. You can be certain of one thing, this chapter will make you a better writer whether you stop after one attempt or continue on to lasting fame.

WRITER'S BLOCK—NEMESIS OR FANTASY?

Back when thoughts of writing were still dreams, story ideas burst regularly into your mind. Unfortunately, you hadn't yet realized how important it was to tuck those flashes of inspiration into a *Potentials File* waiting for the day you finally decide it is time to stop dreaming and start writing. So there you sit, facing a blank computer screen, wondering where you go next. Or, maybe you're lucky enough to start out with a very specific idea, but find you just can't bring it to life. That villainous computer screen stares back, taunting you with the subliminal message that you can't make the leap from thought to reality. That's when too many wanna-be writers—and occasionally even experienced ones—fall back on the universal crutch, *Writer's Block*.

WORDS OF WISDOM

Roy Blount, Jr, author of *Crackers and One Fell Soup* is quoted in *The American Directory of Writer's Guidelines:* "I think writer's block is simply the dread that you are going to write something horrible. But as a writer, I believe that if you sit down at the keys long enough, sooner or later something will come out."

I consider writer's block nonsense. Writing is no different from any other challenge. The toughest part of any task is getting started, and that's certainly true of writing. As Roy Blount suggests, the answer is to stop thinking about the enormity of the task ahead. Stop searching for a starting point, and just plunge in. Get started. No matter how poor the opening few paragraphs may seem, don't stop. Don't turn back. Keep writing, and before long you will find it all suddenly comes together. This approach will certainly require you to return later and clean up those initial sentences. Perhaps even do a major revision on your opening. But you are now on your way. After all, there's another truism, even if the great Yogi Berra never mentioned it: "If you don't start, you'll never end!" I am sure you learned that well during your years in the business or professional world. Writer's block is nothing more than a stumble that can readily be overcome and even avoided completely with proper preparation. Let's look at how a writer prepares him/herself to avoid this troublesome blockage.

WRITE WHAT YOU KNOW

I am sure that you have heard this admonition time and again. It makes sense in many ways. You need facts to be able to create a successful book whether it is fiction, how-to, history, true crime, travel or any other category. To be convincing, an opinion piece or essay must be grounded in fact, and demands the writer have an accurate knowledge of the subject. In a memoir, you write about the realities you remember or learn from others. To give the facts greater meaning, you then analyze the *why* of the events, the significance of important turning points in your life or in the lives of the other persons you write about. Regardless of the category in which you choose to write, it is critical that you know your subject intimately. We retirees enjoy a distinct advantage in this area, for we bring a lifetime of experience with us when we face the computer.

When writing a novel or short story, you are able to let your imagination run free. However, it still requires an intimate knowledge of the locale in which you place your story and the background of the characters with whom you people it. If readers detect errors of fact, inconsistencies that don't ring true, the flow of the piece will be interrupted. Readers will lose both interest in the story and trust in you as an author.

No matter what category or genre you write in, fiction or nonfiction, it is imperative that you are factually prepared before you sit down at the computer. Accomplishing that is far easier if you choose to write about a subject with which you are already familiar, and then go on to validate and expand your knowledge with research. You sit down to write, armed with the detailed preparation you have completed, and writer's block is foiled once again.

Writing about things you know has added advantages. When you are personally familiar with a subject, it is far easier to find an exciting and different angle (or hook as most editors call it) to make your story distinct and probably superior to others that have already reached publication. Because editors and publishers are often leery about working with new or first-time writers, you stand a much better chance of landing an assignment or selling your book idea if you can convince the editor that your lack of experience as a writer is offset by your exceptional familiarity with the subject you are writing about. That's your great advantage! Certainly a trout fisherman with years of experience is far better qualified to tell readers how best to tie a *Greased Lightning* than I am. However, none of this precludes you from writing on a subject you know only peripherally if you are willing to do the intensive research required to develop the command of the material that a well thought out book demands.

WORDS OF WISDOM

Donald Maass, author of more than 17 books, draws this telling analogy in *Writing the Breakout Novel*: "Have you ever been trapped at a party talking with someone who has nothing to say?...You mentally work up excuses for slipping away. Experienced partygoers know how to disengage smoothly. So do readers. When they run across a novel that has nothing to say, they snap it closed...or perhaps hurl it across the room."

SELECTING A SPECIALTY

Ask yourself what subject interests you most, and about which you are most knowledgeable. It may be astronomy, retailing, rock music, carpentry or baseball. It matters little what the subject is. There is always a market for an article, and probably even a book, if you are fully conversant and up-to-date with the material or at least know how to research effectively, understand what you find, fill in the gaps and add your own unique viewpoint.

An excellent way to begin shaping the thrust of the article is to pose questions to yourself that you would want answered if you were the reader. Or think of questions that others have asked of you on the subject.

Maybe your preference is a more personal approach to idea generation. If so, create an outline of the most memorable experiences of your life. No, you're not necessarily going to write an autobiography or even a memoir. But you may dredge up some very intriguing topics for your next story or article or possibly a book. Here are a few examples to get your thought processes churning.

a. You were an adopted child. Your story can be personalized as your own life experience or analyzed in a third person article. Both fiction and nonfiction on this subject are almost always saleable if properly written.

b. Your Grandfather was a Native American. Indian lore always provides a fascinating topic. The way in which your family and you preserved your cultural identity while growing up in the mainstream could make a fine piece.

The list goes on and on. Your Mom died of cancer at too young an age (hopefully not), you experienced a particularly nasty divorce, you have enjoyed a remarkably affectionate and happy marriage in this age of constant breakups, you happen to be seven feet tall…there are endless possibilities and they all offer vast potential for articles, stories and as the basis for the protagonist's problems in the novel you are about to write. Best of all, you know the topic intimately, and are able to write well about it.

WORDS OF WISDOM

Lawrence Block, Grand Master of the Mystery Writers of America, states in his book *Writing the Novel From Plot to Print*, "Maybe you've endured something that strikes you as the raw material for a novel…Colorful or bland, anyone's life can be turned into arresting fiction if it is incisively perceived and dramatically portrayed."

TRAWLING FOR IDEAS

If you prefer to avoid personal subjects, visit your local library. Select a source book like *Writer's Market*, the excellent directory of periodicals you were introduced to in the last chapter. Peruse the index. When you have sorted out those topics that capture your interest, turn to the section that lists periodicals on the subjects you have chosen. The listings you find there narrow down the general topic to the specific aspects emphasized by each individual magazine, and may help you further crystallize your ideas. This approach isn't applicable to article writing alone. The wealth of subject matter in *Writer's Market* can be used effectively to trigger ideas for books as well. Used properly, this extensive catalogue of consumer periodicals and trade journals is a superb source of ideas and topics for any category of writing. If your interest lies in writing articles, *Writer's Market* will also provide you with an excellent list of editors to whom you can send queries and articles on the subjects you choose. In addition to its listings of periodicals, this "must-have" directory contains a listing of key literary agents and publishers for book queries.

A source like *Readers Guide to Periodical Literature* is very helpful. Using it allows you to kill two birds with a single stone. Not only does it pique your interest in a variety of subjects, it also allows you to see just what has been written on each subject, when and by whom and in which periodical.

The Internet is a treasure trove of ideas for articles and books. Those of you who have already taken advantage of this unique compendium of information know that by clicking onto one of the major search engines and entering a subject, endless variations on the topic will appear, offering a diverse menu of story possibilities.

A superb source of ideas that serves many a freelancer well is the daily newspaper. Weekly community papers are also excellent idea generators. But always remember this distinction: Newspapers chronicle events as they happen. You, as a freelancer, also chronicle events, whether factually or by adapting them to fiction. The difference is you are not restricted by time as is the harried newspaper reporter who regularly faces same-day deadlines. That allows you to probe more deeply. To put some real flesh on the piece (through research or in the case of fiction by calling on your imagination) and to write something very different from what appears in the concise, matter-of-fact columns of a newspaper.

CLIP, CLIP, CLIP

When you search a newspaper or magazine, you must read it in a very special way to gain maximum benefit. Keep pencil and scissors handy. Whenever an article piques your interest, clip, date and file it by subject. Don't neglect the classified pages. You'll be surprised to find how advertisements for odd jobs, personals, notices and even the lost and found can be great sources of ideas.

In an article in the *Handbook of Magazine Article Writing* writer Stan Bicknell explains that he uses clips not only to generate story ideas, but also for background information on subjects he likes to write about. These running files serve as a rich resource when he sits down to produce an article related to that subject.

WORDS OF WISDOM

Well known author Stan Bicknell writes in the *Writer's Digest Handbook of Magazine Article Writing*, "For nearly 15 years hardly a day has passed that I haven't taken up shears and cut out one or more news and feature stories from the daily papers…The chore takes only a few odd minutes, but I consider it the most important thing I do."

Whatever the publication, CLIP, CLIP, CLIP. Just as a writer can never read enough, he/she can never clip enough or save enough. Don't overlook the Internet, an endless source of information on so many subjects. Print out what you find. Whether the clip is a new idea or a follow-up on something you previously found interesting, be sure to file it. You will find yourself continually adding updates to the file of a single story idea. When you are ready to write, the complete trail of the story's development awaits you in the file, ready to draw upon.

EASY TO FIND

How do you organize a functional clip file? That's really up to you, for no one knows better than you what system will make retrieving the information easiest. Whether you store the clips in a wood paneled file cabinet, an inexpensive cardboard or metal file from a stationery store or just a milk crate or cardboard box rescued from your corner liquor vendor, your file folders must be labeled and sorted alphabetically by subject. Organize the file to provide you with the simplest and fastest retrieval possible. Those of you who are adept at computer operations may prefer to sort and scan the clips into your computer, eliminating the need for a file cabinet.

As you search for subjects, always remember: no topic will be rejected simply because it has been used before. There are very few new ideas, just new and novel treatments. Here's an example. Several years ago I was vacationing in the Southwest for a short period of time. While there in the land of Indian reservations and extraordinary archeological sites, I was unexpectedly inspired to craft a piece on Native American lore and culture, a topic that's been written about countless times. A subject that predates Columbus. Ahhhh! That was the hook. The story offered a look at the people who inhabited this land long before the arrival of the Pinto or the Nina or even the Santa Maria. The year I wrote the story happened to be the much publicized 500th anniversary of Columbus' landing. Needless to say, the story sold well.

Now that you have solidified the type of writing you want to do, as well as the subject and the angle you intend to use, it's time to head for the computer. No reason to be shy or afraid. Digesting the following chapters on the fundamentals of each of the seven categories of writing we retirees seem to prefer, will provide you with more than enough ammunition to craft respectable, salable work. Let's begin with the novel.

WRITING YOUR BOOK

CHAPTER 3

THE NOVEL

Some years ago, the great writer Somerset Maugham declared, "There are three rules for the writing of a novel. Unfortunately, no one knows what they are."

While Maugham's words may sound flip, there's a great deal of truth to what he said. Nonetheless, successful patterns do exist to help you organize, pace and enrich your novel, and we will share these with you as we wend our way through this chapter and the next. But first I want you to ask yourself the question, "What exactly is a novel?" Aside from the simple answer that a novel is fiction, have you really thought about the question? How is a novel constructed? What differentiates one from another? I'm sure you've read many novels, and equally sure you raved about at least one title to your friends, insisting they read it. But after reading just a few pages of another, you slammed it shut and warned those same friends to cross it off their list. Why? In both these scenarios, the books were novels. So why did you, an avid fiction reader, react so differently to each? That's the question this chapter hopes to answer, because in that answer lies the secret of crafting a first rate novel.

THE FICTION LADDER

We certainly know that your personal preferences, background, experiences all play a role in your likes and dislikes. But when you read a book even more important is the ability of the author to attract you with a challenging or intriguing first page, and maintain your interest through a pattern of continuously escalating challenges and tensions until a final resolution is reached. The opening paragraphs set the major goal for the protagonist. In the mid-section of the book he/she faces obstacle after obstacle that must be overcome to reach that goal. When you read your next novel, I want you to be keenly aware of this force, this movement, for it is the key to a successful novel. Think of it somewhat like a "literary ladder," and watch as it progresses step by step: Challenge, conflict, tension, momentary relief. That sequence occurs over and over again until the final resolution is reached and the book ends with the protagonist either accomplishing his/her goal or wallowing in defeat.

While there are wide variations, the series of scenes on which most novels are based don't necessarily conform to chapter breaks. They are entities within themselves. Several—or none—can occur within a single chapter. The protagonist, eager to reach a goal, is beset with challenges that make that goal seem unattainable. But each time, after some degree of anguish, the protagonist overcomes, and plunges headlong into the next obstacle, keeping the reader continuously rooting for his/her success. Of course, a degree of subtlety is needed to make this progression palatable. You can't just overwhelm your reader with a heavy-handed crisis over and over again. Often-times the crisis is implied, not concretely stated. You, the author, are the best judge of the tempo you need to hold your readers' interest without overwhelming them.

WORDS OF WISDOM

Crawford Kilian of Capilano College in Canada writes on his web site *www.steampunk.com*: "If your novel or short story is going to work, it's going to need all the right components. Used without imagination or sensitivity, those elements may produce only formula fiction. But, like a good cook with the right materials and a good recipe, you can also create some pleasant surprises. (It all has to do) essentially, with bringing your characters and readers from a state of ignorance to a state of awareness: Can our heroine find happiness as a journalist? We don't know, but we'll find out."

BUILDING AND SUSTAINING TENSION

Let's imagine a very simplistic example. As we begin reading, we discover that John, the protagonist and a devoted drinker of orange juice, has just learned that an unsafe chemical is used in the commercial preparation of the juice sold in supermarkets. A health nut, he decides to convert to fresh-squeezed. Because he lives in Florida where orange trees grow in backyards, there is no need for stores to carry fresh juice, a costly item to prepare. Therefore the first obstacle he faces is his inability to find a store that offers it. Finally, his extensive search reveals the one grocery store in the region that does. Relieved, he heads there and buys two quarts. Second obstacle. His joy quickly turns to anger as he discovers that the juice is not quite as fresh as he imagined. The first quart turns sour days before the expiration date stamped on the container. He returns the last quart, and is offered a replacement along with the store manager's apology. Third obstacle. This time the juice remains tasty to the end, and John assumes he has found the solution to his craving until Ruth, an acquaintance at work, shows him a survey of food stores that condemns the fresh squeezed juice they sell. Testing revealed contaminants, attributed to unsanitary preparation, in 97 percent of the juice. John immediately throws out the remainder of his juice supply. Fortunately, he lives in Naples, Florida, and drives to the closest citrus grove, and has them prepare several quarts for him. Fourth obstacle. The prices are so high, he uses this solution for a month or so, but knows he can't afford to continue. And on and on the story builds, always focused on John's quest. At last he decides to plant his own tree, but the yard is too shady. He removes a shade tree, and finds a soil problem. Ultimately, John's perseverance wins out, and the novel ends happily as he gulps down the first harvest from his own Valencia tree.

This, of course, is brazenly naive. I used the example only to demonstrate that the most mundane issue can be intensified by a series of recurring challenges. The reader is motivated to turn page after page, breathlessly waiting to learn how the hero overcomes each challenge. In the case of a compelling novel, success doesn't breed success at once. After several pages of tension-free reading, each success quickly gives way to the next obstacle, ultimately achieving resolution by page 300 or so. Reading a novel with this awareness, will help you understand far more clearly what I am about to tell you or what you will find in the many excellent books listed in the Appendix that have been written to teach you how to write a novel.

Bear in mind that when I talk about tension it is not necessarily a high-pitched, blatant conflict. As suggested above, tension can be presented in a far more subtle manner. Its task is to impel the reader to turn the page in search of a resolution. The very first paragraphs of the opening must capture the reader, and then build on that interest. One of the great classics of contemporary prose is Pulitzer Prize winner *To Kill a Mockingbird*. Author Harper Lee opens her novel with the sentence, "When he was nearly thirteen, my brother Jem got his arm badly broken at the elbow." Following a brief description of the break and its lasting consequences, she continues, "When enough years has (sic) gone by to enable us to look back on them, we sometimes discussed the events leading to the accident. I maintain that the Ewells started it all, but Jem, who was four years my senior, said it started long before that. He said it began the summer Dill came to us, when Dill first gave us the idea of making Boo Radley come out."

Very quietly and with little emotion, Lee has snagged her reader. There is a modest conflict in the different recollections of the protagonist and her brother. She has made us wonder who Dill is and why "Dill came to us." We want to understand why it was important to make "Boo Radley come out." The characters' unusual names, Jem, Dill and Boo Radley, add to our curiosity and our fascination. There is certainly enough intrigue to allow Lee to follow this with almost four pages of beautifully crafted background material before describing the actual day that "Dill came to us" and launching into the meat of the story.

FREQUENTLY ASKED QUESTIONS

Before we plunge into the techniques of actually crafting a quality manuscript, let me first give you answers to some of the questions that are probably dominating your thoughts. Budding novelists regularly ask these of me at social events and whenever I speak on the subject of writing a book.

a) *How long should my book be?* It should be as long as needed to make the story work; long enough to convey what it is you want the reader to learn, yet short enough to hold the reader's interest. Granted that is a vague response, but the only one that is truly accurate. To accomplish this, the majority of novels fall between 250 and 400 pages of printed text.

b) *Is there a best length for a chapter?* The answer is No. Some will be longer, others shorter. The level of comfort the writer feels as the book develops will determine the length of each chapter. Average chapters in manuscript usually fall somewhere between 10 and 25 typed pages. This translates to roughly 2500 to 6200 words. Let me emphasize again that chapters do not have to conform to the scene pattern that we talked about earlier. There can be no scenes or many in a single chapter. The most important concern is to recognize that the end of a chapter is the most common stopping point for a reader. He/she is most likely to put down the book at that point. Therefore, it is crucial that we end a chapter with a definite impetus to continue. Often that means ending the chapter with an unresolved conflict. If the protagonist is frustrated and searching for a resolution, the reader will be eager to discover the choice the hero finally makes. That will motivate the reader to pick the book up again if he/she stopped at the end of a chapter because of other obligations.

c) *How about paragraph length?* Again, need determines the length. In a single book, you might find paragraphs of 30 lines or more and others that are just four or five lines long. It matters only in terms of pace, a subject we will discuss later. The average, however, seems to be about 10 to 14 lines, but again this is highly flexible and often is determined by pace. Length of paragraphs and sentences is generally geared to the subject matter you are writing about. For example, a tense, action-packed segment will have short graphs and clipped sentences. In a more contemplative narrative, the pace will naturally be slower and more relaxed.

d) *How should I format my manuscript?* Most editors and agents feel that ragged right is the easiest format to read, and many insist upon it. That means your copy is flush and even with the left margin, but lines end with full words on the right whether even or not. The simplest way to accomplish this on your computer is to go to the upper bar and click on the diagram that illustrates flush left. It is the first icon, just to the right of the underline "U."

e) *How can I know the number of words I have written?* That's easy. You may remember that we talked about this far back in the earlier chapters of this book. If you are working on a current PC—and I certainly hope you are—click on Tools in the top menu. The first tool to appear is Word Count. Clicking on that will give you the number of words written thus far in the file you are working on. To count on your own, estimate 250 words per each double spaced page written in 12 point type.

f) The last universal question among start-up novelists is *How much should I expect to write each day?* The answer from most writers seems to be an average of three to 15 pages. However, if you are on a roll, don't quit just because you reached 15. Don't sacrifice the momentum. Conversely, if you can't reach three good pages, write anyway. You can always go back and rewrite, edit or toss those pages away. So the real answer to the question is the same as it was for several others. There really isn't an answer. It depends on you and your comfort.

The majority of writers prefer to work in the morning when they are at their freshest, and then pursue other activities for the rest of the day. That was the choice of greats like Hemingway and Michener. Far more important than the number of pages is the consistency of your work schedule. Whether you choose to write in the morning, afternoon or wee hours of the night, you must do it regularly to maintain the continuity your novel requires. However, it is equally important to break away from your desk and enjoy a rounded, interesting day to keep you stimulated. Hemingway headed to his boat most afternoons when his work was finished. If you spend too much time at the computer, writing can become drudgery.

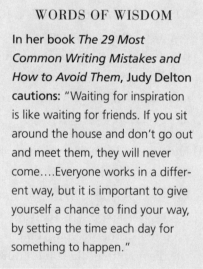

WORDS OF WISDOM

In her book *The 29 Most Common Writing Mistakes and How to Avoid Them*, Judy Delton cautions: "Waiting for inspiration is like waiting for friends. If you sit around the house and don't go out and meet them, they will never come....Everyone works in a different way, but it is important to give yourself a chance to find your way, by setting the time each day for something to happen."

CRAFTING YOUR NOVEL

We're going to break our discussion of craft into seven sections, all essential elements in creating a first-rate novel: Theme, Structure,

Plot, Pace, Viewpoint, Character and Description. The sequence in which I have listed them doesn't necessarily reflect the degree of importance of each; it simply makes sense to begin with the broader aspects like theme, structure and plot. So let's start with theme.

THEME

Most people who make the effort to write have something to say, and it matters little whether they prefer to relate it in a nonfiction or fictional format. In turn, readers too have opinions. They turn to books to have their beliefs validated or occasionally to discover that another point of view may be preferable. Expressing an opinion can be accomplished in many ways. Incorporating it in your novel is far more civil than presenting it as a polemic…and under some circumstances more convincing as well. The danger for a beginning author is that he/she may preach instead of tell (a spin-off of the "show don't tell" rule of quality writing that you will hear much more about in the next chapter). You must allow the choices your characters make and the actions they take to illustrate your theme.

You already know from the earlier paragraphs of this chapter that scenes are built around conflict and the need to make choices to reach a resolution. This requires beginners to exercise great care that their passion for the theme they have chosen for their book doesn't box the protagonist into a corner, leaving him/her with only one moral choice to avoid mortally blemishing his/her reputation. Having no other

WORDS OF WISDOM

Once again Donald Maass offers outstanding advice in his book *Writing the Breakout Novel:* "Enhancing motivation is what you will need to do if you want to give your protagonist the inner fire that, developed step-by-step through your manuscript, results in a powerful theme…When high motives are made believable and integral to a given character, it is like sending a ten thousand volt electric current through your novel."

alternatives may block any further movement of the book or in some cases cause the reader to feel that the choice was out of character and therefore unbelievable.

To avoid forcing your protagonist to make a decision that is unrealistic or out of character, you must think through the entire sequence of the book from the opening paragraph and steadily develop motivation that will not conflict with the code of ethics he/she possesses nor with your convictions as the author. That way, the action that builds always remains consistent with the protagonist's character and with the novel's theme. Equally important is that the protagonist be firm in his/her convictions. A wishy-washy character who is unsure and doubting of his/her own beliefs will fail to gain a reader's support and probably turn the reader away. This doesn't mean that the protagonist can't have a serious debate within him/herself or even with others while deciding between several paths to follow. Real life persons often waver in their decisions before ultimately choosing well. A character's temptation to violate his/her beliefs is fully acceptable. It contributes to building tension and character, provided the final decision conforms to the individual's true nature. Readers seldom have tolerance for one-dimensional characters who are unbending, rigid and consider themselves infallible.

STRUCTURE
While to many they seem to be the same, there are subtle differences between *structure* and *plot*. Once you have thoroughly massaged your theme and understand it well enough to fashion it into a novel, it is time to think in terms of structure. In his highly informative book *Scene and Structure*, Jack Bickham defines structure as "Nothing more than a way of looking at your story material so that it's organized in a way that's both logical and dramatic." He goes on to compare it to the internal framework of a house, the 2 X 4's, braces and other supports, but cautions that "structure is a

process, not a rigid format…not static, but dynamic."

The essence of structure is "cause and effect" or expressed a different way "stimulus and response." In real life, events can and do occur randomly or by coincidence or even fate. They cannot in your novel. In fiction there must be a reason why things happen to make them credible or you will lose your audience. For the novelist, this requires placing adequate background material in the story, developing the character's persona and creating a context in which the protagonist or other individuals take action that is understandable and realistic.

THE SCENE

It is here that we must examine the role a *scene* plays in the overall structure of a novel. Following Bickham's earlier comparison to constructing a house, if the structure is the frame of 2 X 4s, then the scenes are the braces that hold the structure—house or novel—together. The scene, much like the scenes in a play, is a segment of the story within which it unfolds. Scenes are in essence the high and low points of the "roller coaster ride" the protagonist takes. Each individual scene contains the moment of conflict, the seemingly irresolvable challenge that confronts our hero, creating tension at its peak. It is an action moment, not one of reflection. As several writing coaches suggest, the scene represents external action, not internal thought and contemplation. The latter typically serves as the break between action scenes, giving the reader an understanding of the circumstances that led to the action of the scene. It allows the reader to peek inside the thought processes of the protagonist as he/she resolves to move forward in another attempt to reach the ultimate goal.

It may seem cruel to some of you, but the goal of a scene as it progresses is to force the protagonist into deeper trouble. He/she should be far worse off at the end than when the scene began. That will excite the reader, and propel him/her onto the next phase of your narrative. Remember "Orange John," the example of scene function you read earlier in this chapter. At each step of his quest to slake his obsession for quality orange juice, the scene ended with another obstacle confronting John. With still another option closed, he certainly was worse off than when the scene began.

A scene begins with the protagonist intent on achieving a specific objective that will help him/her reach the ultimate goal that was described early in the novel's opening chapter. Again, I have to stress, be sure that each scene is constructed with its own immediate challenge that must be overcome on the path to the ultimate goal. When that happens, the protagonist is chagrined and the reader eagerly turns pages to discover what action he/she will now take, if any. And so the movement continues in this uphill, downhill pattern, broken, of course, by narrative, description and introspection.

Donald Maass, whom we have quoted frequently because I consider his book *Writing the Breakout Novel* priority reading for any future novelist, explains, "A well-constructed scene has a mini-arc of its own: a beginning, rise and climax or reversal at the end." He goes on to say, "Whatever drives the main character…make sure it is an inner conflict as powerful as any outer conflict could hope to be: Urgent, unavoidable and full of an emotional appeal that anyone can feel. (Therefore) breakout novelists frequently use exposition—that is interior monologues in which there is no action—not to propel their protagonists in different directions but to deepen dilemmas and increase tension."

Jack Bickham uses the term *sequel* for this period in which overt action cools off, explaining that it begins when the scene ends. He explains that the protagonist then "is plunged into a period of sheer emotion, followed sooner or later by a period of thought, which sooner or later results in the formation of a new goal-oriented decision, which in turn results in some action toward the new goal just selected." So you see that both of these accomplished writers agree that the progress of the book continues from disaster to thought to action and back to the next crisis, much like the roller coaster we have compared it to. Naturally, this is the structural outline of a book at its most simple level. The addition of subplots, other characters and new movement makes it much more realistic and believable.

PLOT

Webster defines this versatile word as "the plan of action of a play, novel, etc." *The American Heritage Dictionary* describes it as "the plan of events or main story in a narrative or drama." Of course, the words "plot" and "plotting" have a variety of other applications. These definitions relate to their use in literary fiction. James Bickham expands those definitions: "It is supremely important for you to remember that a master plot is *not* a fill-in-the-blank proposition, and it's not set in stone. It's nothing more than very general description of the way *one* writer might write *one* novel—the kinds of events he would hope to have happen and generally in what sequence." I frequently make a comparison with the human body. Plot is the skin in which the bones of the book are wrapped. It holds the structure (the sequence of scenes) together by incorporating motivation, ambition, determination, all of the inner feelings that drive the protagonist and make the sequence of events plausible.

What do all those fancy interpretations really mean? In the simplest terms, plot is what occurs to transport the protagonist and the reader from the opening of a book to its conclusion. It is represented by the scenes—the ups and downs—as the protagonist advances towards his/her goal. It is the flow of action created by the intensity of the protagonist's desires. That forces the novelist to consider factors like motivation, justification and personality when producing a quality novel. Pulitzer Prize winner Jane Smiley offers this sage pointer in her book *13 Ways of Looking at the Novel*, "Fiction is not so much about what happens as about how it happens; how it happens is intimately bound up with who does it."

Now that you have a grasp of the action your novel must incorporate, let's move on to the next chapter to understand the Pacing of that action and the basics of Character Development, Description and Viewpoint, for these are the elements that help us understand the "how" that Jane Smiley talks about.

CHAPTER 4

THE NOVEL (CONTINUED)

VIEWPOINT

Stop and think carefully about the story you are about to tell. Before you ever place a word on paper, analyze it from the point of view of each important character, not just the protagonist or antagonist. That will help you determine the primary Viewpoint from which you should write. The story can be told by any one of your main characters or by you, the author. This exercise will help you select the person best qualified to serve as narrator.

The tale can be told in the third person (he, she, it, etc) or in the first person (I). The latter, however, is somewhat more restrictive. An "I" narrator cannot possibly know and relate what each of the characters is thinking, and can only tell the story from his/her personal observation. If that narrator is one of the main characters, and he/she certainly can be, the novelist must be very wary. This is an invitation to skew the story and destroy its objectivity. Since using a first person narrator can be limiting, the author should strive to occasionally reveal the thoughts of others by temporarily shifting the viewpoint to another character. But beware of doing this too freely. It can become extremely confusing for the reader. A far better solution is to reveal the thoughts of these secondary characters through their own words (dialogue) and actions. I strongly recommend to start-up novelists that they use a third person viewpoint (author as narrator) until their skills have become more sophisticated. After all, you, the author, know what is going on in every character's head although you are not a visible player in the story.

It is essential that the reader should be able to identify with the protagonist, whether in a supportive or antagonistic way. While the emotion needed to sustain the reader's interest will surface whether the protagonist is liked or disliked, it is far better if the reader champions him/her, agonizing each time he/she stumbles and cheering when he/she recovers. Most writers and academics agree that books that end with the reader rejoicing because the protagonist ultimately prevails stand the best chance of success.

PACE

You now understand how segments of the book, particularly the "highs" of each scene, create the tension and excitement that propels the reader on. But despite our need to maintain his/her interest, no reader can withstand the emotional pounding of continuous highs without respite. Although forward movement must always be maintained, the speed should vary. That is the key to pacing. When you offer the reader a peek into a character's mind or provide some enriching description or background material to make the character's actions more believable, the pace will obviously slow and tensions diminish.

However, you cannot afford to lose the vibrancy of the story line, so it is crucial that your narrative adds something new to the reader's understanding of your characters or of their environment. That way, forward movement, so vitally important, continues. If in some manner the narrative offers or implies a modicum of tension, so much the better.

While pace should, indeed must, change in a well structured book, there has to be a solid reason for the switch, and it should be reflected in the tone of your writing. Your sentences can turn staccato or flow lazily like a winding river to complement a change in the action of the book or of a specific character. Using active or passive verbs will vary your pace. Active verbs speed up pace; passive slow it down. The length of sentences as well as the number of syllables in the words you choose will affect pace. The judgment of whether to crank up the pace or slow it down is yours alone to make. However, always be on high alert for an artificial change of pace that results from a break in your writing schedule. The longer you are away from the computer the more difficult it is to regain proper pace and effectively move the threads of the story forward.

WORDS OF WISDOM

Jack Bickam in his book *Scene &Structure*: "You can control the pace of your novel at every turn by how you handle your scenes and sequels. If it seems to be going too slowly, you need to build your scenes and possibly trim or cut out some of your sequels…If it seems to be going too fast, you need to do the opposite."

CHARACTERIZATION

The renowned editor and writer William Sloane once said, "The reader reads fiction more for its people than for any other element." The essence of fiction, of course, is the way in which events affect the characters and their interaction with one another. As we have emphasized again and again, the success of a novel depends upon the emotion aroused in the reader by the people he/she is reading about.

More than two millennia ago, the brilliant Greek philosopher Aristotle endorsed the importance of human emotion in drama. In the *Poetics*, his famous treatise still read and admired today, he countered the call for censorship of plays by stating that exposure to the heightened emotions of

Greek tragedy was beneficial and cathartic and freed the spectator's (in our case the reader's) mind from unhealthy inner feelings. If alive today, he would strongly approve of the challenge-resolution sequence that we discussed in the earlier sections on structure and plot. But to develop that level of emotion in our readers and allow them to experience the catharsis Aristotle speaks of, our characters must be strongly defined and real enough so that the reader can feel compassion for them, indeed at times even identify with them.

Carefully observing and listening to the people about you will help you sharpen your ability to draw lively characters. Keen eyesight and sharp ears are the writer's invaluable tools. With a little practice you can use them to fullest advantage. As you see or hear something that helps you create a person who will "live and breathe" in the mind of your reader, jot it down. File it away as a resource to draw upon when it fits the image you are creating.

WORDS OF WISDOM

In his fine book *Show, Don't Tell*, William Noble points out:
"Reality and fiction are never so closely entwined for us as when we're dealing with characterization. It isn't only the sense of identity we feel, it's the fact that characters—people—are what give a story life. Dead characters make dead prose."

HUMANIZING YOUR CHARACTERS

There must be a reason for every action taken by any one of the characters in your novel. Motivation is the key to making action believable, and it will always be found buried in the characters' past. Therefore it is crucial that you know the people you create intimately. Before putting pen to paper, you must probe their past as if you were a government agent conducting a top security clearance. Prepare a chart outlining their education, hobbies, work history, geography, religion, friends and enemies, family relations, physical characteristics, emotional persona, outstanding traits and more. You will find yourself referring to this chart time and again as you progress through the book.

As you design your characters, don't forget that they must possess some flaws, some vulnerability, the human failings that all of us suffer from, or they will not be accepted by the reader. Conversely, you cannot strip a character of all strength, making him/her so weak that he/she can't or won't fight back. In that case, you will have no story to tell because the character will never be able to meet and overcome the challenges with which he/she is confronted.

Stop and think back for a moment to discussions you and your friends have had about books that you read. What is it that captured the bulk of the conversation? I suspect every one of you will answer the characters and their actions because that is what a book is all about. People. What they do, what they say and how they interact. The plot is only as interesting as the characters who people it. They bring your story to life.

As you reflect on some of the fictional characters in books you have read, certain features stand out in your mind. You may recall how pretty she was. It may very likely be emblazoned in your memory because of the disfiguring scar on her right cheek, the result of fighting off a rapist's attack. Or perhaps you recall the odd stride of a retired hockey player who had broken his left hip and leg several times. Whatever it might be, it was a distinctive feature that embedded the character in your memory. I want you to store in your mind the words of Monica Wood, the perceptive author of *Description* whom we will hear more about shortly. She has stated this so well. "Sometimes it takes only one or two details to light up a character for your readers. These precise illuminating finds are the 'telling' details of fiction, for they stretch beyond mere observation to give the readers a larger, richer sense of character…The right details, inserted at the right times, allow your readers access to a character's inner landscape, to his or her peculiarities, fears, and compulsions that cannot be easily explained."

Actions speak better than words in fiction, just as they do in life. One way to make your description of a person more interesting is to include some form of action. For example, change the simple statement, "John had thick brown hair" to "John's fingers disappeared as he ran them through his thick brown hair."

Let's look at another example. Joe has just finished a grueling marathon. Of course, he is tired and sweaty. The reader expects him to be, and therefore stating the fact in those general terms is dull and boring. Draw a specific picture for your reader. "Joe's body, normally erect and animated, sagged as he struggled to return to normal breathing. His soaked shirt, now several shades darker, clung to his body. Strands of hair were glued to his sweaty forehead."

DESCRIPTION

Just as motivation makes your characters and their actions credible and allows your readers to feel sympathy or contempt for them, it is the task of description to turn fictional characters into real people and to create the verisimilar settings in which they function: People you can touch and places you can visualize. In that way, you bring your readers directly into the story, eliminating detachment and to a great degree enticing them to become participants in the events you are relating.

The importance of description is hardly a new concern. In his *Poetics*, Aristotle, the ancient Greek philosopher whom we met earlier in this chapter, credits description as giving "metaphorical life to lifeless objects." Good description creates an image that allows readers to grasp more fully each important element of your novel whether it is one of your characters, an object or the surroundings in which the story develops. It can unfold in a variety of ways, and goes far beyond just visual details that too often are the extent of the beginning writer's tool bag. Much can be revealed by what a character says and the manner in which he/she says it. We will soon talk more about dialogue and how it can become an excellent source of description. Meanwhile, think of all the senses that real people employ every day. In addition to speaking, they see, they hear, they touch, they feel, they smell. Employing each of these senses in your writing can add to your readers' ability to identify with your characters, because these functions are very natural for them and are used throughout all of their waking hours.

WORDS OF WISDOM

William Noble writes in his book *Show, Don't Tell*: "How do we personalize a story so it gets under the reader's skin? How do we touch the reader's sensitivities? We do it by allowing the reader to feel what's happening…(and) to provide the reader with solid information so he or she will grow comfortable with what we want them to identify with. The more they come to know, the greater the chances they will identify, and that's when we get our sympathetic reader."

Exercise caution when filling out your narrative with description. Too much can slow down the action of the book; too little can make your characters robots, not real people. Monica Wood, whom I quoted earlier, warns, "There is no greater (nor more annoying) motion-stopper than immobile chunks of physical description. A head-to-toe tour of a character's appearance, clothing, etc., before we know any thing else about him, is at best ineffective and at worst counterproductive…it stops the natural flow of the story."

Frankly, there are no set rules that determine when you are boring your reader with a surfeit of unneeded information or when inadequate information makes it impossible for the reader to envision a person or place. The decision is instinctive. You, the writer, must be able to determine when enough is enough and therefore just right.

BE SPECIFIC

It is important to be specific in what you write. Generalities don't support meaningful description. Once again, Monica Wood very cleverly sums it up, "Avoid details that call to mind *anybody*, and use the ones that call to mind *somebody*." A flower isn't simply *pretty*. It is *red*, and it is *tall, moist, fragrant, swaying in the gentle breeze, dainty, scalloped* etc. Only by offering him/her a very specific portrait can a reader visualize and identify. Wood's excellent book *Description* is listed in the Appendix. It is well worth reading.

McClanahan goes on to state in her excellent book on description, "Since words are our only tools (in contrast to painters) we cannot afford to be imprecise, to say *knife* when we mean *scalpel*." She points out that while a writer cannot afford to waste words on unneeded description, it is necessary to offer readers enough of an understanding of the personae and the scene to make them comfortable. They then are able to sit back, kick off shoes and meld into the story, reacting

WORDS OF WISDOM

In her book *Word Painting*, Rebecca McClanahan explains: "Use only those adjectives that call forth the qualities of the object; avoid adjectives that label or explain. Words like lovely, old, wonderful, noteworthy or remarkable are explanatory labels; they do not suggest sense impressions. Adjectives like bug-eyed, curly, bumpy, frayed or moss-covered on the other hand are descriptive."

intimately to the people and the place and the action. That is the test of well crafted descriptive writing.

TWO HELPFUL TOOLS

Let's take a minute to look at two techniques that describers regularly use: simile and metaphor. Indeed, simile is used so frequently in our everyday conversation that many phrases have become part of the American lexicon. Think of the number of times you have used or heard phrases like *Hungry as a horse*, *Tough as nails*, or *Sings like a bird*, among many others.

How do these two fundamental descriptive tools differ? The simile uses words such as *like* and *as* in a simple comparison of one thing with another. It "shows" instead of "telling" because it likens a person, object, whatever, to another. Metaphor goes still further. More than just comparing, this tool describes by ascribing some of the characteristics of another person, object, etc to the person, place or object that is being described. It creates an image and invites the reader to use his/her own creativity to expand the image further. Let's view the two tools in actual use:

Simile: David is as lithe as a deer.

Metaphor: Running with the speed and grace of a deer, David effortlessly bounds over the hurdles.

As you can see, both do offer a comparison, but the metaphor actually immerses the character into the essence of the object or person to which he/she is being compared. It draws a much fuller picture for the reader than the simple comparison a simile offers.

Earlier, we talked about "showing" as opposed to "telling," so I will not go into extensive detail here. Both have their use and their place in well written fiction, and both are substantial tools for the writer to use. But you should be cautious and judicious in their use. Too much telling can become dull and repetitious, particularly if you use the technique on a number of characters. Too much showing can overwhelm the reader and blow a character (if not the protagonist) out of proportion. It is wise to follow William Noble's advice in his book *Show, Don't Tell*, "Writing is not a mirror that picks up every facet of our lives; it is a telescope which focuses on certain experiences and molds them. Writing picks and chooses from life."

DIALOGUE

Dialogue is one of the most effective tools a writer can use to allow the reader to penetrate a character's being. Mode of speech offers a great deal of insight into a person's mindset. Pace, articulation, accent all contribute to an understanding of an actor in your fictional story just as they do in life. Speech is a very effective tool to help differentiate one character from another. As an exercise, read an exchange with no attribution between several of your characters to determine whether their speech is distinctive enough to identify each as he/she speaks. Done well, dialogue reinforces a character's distinctive persona and lifestyle. Dialogue can be used effectively in place of narrative to enhance description. Just as his/her speech helps define the speaker, insightful dialogue can also be used to describe another person or a setting without slowing the narrative with dull exposition.

Think of different books you have read and try to recall the way in which a character's speech helped you to draw an accurate and believable picture in your mind. Perhaps one of the finest examples in modern literature can be found in J.D. Salinger's classic *The Catcher in the Rye*. Holden Caulfield, floundering after he has been asked to leave several prep schools, serves as both the narrator and the main character of the book. The young man's discourse, a monologue that lasts for hundreds of pages, is a brilliant reflection of the manner in which a teenage boy of that era would phrase his thoughts.

You must insert distinctive speech mannerisms that reflect the persona of the character who is speaking. You wouldn't allow a cowboy to speak with the same clipped British accent and perfect grammar of an Oxford professor. Use an identifying mode of expression, but be careful not to overdo it, an error beginning writers tend to make. Overworked speech patterns can bore a reader or seem unrealistic when they are read, as opposed to heard. (One of the most remarkable recent examples of using ethnic dialogue extensively can be found in Zadie Smith's *White Teeth*. Without ever turning off the reader, this outstanding first novel uses a mixture of Jamaican patois, Bangladesh, Indian and British accents to capture the mixed urban scene of London.)

WORDS OF WISDOM

In *How to Write & Sell Your First Novel*, the authors Oscar Collier and Frances Spatz Leighton point out: "What brings the plot to life is the characters. What brings the characters to life is dialogue—with each character having his own way of talking. Someone once said if you can't tell which character is talking, if they all sound alike, none of them is talking, it's the author who is talking."

Never forget that a character's dialogue can change as mood changes in response to events that are happening around him/her. Although consistency is primary, as the author you must also be aware of circumstances that can momentarily alter speech patterns. I find that one of the best ways to test my dialogue is to speak it as it appears on the computer screen and determine whether it flows naturally and fits the character and the circumstances.

Real-life people talk in fragmented sentences. They often pause as their thoughts are collecting. Sometimes they offer silly or off-color humor. Even profanity, if used judiciously, can help define a character. (Once again turn to Zadie Smith' *White Teeth* to view an example of what would be profanity overkill in the hands of a lesser author.) Don't overlook the importance of body language in defining your characters. Their expressions and their actions while they talk reveal a great deal about what they are thinking and therefore who they are. There are times when a character can respond to another's comments with body language alone: a shrug, a grimace, tears, laughter, turning away, etc. Incorporate all of this in your story to mold your characters into real people.

Just as people look different, they speak differently. This distinction makes it easy to eliminate identification tags without confusing the reader (John said, Ruth answered) in well-written exchanges of dialogue. Whenever tags are used, try not to overdo the use of descriptive verbs (screamed, whimpered, whispered, etc.). The "tried and true" verb *said* should be the most commonly used in any tag. That way, when the added emphasis of a descriptive tag is used because it is needed for additional impact, the effect will be far greater.

Be wary of boring your reader by allowing your characters to discuss something that has already been revealed unless they are able to add a new perspective or relevant new

WORDS OF WISDOM

Lewis Turco states in his book *Dialogue*: "A writer can learn the rhythms of speech in two ways…By trial and error one can develop an "ear" for dialogue, or one can study language formally and learn about its rhythms the way a poet learns, by "scanning" it and developing an ear according to a program of study."

information. Don't try to present lengthy amounts of background material through your character's conversations. That too can become boring unless there is concurrent action happening to maintain the reader's interest. Remember always, as author William Noble cautions, "Dialogue must advance the story; dialogue must develop character."

TALK AND ACT

An effective way of presenting dialogue is to have your character involved in some activity while he/she is talking. In real life, we are usually involved in some activity while we talk. We may be walking, driving, eating, knitting, pursuing any of a variety of tasks while conversing. Oftentimes our surroundings influence our speech. We may be at the zoo, walking in the countryside, watching an opera. As we talk and something catches our eye, we divert for a moment to mention it. Using some or all of these techniques makes your dialogue much more real and convincing.

WORDS OF WISDOM

In her book *Description*, Monica Wood points out: "Conversations do not occur in a vacuum; the speakers are usually doing something else… (and) physical surroundings can influence what characters say…To make a scene come alive, you must attend to the context of the conversation….Most dialogue needs some descriptive interruption in order to make its full impact."

Ms. Wood goes on in her book to explain that these "descriptive interruptions" can range from a three word dialogue tag (he said angrily) to a "narrative break—a full paragraph (or longer) describing a tent site in the middle of a conversation between two campers."

While complete books have been written on creating a novel—and I urge you to read several of the excellent ones listed in the Appendix under

"Fiction"—the two chapters you have just finished should give you a very solid launching pad for moving forward with your book. Now we'll shift gears from fiction to nonfiction to grasp the basics for creating sparkling nonfiction classics.

CHAPTER 5

THAT'S MY BOOK

For those of you whose goal is marketing a nonfiction book, these statistics from the publishing industry should bolster your confidence substantially. Nielsen Book Scan reports that the U.S. publishing industry posted a 9.3 percent jump in book sales for 2005, but even more exciting is it's finding that adult nonfiction sales grew 9.2 percent, almost doubling those of adult fiction during the year. If you still have any doubt about the importance of nonfiction in today's literary world, click on the Google search engine. You'll discover thousands upon thousands of listings for this topic.

Of course, the nonfiction category covers a huge range of subjects, and you'll be limiting yourself to just one when you launch your new career as a first-time author. Nonetheless, the readership trend toward nonfiction bodes rather well for your chances of reaching publication. Think carefully about the niche that best suits the book you have in mind. *The Complete Guide to Writing Nonfiction* compiled by the American Society of Journalists and Authors lists more than 20 specialties under the nonfiction heading. The choice extends from how-to's to true crime, from hobbies to nutrition, gardening to sports and on and on. If you break down trade journals into their individual industries, you'll come up with many, many more.

WORDS OF WISDOM

Glen Evans, the editor of *The Complete Guide to Writing Nonfiction*, states: "The specialized markets take a backseat to none. They have millions upon millions of readers, and are often more stable and enduring than the huge mass-circulation general giants."

ENSURING YOUR BOOK'S SUCCESS

Most books have their genesis in—or at least some relationship to—the author's life experience. Indeed, it is likely that the book you are contemplating is in some way the product of your own past. Something you did, observed or that actually happened to you made an indelible impression or simply has always interested you. It has stirred inside your head for some time either consciously or unconsciously, begging to be developed into a book, but you had neither the time nor the know-how to write it.

On the other hand, if you are not that lucky, and are finding the process of selecting a subject a bit sluggish, there are places to turn to for help. Thumbing through the long list of periodicals in the *Writer's Market* should jumpstart your thinking. Wandering through your neighborhood bookstore's shelves of nonfiction works will certainly help. Try emptying your mind completely in a silent corner where you won't be disturbed. One by one, think hard about the issues, causes, concerns, events that have meaning to you. Evaluate each by imagining yourself as the reader seeking information. What would you want to know about the subject? Then determine what it is that you can offer the reader that will be of substantial value and justify the hours needed to read your book. Don't be frightened off because the subject you choose has been written about before. New subjects are few and far between, but treatments of the subject can differ greatly and be fresh and vibrant.

What is so new and exciting today is the expansion of subjects available to you. The world of technology has exploded. Medicine has made vast leaps forward. Environmental concerns, personal nutrition and health have taken center stage. Ethics in politics and warfare dominate our current thinking. A perceptive writer will never run out of ideas. The trick is to find one that excites you and evokes real passion, enough to sustain you through months of writing a full-length book. It is a major undertaking, and you will need that kind of ardor to carry you through the many days of dedicated, often lonely, work that lies ahead. Think carefully about your choice. You must be knowledgeable on the subject, but you don't have to be an expert to write intelligently about it. If you have enough familiarity with the topic to employ solid research to supplement your blind spots, you should be able to satisfy a reader hungry for information. Before you finalize your decision to move ahead on the project, devote several hours to a preliminary search. It will show you what sources are available to further your knowledge, and that will help you determine whether it makes sense to continue on. If you have done your research well, people will begin to recognize you as an expert.

FIVE KEY QUESTIONS

Carefully evaluate what you have found by answering these questions:

a. Does the specific approach you intend to use offer enough material to fill a full length book?

b. Should it be limited to a magazine article?

c. How broad is its appeal?

d. Is the audience for the book large enough to interest a publisher?

e. What is different about your approach that will make your book unique?

Once the answers to the questions above validate your choice of topic, it is time to begin the intense research that will make your book a success. Nothing is more important in a nonfiction book than its content. That means you, the author, must supplement your personal knowledge and experience with adequate research to make you an authority on the subject of the book. It goes without saying that the material you include must be timely and interesting. The quotations you include must be exact. Facts and figures, whenever used, must be double checked for accuracy and the information presented in a logical, organized manner. Even more than in fiction, which readers purchase for entertainment, the title and opening paragraphs of a nonfiction book must assure the information seeker that there is a real benefit to be derived from reading your specific book through to its end.

Carefully check *Books in Print*, Amazon, Barnes and Noble and other bookstores to analyze the competition and determine whether everything you have to say has already been said in print. Hopefully not. Moira Allen, Editor of *Writing-World.com*, offers this sage advice, "One final thing to watch for, of course, is a book that is "exactly" like yours. If your book has already been done, your chances of selling it are slim. Keep in mind, however, that there is room for a great deal of variation on a single topic. No matter what has been written on a subject, there's usually room for a different angle, an analysis of a less-explored related topic, or a different viewpoint."

WRITING IN THE AGE OF SPECIALIZATION

The literary world has changed. Nowhere is that more evident than in the demise of some of the large circulation consumer magazines that carry general content while most specialized periodicals remain healthy. That trend is reinforced by the 9.2% increase in readership of nonfiction books that we spoke about in the opening paragraph of this chapter. In this age of specialization, more and more people turn to nonfiction to learn. That is one of the reasons why I spoke earlier about developing recognition as an expert in a specific field. Many journalism schools are now urging their students to specialize. At my own alma mater, Columbia University, the journalism curriculum has recently incorporated several new courses in specialized writing.

The trend toward specialization is good news for both beginners and veteran freelancers. Many of you retirees are highly knowledgeable in a specialty, probably the field in which you have worked for so much of your life. Your chances of breaking into the publishing world are greatly enhanced by that expertise. If you are ready to commit to a full-time career as a freelancer, it may make sense to be a generalist and avoid missing any opportunity that might come your way unexpectedly. With a strong talent for research, you should be able to write credibly on all but the most technical subjects. But even a generalist should cultivate a particular expertise in one or at most two areas. As a newcomer to writing, it is important to build a reputation as an expert. You can start by writing print articles, eZines or even short eBooks on your chosen subject. When you reach chapter 20, you will learn how to produce your eWork and how effective ePublishing can be.

WORDS OF WISDOM

Morris Rosenthal, the publisher of Foner Books (*www.fonerbooks.com*) offers this sage advice: "Writing a nonfiction book requires the ability to write nonfiction. This means you either have to know enough about a subject to write a book, or you have to know how to research a subject sufficiently to write a journalistic style book. I'm not talking about writing skill here, I'm talking about knowledge of and experience in the subject. Otherwise, you might believe you're writing a nonfiction book, but a knowledgeable person reading it would recognize it as bad fiction. There's a lot of really bad fiction written under the guise of nonfiction, generally for a profit motive. Do everybody a favor and write what you know. You'll come out better in the end than if you just pick a hot topic to write about."

RESEARCH RULES ALL

Regardless of the topic you choose or how stylistically you write about it, the success or failure of your nonfiction book will depend on the quality of the research you undertake. Without the facts uncovered during an in-depth program of research and the opinions you obtain by interviewing experts, the book will have little credibility. While you might be able to sustain an op-ed essay or possibly a short magazine article relying on just your own knowledge and opinions, your book will fall apart if it isn't bolstered by more. When you arrive at Chapter 22, study it carefully. It will walk you through the essentials of solid research and interviewing.

Jenna Glatzer, Editor in Chief of Absolute Write (*www.absolutewrite.com*) and a prolific author, counsels, "*Write what you know* is a very good starting place. But that's all it is. It's a place for you to go to get your feet wet, and a place to come back to when the tide gets too high. But it's not a place to stay for very long. A better piece of advice is *Write what you WANT to know*…Think of freelance writing as your own opportunity to learn about all the things you ever wanted to know, and don't worry if you're not yet an expert." Note that Glatzer has included the word "learn" because that's what you do when you research properly and the only way you will qualify yourself to write well about a subject. Actually, this learning process is a great part of the fun of freelancing. Each time you tackle a project, you learn something new.

ORGANIZING BY CHAPTER

The next essential step is to organize the wealth of information you have uncovered from your research, and create a logical, flowing structure for your book. This can range from a very formal outline, the kind you learned to do back in grade school, to something far looser. There are a handful of gifted writers who manage to juggle all of their research findings in their heads, but I strongly recommend using an outline. The way you organize depends on the type of book you are writing: I.E. chronological for true crime and for most histories and biographies; development of a concept for self help; the step-by-step approach of an assembly manual for how-to books. Before I begin to write, I first sort the information, assigning it to specific chapters, and then plan my structure based on the chapter headings I develop.

Once the overall structure has been determined, the internal content of each chapter must be planned as well. Once again, before I start to write each chapter, I amass far more information than I can possibly use, and organize it as the basis for actually crafting the chapter. By doing this, all aspects of the subject are covered, and I have the luxury of selecting those that I think are most important and most pertinent to my readers. I insert the most germane and informative quotes I have found. At the same time I often incorporate my own thoughts and conclusions about the research material by writing one or many paragraphs of commentary. These frequently end up unchanged in the final text. This "creative" combination of selection (the input from my research) and deduction (my own conclusions based on what I discovered) helps distinguish my work from that of other authors and makes the book uniquely my own.

WORDS OF WISDOM

Writer-editor and co-owner of Excalibur Publishing Inc Sharon Good, writes: "People are always looking for ways to enrich their lives and improve their skills. That keeps self-help and how-to books in demand. No wonder then that agents and editors are always looking for unique, well-constructed books in these genres. To write a successful self-help or how-to book, you must win readers' trust by convincing them that you understand their problems and will offer ways to resolve them. You must also provide tools and techniques to further readers' knowledge and skills, and resources for further study or growth."

All of this is part of the creative fun of writing a book. It begins with the thrilling moment your concept finally gels so you can grasp it and move on. You expand your knowledge while you research, and that is equally exciting. Few moments are more exhilarating than when those facts fall into a structure and you can finally envision the book you have struggled to create. Only the task of writing remains, and that is not just stimulating; it is gratifying as well, as the words flow to express your thoughts. If you have done your research and clarified your thinking on the subject, the words do flow easily. Chapter by chapter the book takes shape until you reach the final reward. Your finished book. The opportunity to share your knowledge and your feelings with others. The chance to guide some in their efforts of self-realization; others as they attempt to accomplish something. They have all turned to you because there is something they crave to learn.

CRAFTING A MEANINGFUL NONFICTION BOOK

The quality of your writing, like the quality of the information you offer, will determine the success of your effort. With just five words, the great Ernest Hemingway offered a world of cogent advice: "Easy writing makes hard reading." Although the variety of books classified as nonfiction is quite broad, fundamental rules of writing are applicable to all of them. Very much like the novel, nonfiction books have their own list of essential basics to heed. Let's very quickly touch on several.

COHERENCE We'll start with coherence because it plays so vital a role in tying your book up into a readable, understandable document. It means including every fact and figure that is relevant, while discarding others that are really extraneous window dressing. There must be coherence whether you are relating the tale of a serious crime or explaining to a wanna-be carpenter how to build a house. This is a tightening process that requires a careful review of your words and sentences, paring out those that are not immediately relevant to the subject and helpful to your reader.

RHYTHM AND PACE While discussing development of a novel, we learned of several factors that are essential if the book is to flow smoothly toward its conclusion. They are applicable to nonfiction as well. The pace of your narrative and the rhythm of the words you use relate to the subject matter. In most nonfiction books, they will remain quite consistent throughout, while true crime books and even some histories and biographies will vary pace and rhythm to reflect tension or excitement because they are stories, as contrasted with, for example, a how-to.

STYLE Your style—some call it tone—must always remain your own. It must flow naturally from inside your brain regardless of what type of book you write. Don't try and be cutesy or funny, if you are essentially a serious person. Don't attempt to copy someone else's style simply because his/her book was a success. Be yourself.

DESCRIPTION Just as "show, don't tell" is crucial to good description in fiction, it is equally essential in a nonfiction book. When your how-to subject is gardening, the yard doesn't have "a lot of flowers." Your task is to set the scene you want your reader to envision: "Begonias line the narrow crushed stone path that winds through circles of bright red geraniums and into the garden of climbing roses that lace the picket fence with dabs of red, orange and yellow." A bit overdone, I admit, but stretched to make my point eminently clear. Similarly, no killer should leave the crime scene simply with "blood all over his hands." The struggle was messy and his shirt is "covered with bloody smears that turned to black as they mixed with his sweat."

When you visit a location during your research phase, make sure to describe the scene thoroughly in your notes. That way when you begin to write, the story will come to life and create a greater reality for your reader. While sitting across from your interviewee, jot down notes on his/her attire and on the surroundings, office or home, and how they are furnished. Study your subject, and note any distinctive characteristics in appearance or actions.

THE OPENING In earlier sections dealing with the novel, we spoke of the need to whet your reader's appetite with the title and first paragraph. As crucial as this is in everything you write, it is absolutely essential in the informational categories of nonfiction: how-to, self help and books to which the reader turns seeking guidance. After scanning the opening lines, if he/she is not confident that reading the book offers a real benefit, you can be assured your book will land back on the store shelf. Author Sophfronia Scott writes on *www.ezinearticle.com*, "Once you've figured out what people want, you have to make it crystal clear that you're going to give it to them. You'll do that with the title and subtitle."

As stated before, the opening and the ending are vital to the success of your book. The opening must propel the reader toward the checkout desk. The task of the closing is to leave the reader with a sense of completion and satisfaction to express to other potential buyers. No publicity is more effective than word-of-mouth.

ACCURACY When editing and revising your book, remember you're not just looking for mistakes in grammar, spelling or punctuation. Absolute accuracy is critically important in nonfiction books. Facts must be re-verified to be certain you got them right. Figures too demand rechecking. Review your notes and/or tape recorder to be certain you have transposed all quotations precisely. You will lose not only readers, but your reputation as well if errors occur.

Don't ever assume that the agent or editor to whom you submit your book or the eventual reader will not sense it if you feel any uncertainty about something you have written. Go back again and again until those nagging concerns are alleviated. Agents, editors and readers are just too darn smart for you to believe they will gloss over glitches in the book.

VALUE YOUR WORDS AND THOUGHTS

Before we close this chapter, I want to leave you with a real sense of the importance of what you create when you write and publish a worthy nonfiction book that brings information, support or guidance to others. The value is shared by both author and reader. In addition to obtaining information he/she needs or desires, the reader develops a potential new source to turn to when in need of more. You, the author, not only enjoy the satisfaction of providing that information, but can take great pride in the respect you have gained as an expert in the field.

Dan Poynter, head of Para Publishing and one of the most respected gurus of the publishing industry, often points out that "Authors are highly valued in our society." See how he supports this contention in his WORDS OF WISDOM, and recall his words whenever you get discouraged. I can think of no better way to close this important chapter.

From here let's move on to one of the most popular nonfiction categories, so unique and so popular that it has created its own niche in the literary world—the memoir.

WORDS OF WISDOM

Dan Poynter: "A book provides you with more credibility than anything else you can do… People think if you wrote a book, you know something. And you probably do. When you think about it, you are writing your book from the very best research plus personal experience… You are earning an advanced degree in the subject. Your book validates your expertise and lends more credibility to what you say. There are many justifications for writing a nonfiction book. Some are fame, fortune, to help other people and because you have a personal mission. Can you imagine doing what you love and loving what you do?"

CHAPTER 6

TELLING IT ALL

Although tales of one's life experiences have always held a prominent place under the literary sun, never before in history has autobiographical writing—especially the personal memoir—attained the notoriety that it enjoys today. Way back in the 4th Century, St. Augustine of Hippo wrote his *Confessions*, a memoir that intrigued the world by recounting his evolution from a young bon vivant in Carthage to one of Catholicism's most influential early thinkers. Long before that, the authors of *Genesis* told the story of their earliest antecedents, Adam and Eve and their offspring. Sooner or later in his/her academic career, every student discovers Samuel Pepys, the son of a tailor who rose to become an advisor to British kings. His name is synonymous with the word "diary," and his chronicles of daily life in London still remain fascinating almost four centuries later. Ulysses S. Grant, the Union General who entered the White House in the 19th Century, produced a remarkable two volumes that today are still considered America's premier military memoir. Personal memoirs, autobiographies and family histories have been an integral part of our culture throughout the centuries, but it wasn't until the 1990's that they captured the fancy of the American masses and began to top the best seller lists.

TWO SIDES OF THE COIN

The change was somewhat of a two-sided coin. It brought the memoir not only great prestige and popularity, but disgrace as well. The genre became the tool by which far too many writers unleashed bitter frustrations. In the spring of 2006, the renowned writer and teacher of nonfiction William Zinsser described the phenomenon to listeners of *National Public Radio*,

"Memoir became therapy with lots of bashing of parents, of people who had done them (the authors) wrong...Decencies that made our nation great have been destroyed."

Unfortunately, shock and awe are triggers to huge sales, and as the 1990's progressed, the parade of decadent memoirs grew longer and more raucous. In the same NPR appearance mentioned above, William Zinsser added, "No family (was) too dysfunctional, no memory too squalid or shameful to be trotted out for the amusement or wonderment of the masses...and to fill the carnivorous maw of talk show hosts." By the turn of the century, books like *Running with Scissors* by Augusten Burroughs both shocked and fascinated the public. It has since been turned into a feature motion picture, and has dominated the best seller lists for weeks despite facing a defamation of character lawsuit and persistent questions of its legitimacy.

WORDS OF WISDOM

Mary Karr. whose *The Liars' Club* was one of the leading memoirs of the mid-90's, writes, "In our loneliness for some sense that we're behaving well inside our very isolated families, personal experience has assumed some new power.Memoir—reliant on a single, intensely personal voice for its unifying glue—wrestles subjects in a way that readers of late find compelling."

It was inevitable that the memoir balloon would implode as it continued to test the boundaries of honesty and decency. And implode it did when literary luminaries were taken aghast by revelations from a little known Internet blog, *The Smoking Gun*, that James Frey had fabricated major parts of his memoir *A Million Little Pieces*. Ironically, those revelations, while injuring the reputation of the memoir genre, catapulted Frey to the top of best seller lists and added big bucks to his personal treasury...a sad commentary on the state of ethical and moral standards in today's society. William Zinsser feels this is a reflection of the fact that there is a "crisis of truth in our country."

Despite all of this, a number of fine memoirs were published during this period and the early years of the 21st Century. In 1999, *Angela's Ashes* by Frank McCourt captured the hearts of hundreds of thousands of readers. While not as widely popular, *Night* by Nobel Laureate Elie Weisel was selected for Oprah's Book Club. Newspaper columnist John Grogan's sensitive and touching *Marley and Me* charmed many thousands of readers as it topped the best seller list for weeks.

CATEGORIES OF PERSONAL STORIES

After reading this brief introduction to the memoir, I hope that you better understand its place in today's literary landscape. Before we get down to the nitty-gritty of guiding you through the development of your own contribution to this delightful genre, it is important that you understand the differences between the principal types of personal stories. A journal or a diary is a private document, designed essentially for your own use. Perhaps you may decide to share parts of a journal written about a travel experience or some other specific event with friends or relatives, but for the most part the content is yours and yours alone. Conversely, a memoir, like an autobiography, is written to be read by others. These are public documents, differing from each other only in their structure. Memoirs have no restrictions of time or place. They can be based on timeline, theme, relationships or even geography. They can begin in early childhood and progress to the present. The significance of events and the impact they created can determine the time, the place and the sequence. Autobiographies generally employ a chronological progression from an earlier date (birth or other significant event) to a later one.

PERPETUATING TRADITIONS

Although it has demonstrated its dark side, the memoir remains an ideal instrument for writers to pass on family traditions and histories as they repolish this tarnished genre. But all memoirists, experienced or new, must always be aware of the fact that while memoirs are essentially the writer's perceptions, memory can mislead, albeit unintentionally. Coursing over decades, impressions can change. Therefore, it is important to validate your memories wherever possible by talking with others who experienced those days. That will help you place the events you recall in proper context. Accuracy is something for which the memoirist must always strive. Equally important, however, is portraying the affect events and circumstances had on you, the author, and on others who were involved. Personalizing the impact of the event raises simple history to a far more meaningful and therefore more interesting level for the reader. This should be the goal of every memoirist. By allowing the reader to share the significance of these events, you are encouraging him/her to empathize more fully with you, the author.

WORDS OF WISDOM

Judith Barrington in her book *Writing the Memoir: Truth to Art* explains: "Rather than simply telling a story from her life, the memoirist both tells the story and muses upon it, trying to unravel what it means in the light of her current knowledge. The contemporary memoir includes retrospection as an essential part of the story. Your reader has to be willing to be both entertained by the story itself and interested in how you now, looking back on it, understand it."

SELECTING LIFE EXPERIENCES

Quite obviously, as we choose the events and incidents that illustrate our memoir, the selection process is highly subjective. Lawrence P. Gouldrup, PhD, explains in his excellent book *Writing the Family Narrative*, "As we experience life, we mentally distinguish between those events and personalities that are insignificant trivia and those that have become important and memorable to us. In other words, we constantly bring our own private experiences into focus by seeing events and people in certain patterns."

I feel that the best that can be expected is that the memoirist makes a robust effort to validate each memory and to place it in a context that gives his/her message real meaning. If you pursue that goal honestly and to the best of your ability, you will earn (and deserve) the respect of your readers and your fellow writers.

Very often, events that took place at the same time as the personal experiences you are writing about, whether they occurred at home, in the state, in the nation, even in the world, have a substantial impact on what you remember and how you recall it. If they are at all relevant, include these events for they will add a far richer dimension to the experiences you relate. A good writer offers his/her audience as many details as possible to give greater meaning to the story. Susan Carol Hauser said it well in her book *You Can Write a Memoir*, "When most of us write, we want to convey more than the details of our lives. We want to convey the meaning of our lives and the lives of those around us."

GETTING DOWN TO BUSINESS

So how does one begin the seemingly daunting task of putting these very personal memories on paper? D.G. Fulford, author and creator of *www.familyhistories.com*, states, "Our minds are filing systems. Everything is in there. The merest cue can call up what we thought was lost. The things we forgot to remember." But how do you find those cues and retrieve those elusive remembrances? You may find this exercise helpful. For one week, devote one hour each day to triggering distant memories. Clear your mind of all other thoughts and distractions, and search your memory for past events, holidays, dinners, get-togethers, unique clothing you wore for a special occasion, vacations, even simple happenings like learning how to tie your shoe, and remembering who taught you how. Who took you to kindergarten on your first day of school? How about that special gift you received? What was the occasion and who gave it to you? These are your cues.

Jot down your new-found recollections, and watch with surprise how quickly the list grows. Eventually these memories will begin to form a theme (or context) for your story, a way of looking at your life and its significant moments. That will help you structure an outline to record your life story in a form that the reader can easily grasp. Much like the ups and downs of the novel that we discussed in the preceding chapter, it will be a chronicle of the challenges you faced and the ways in which you overcame them.

QUESTIONS TO ASK YOURSELF

You must answer several basic questions before you begin to put words on paper or even develop the outline, and always keep your conclusions prominent in your thinking. What audience are you writing for? Are you limiting the book to just intimate relatives and close friends? Or are you aiming for a larger audience? Are you gearing toward one sex or the other…or both? What age bracket are you targeting? Audience is particularly important when writing a memoir, for you may want to reveal certain intimacies only to select audiences.

Next you must pre-determine the shape or format of your memoir, particularly the viewpoint you are writing from. (Remember the importance of viewpoint when we discussed the novel?) Are you reaching for a total retelling of the family history of which you are only a single part? Or do you want to write about YOUR life and the influences of family members and others upon it? Think of this decision as the difference between a symphony performed by a complete orchestra or a concerto in which you are the central figure while the orchestra simply offers a frame of reference to enhance your performance. Or perhaps it is neither. You may simply want to highlight some specific events because they mattered so greatly to you. Even though this may result in a looser structure, the viewpoint you write from still remains YOU.

Denis Ledoux, author and director of *Soleil Lifestory Network* (*www.turningmemories.com*) suggests you ask yourself the question "Who is writing your memoir?" He points out that this is not a trick question. It is very a serious one because "you have many parts (of you) vying for authorship of your memoir, each insisting on setting the tone and theme of your story." Ledoux wonders whether you will be the hero surviving all odds or the suffering martyr or possibly even the saint who sacrifices self for the good of family. He points out, "Which part you allow to be the narrative voice of your story will shape the message (theme) you ultimately make."

WORDS OF WISDOM

In his book *Writing the Family Narrative*, Lawrence P. Gouldrup, PhD, states, "Family literature is that piece of writing—prose, poetry, or drama—that emphasizes the family and sees the individual as a part of the larger family unit whether over one or several generations. It does not casually touch on the family; it focuses on the family and sees its subject as units within the family."

INTEGRITY AND OBJECTIVITY

While we talked a bit earlier about integrity in the memoir, it is of such great importance that it must be stressed once again, particularly in view of the recent frauds and fantasies that have come to light. Your recollections must be honest; they cannot be manufactured or twisted just to titillate the reader and sell more books. This is not to say that you can't include salacious material or episodes that were distasteful, even odious, if they are pertinent to the story. But they must be factual and they must be consistent and relevant.

Objectivity is extremely important. It allows your reader to understand the significance of events, persons and places in your tale. Anger and vengeance should never dominate a well written memoir. It is far too easy to fall into the trap of using your writing for revenge. Conversely, if the circumstances are a legitimate condemnation of someone else, have the courage to reveal them as long as you are not doing it purely out of vindictiveness, conscious or unconscious, to "even the score" for something that happened decades ago. In *Angela's Ashes*, Frank McCourt didn't hesitate to present his father as a drunk who abandoned the family, despite the fact that young Frank had a great affection for his Dad.

WORDS OF WISDOM

In his excellent book *Writing About Your Life*, memoir master William Zinsser cautions, "The only pertinent question about any memoir is: is it a good book or a bad book? If you use memoir to look for your own humanity and the humanity of the people who crossed your life, however much pain they caused you, the readers will connect with your journey. What they won't connect with is whining. Dispose of that anger somewhere else. Get your intention clear before you start and tell your story with integrity."

CONSIDER THE REACTIONS OF OTHERS

When the memory of an event is pivotal to you, make it equally significant to your reader by bringing it to life with enriching detail and images. Convert the simple snapshot to a carefully framed art photo. The recollection of a moment is the snapshot we retain from childhood. But there is likely much more to that image that our immature sensibilities never recognized. Now, as adults, we must add a new dimension to that egocentric memory, looking at it from the perspective of everyone involved. For example, you vividly remember a special birthday party at which something went wrong, and you exploded in anger. But you will find many other consequences of that event when you reach beyond your own limited perspective and consider the reactions of others. What about your parents' embarrassment at your behavior? Or your guests' astonishment? The secret to a powerful memoir is placing more catholic flesh on the skeleton of an egocentric childhood remembrance.

Try this example to make the point even clearer. A photograph of you standing in your best dress, covered with a mix of mud and green grass, reminds you of a traumatic childhood incident. You recall your anger when your brother tripped you while the two of you played outside, awaiting the family's departure for an uncle's wedding. But there were many reactions that contributed to that scene and will enhance its retelling: Your mother's upset, your father's concern about missing the ceremony, your brother's fear of a spanking. All of these make that scene so much more real and identifiable to your reader.

WORDS OF WISDOM

Susan Carol Hauser in her book *You Can Write a Memoir* recalls the first bus ride to school, "When I first wrote the scenario about the orange school bus, I expected it to be useful to talk about the vulnerability of children…(Then) I found myself expanding the memory. As I did, my mother started to come into focus, and I realized she also has a story to tell about that moment. As I think about it now, I realize that she might have felt more alone than I did…As children we feel so much but are able to feel so little for others. "

INVITE YOUR READERS IN

Description is every bit as important in writing a memoir as it is in a novel. Properly done, it develops an intimacy between the reader and the characters of the book and helps the reader relate to the incidents you are revealing. You've heard the epigram, "The proof is in the details." Similarly in writing, "The richness is in the details." Add to that the second adage, "Show, don't tell," and you have the formula for a successful memoir… indeed for success in any type of writing, as you saw in the previous chapter on the novel. To refresh your memory, "Show, don't tell" means demonstrating what is happening through action, metaphor, simile, comparison or other techniques of description. It avoids leaving the reader dissatisfied with a colorless adjective. Showing transports the reader to the scene and helps him/her empathize with your characters, perhaps even compare the incident you relate to one he/she recalls from his/her own life.

This intimacy comes from two sources: (1) giving meaningful context to the event, as we discussed above and (2) describing the environment and the people involved in the event in adequate detail to allow the reader to visualize both and relate comfortably to your characters. Here is a simple example of showing, not telling as you describe a character. "John entered the house, his mane of white hair tousled by the wind outside. He grimaced as he tried to lift his arthritic right arm to smooth it down." This offers the reader a far more graphic impression of John than a simple statement that he was old and arthritic.

RESEARCH, RESEARCH, RESEARCH

Research, of course, plays a major role in developing your memoir. While the history you write about reflects your own personal experiences, there are times when research is necessary to verify a fact, to establish the background and motivation for an incident or depict a location accurately. Whatever your need, research can satisfy it. Personal interviews are always helpful, and as a bonus, often unearth additional cues to jog your memory. The Internet, of course, has become an invaluable tool for researchers. The library, genealogical charts, public records (birth and marriage certificates, etc) can all provide you with needed information. Good research techniques are the same regardless of the genre in which you are writing. For a memoirist they are essential. Chapter 22 will discuss them in greater depth.

THE "NEW BOY" ON THE BLOCK

Before closing this chapter on memoirs, I want to introduce you to "Creative Nonfiction," a relatively new term you will hear more and more often. It is an approach to writing that is particularly applicable to memoir creation. Lee Gutkind, a professor of English who founded and serves as editor of the journal *Creative Nonfiction*, describes this increasingly popular methodology as "Dramatic, true stories using scenes, dialogue, close detailed descriptions and other techniques usually employed by poets and fiction writers about important subjects—from politics, to economics, to sports, to the arts and sciences, to racial relations, and family relations. Creative Nonfiction heightens the whole concept and idea of essay writing. It allows a writer to employ the diligence of a reporter, the shifting voices and viewpoints of a novelist, the refined wordplay of a poet and the analytical modes of the essayist."

You now see this writing trend used with increasing frequency in your daily newspaper. While the former approach to news writing was a straightforward formula that spat out "who, when, where and how" in machine gun fashion in the first few paragraphs, today's news columns often read like short stories, filled with anecdotes, descriptions and other devices, formerly the exclusive province of poets and fiction writers.

On *Poynter Online*, the web site of the renowned journalism center in St. Petersburg, Florida, Chip Scanlon describes the technique very simply, "Creative Nonfiction is the latest name for fact-based writing that can perhaps be best understood as the union of storytelling and journalism." It is an ideal writing tool for memoirists who are weaving their life experiences into what they hope will be a tale that is fascinating to others. For those of you who are interested in learning more about this new method, I have listed several good resources in the Appendix.

THE BENEFITS TO YOU

Perhaps the best way to close this overview of the memoir is to offer you this insightful WORDS OF WISDOM by Pulitzer Prize winning author Annie Dillard when discussing her autobiography *An American Childhood*. It illustrates how important it is to plan your memoir carefully, stay on track and maintain context. But even more significant is the personal benefit to you, the writer, that comes from probing your own life and discovering who you really are.

Now that we have been introduced to the three most popular categories of books in the opinion of most retired wanna-be authors, it is important to recognize that writing your book is just the first step in introducing it to the public. Let's now look at the next critical steps: the many options now available to publish your manuscript and the most effective techniques for marketing it.

WORDS OF WISDOM

Annie Dillard talks about her book *An American Childhood*:
"In the course of writing this memoir, I've learned all sorts of things…about myself and about various relationships…I leave out many things that were important to my life but of no concern for the book. You have to take pains in a memoir not to hang on the reader's arm like a drunk, and say, 'And then I did this and it was so interesting.'"

PUBLISHING & MARKETING
YOUR BOOK

CHAPTER 7

A WALK THROUGH THE BOOK PUBLISHING MAZE

It takes far more than a simple roadmap to find your way through the confusing world of publishing today. Major publishing firms—names you readily recognize like Penguin and HarperCollins—have become massive corporate entities, gobbling up many of the other traditional publishers that competed with them. In the 1980's, Bertelsman Book Group, a German firm founded in 1835 began what its web site calls "colonization of the US." And colonize it did in the publishing, music, broadcast and entertainment fields. Beginning with Bantam Books, the world's largest paper back publisher, Bertelsman swallowed up Random House, Doubleday, Knopf, Crown, Ballantine and a number of prominent companies in related industries.

The traditional community of dedicated editors and publishers consolidated into an industry in which bottom-line considerations too often trump quality and diversity. With this shift in the majors' orientation from pride-in-product to financial performance, new writers or those who don't conform to the proven formulae for high level sales find it exceedingly hard to break in. There are always exceptions to any rule, and an occasional rookie does rise to the lofty heights of the best seller list. But those successes are rare.

Many smaller, independent publishers remain committed to the standards and goals of yesteryear. Unfortunately, the companies in this under-$50 million in revenue category don't yet have the clout that the majors wield in the literary world, but they are often more welcoming to new authors. It is reassuring that in May 2006, the Book Industry Study Group, which monitors trends in the industry, described this under-publicized segment of the market as "sizable and growing with surging numbers."

DESIGNED TO MEET YOUR NEEDS

However, all is not negative. The world of publishing has experienced giant leaps in technology over the last several decades. Innovations never before imagined now meet the needs of fledgling authors far better than traditional publishing has. Because they make quick turn-arounds and short press runs possible, they are particularly helpful to first-time senior authors who want to write memoirs, poetry and other materials for limited distribution to just family and friends. Books can now be turned out in any quantity needed, instead of burdening an author with a costly press run of 1,000 or more copies that will rot in the garage. Prior to development of these new technologies, shorter runs were economically unfeasible with per-copy prices reaching astronomical levels. These innovations have also spurred interest in self-publishing by making it easier and less costly.

Let's take a moment to look at the basic technology of printing. If your press run goes beyond 2,500 books *Offset printing*, the technique used for many years, is still the most economical choice. This system prints from plates that are prepared in a complex pre-press operation. Before all elements of an offset press are adjusted properly—ink, plates and the speed of the press—as many as one hundred copies of a book may be discarded due to poor print quality.

By contrast, the new digital presses are able to produce minimal quantities to meet the specific needs of a purchaser "on demand." So the thousands of dollars tied up in unsold books are a relic of the past. Printing perhaps 25 or 50 copies was unthinkable a few years ago, yet that quantity is ideal for many senior writers. Of course, the per-copy price will be substantially higher than if your print run is larger, for it takes the same effort and time to set up the press initially whether you print 50 copies or 500. There are custom printers available who will turn out runs as small as 10 copies. Longdash Publishing in New Jersey (*www.longdash.com*) sets a flat price for printing as few as ten books. The company offers a number of additional pre-print services that range from editing to cover design, *formatting* (preparing your text for printing) and obtaining an *ISBN* (the International Standard Book Number that identifies your book), all of which make a first-time author's life much easier. Each additional service is priced individually.

All of this means it is now possible to turn memories into a finished book, either hard cover or paperback, as attractive in appearance as the big sellers you find in a bookstore. Imagine your memoir or a collection of your poetry or essays, your most cherished personal thoughts, bound professionally, and ready to place on the shelves of dear ones for generations to come. Those of you who harbor dreams of seeing your name on the cover of a novel also benefit from this new technology. If you attempt the traditional publishing path, chances are you will join the ranks of the thousands of other hopefuls, collecting enough rejection slips to paper your office walls. Digital printing, often called *Printing-on-Demand* (POD) and its sister system *Publishing-on-Demand* (publishers who offer full services for a fee, also called POD because they usually utilize digital printing technology) offer the opportunity to shepherd your book into print at reasonable costs and in realistic quantities. In this chapter and the next, we will concentrate on understanding the new innovative

WORDS OF WISDOM

In her book *Writing .Com,* Moira Anderson Allen suggests: "For many writers, POD Publishing offers the best of both worlds. Since books are printed only when ordered, POD publishing avoids the massive up-front cost of printing several thousand copies. Customers, however, can still obtain a copy of a book, complete with a professional cover and well-designed layout."

systems mentioned above. Chapters 9 and 10 will walk you through the traditional approach, analyzing each stage of the process from the earliest days of querying a publisher or literary agent to the joy of seeing your masterpiece on the shelf of your favorite bookstore.

PUBLISHING-ON-DEMAND

Although traditional publishing houses are by far the most prestigious and have long dominated the industry, they often don't suit the specific needs of an author. Either publishing-on-demand or self-publishing using digital print-on-demand technology may well be the better path to take for any of several reasons. The principal benefit, as mentioned above, is the ability to print a short initial run, and then fill in with additional copies as needed. If timeliness is a consideration, because your book is geared to an event or if it is not produced quickly its effectiveness may be lost, traditional publishing may be unsuitable. It is usually a long, slow process, as you will see when we discuss it further. POD technology can produce a book within just a few weeks.

If you self-publish and hire a digital printer, the down side is that all of the preparatory work will have to be done by you. Many authors don't object to that. Indeed they prefer to control every step of the book's production. In addition to editing and formatting your text, you will have to arrange for cover design and, of course, select a printer. There are other headaches as well. For example, the time consuming chores of filing for a barcode, ISBN, Library of Congress number and negotiating contracts with book distributors to place your work in retail stores.

For a beginner seeking professional support, there is great advantage in using a POD publishing house. All of the nitty-gritty chores will be done for you by employees of the company. If you wish, they will even edit your book for a fee. Of course, the price you pay is based on the number of tasks you ask them to perform. So let's take a closer look at the pros and cons of the process.

POD PUBLISHERS

POD houses, once considered unacceptable by the publishing establishment, have gained greatly in prestige in the last five years. No longer do literati sneer that these are businesses preying on inexperienced writers, although as in other fields, POD too has its share of charlatans. You must be careful to avoid them by studying each publisher's literature and contract carefully and speaking with others who have used them. Some authors who have published with POD houses have won prestigious prizes. A handful even reached the best seller level. In her popular web newsletter, well known author and coach Marcia Yudkin recognizes the downside of POD, but feels in many cases the good outweighs the bad. She points out that the stigma attached to digital publishing has faded, and uses as one example the acceptance of POD books by book clubs.

There are dozens of POD publishers currently listed on the Internet. They offer a variety of deals. Most are legitimate and will produce exactly what they offer. But be aware that this is a business, and even for the most ethical of these publishers, the bottom line usually tops their list of priorities. Among the best known in the United States are Author House, formerly First Books, (*www.authorhouse.com*), Xlibris, a partner of Random House Ventures (*www.xlibris.com*) and Iuniverse (*www.iuniverse.com*). In Canada, Trafford (*www.trafford.com*) has a strong reputation. The POD houses listed in the Appendix are all considered quite reputable.

WORDS OF WISDOM

www.yudkin.com by Marcia Yudkin: "With quick access to book buyers, environmental friendliness, creative control and minimal upfront investment, I'm seriously considering publishing-on-demand for books I could easily promote online and sell by mail or through seminars."

Now that the technology is becoming more popular, competition among the growing number of POD publishers is becoming fiercer. They offer clients bonuses ranging from a free or discounted web site to reduced price advertisements in major book periodicals. Before being seduced by these benefits, read and evaluate the offer carefully. Almost every POD publisher promotes the high level of control its authors exercise over the production and distribution of their book. For example, the home page at Author House states, "Unlike some book publishers, Author House authors retain all rights and control decisions around the publishing and marketing of their book. You determine how many and when copies of your published book are printed and you select your own royalty schedule. When your book is finished, it's available for order at 25,000 retail outlets worldwide, on the Internet at Amazon.com, Barnes andNoble.com, and through the AuthorHouse online publishing company book store."

That's a very enticing invitation, but perhaps a bit misleading, although you will find it paraphrased on almost every POD publisher's promotional literature. First you must understand that the ISBN number, which controls the flow of revenue from your book sales, belongs to the company, not to you. Therefore the publisher can set the basic financial parameters, assuring that a healthy share of any sale stays with the company. While it is true that authors "control (*some*) decisions" and "select their own royalty plan," as the POD companies assert, they are very restricted in their choices because the POD house sets a high profit level for itself, leaving the author with a very modest return. The royalty chart you will see later in this chapter will demonstrate this clearly.

Unfortunately, the high per-copy cost that results from this system leaves little opportunity to mount discounted promotions or work out contracts with high volume users like airport bookstores or chain pharmacies and discount stores. Profitable bulk sales are seldom possible when using a POD publisher. Authors can buy copies of their own book, but at a modestly discounted price. Nonetheless, Author House is a highly respectable operation, as attested to by the fact that it currently claims to have more than 27,000 titles in print with relatively few complaints.

The web site of Science Fiction & Fantasy Writers of America (*www.sfwa.org*) lists a number of shortcomings that authors should be aware of when choosing a POD publisher. Some POD houses accept just about everyone who submits, giving the industry the stigma of producing books of poor quality. POD prices are high to allow the publisher to make a profit, often doubling the price of a self-published book. The majority of POD houses do not accept book returns from retailers. As a result, many independent booksellers will not accept POD books. (Author House recently pioneered a program of returns if the author pays an additional fee, and a growing number of other POD houses are now beginning to adopt similar programs. But again, a high fee is charged to participate in this program.) The marketing and promotional programs sold by most POD houses are generally quite ineffective. So while POD houses offer tremendous benefits to first time authors when used judiciously and have an increasingly important role to play in today's publishing world, it is essential to screen carefully before you commit.

CHOOSING A POD PUBLISHER

Step one is to go to the Internet and research under the heading Publishing-on- Demand to find the companies that best meet your needs and standards. Contact them for detailed brochures. They will offer you a variety of programs. The most basic includes publishing a paperback or hard cover, obtaining the needed registrations and placing the book with a distributor, who serves as middleman between the publisher and the retail stores. Pricing is based upon length of the book. A 70,000-word manuscript will probably end up becoming about 300 pages in print. But again, that depends upon the type face, size of page and more.

Mark Levine, President of Click Industries (*www.clickindustries.com*) which offers various services to small business entrepreneurs including writers, has published *The Fine Art of Self-Publishing.* You will find it in the Appendix under self-publishing. Mr. Levine evaluates 48 POD publishing houses, analyzing their contracts and the services they offer. He also ranks the companies by quality with separate chapters listing outstanding, pretty good, just okay and publishers to avoid. You might also click on *www.booksandtales.com/pod/podpublish.htm.* This informative web site lists 30 different POD publishers without evaluating them. However, it offers basic information on contracts, pricing, royalties, distribution and more.

BEWARE OF PROMOTIONAL PACKAGES

A variety of marketing and promotional programs are offered by POD houses for an additional fee. Most of these involve nothing more than mailing out press releases about your new book and supplying some book-marks and postcards. They sound enticing, particularly because you don't believe you have the ambition or the resources to take on this task. Promotional packages are extras, and you are under no obligation to buy them. So don't let this deter you from going the POD route. The extensive support offered by a POD publisher in shepherding your book through the production stages and then bringing it to market can be of great value to the start-up writer. I can assure you that after studying Chapters 12 and 13, both devoted to marketing and promotion, you will be able to mount a productive and cost-effective campaign on your own.

The canned press releases sent out by the POD houses are essentially worthless, and you can probably buy the promotional materials (bookmarks, postcards, etc) they offer from a local printer for a lot less money. Frankly, I don't believe any of the promos sold by the POD houses are worth the investment, but promotional activity is essential if you are looking for sales beyond just your own friends and relatives. You can do it yourself or hire one of the many outstanding literary promoters that are available. They are expensive, but far more effective than the scatter-shot approach of most POD publishers. You can locate them on the Web, but be careful to hire only those with experience in promoting books. You'll find tested professionals listed in the Appendix.

POD ROYALTIES

You will also have to decide the percentage of profit you wish to receive as a *royalty* (the proportion of the profit kept by the author). While additional income may not be your primary motivation for writing, it certainly is a welcome bonus for retirees on fixed incomes. Some POD publishers permit your return to be as high as 50% if the book is sold directly through their own web site. BUT when calculating the percentage you want, realize that the POD house has established its own profit base and will not reduce its level of profit to accommodate your desire for a higher royalty. Since the royalty you choose determines the retail price of the book, the higher the royalty you request, the higher the retail price. For books sold through channels other than the POD house's web site (bookstores, etc), the house allows the author to choose a royalty of 5%, 10% or 15%. However, even the lowest percentage is based upon a price that is usually higher than the standard pricing of a comparable book marketed by a traditional publisher, although it returns a meager royalty to the author.

As an example, a 300-page trade paperback that normally sells from $10.95 to $12.95 would probably be priced at $14.95 at a 5% royalty, returning a "massive" 74 cents to the author. At 15%, the retail price would jump to $18.95, making it essentially unsalable. However, many of these considerations have little meaning for those of you whose work will be distributed to a very small group, and probably given away at no charge. The author's price when purchasing his/her own book is usually discounted by simply deducting the normal royalty amount from the selling price. This chart, produced by one of the major POD publishers for a 300-page paperback, will give you a clearer picture of the royalty program.

BOOKS SOLD ON THE POD HOUSE'S WEB SITE

Royalty % to Author	50%	30%	20%	10%
POD House Website Price	$17.50	$12.50	$11.50	$10.50
Payment to Author	$8.75	$3.75	$2.30	$1.05

BOOKS SOLD THRU RETAILERS

Royalty % to Author	15%	10%	5%
Retail Store Price	$18.95	$15.95	$14.95
Payment to Author	$ 2.84	$1.95	$.74

You can see clearly that even though you paid upfront for the production of your book, the POD house keeps an unbelievably high share of the profits from retail store sales, in the $14 to $19 dollar range. If the house sells your book on its own web site, its profit is reduced to $8 or $9, but still is substantially higher than the author's share.

EBOOK PUBLISHING

The growth of computer technology has made possible a completely new form of publishing. Some of you may already be aware of eBooks, even be readers of this amazing innovation that is growing at a steady pace. Many avid readers who have grown up holding an actual printed book in their hands, hardcover or paperback, consider these newcomers "virtual books." But they are very real and already quite popular. The International Digital Publishers Forum reports that the eBook industry posted a 23% increase in revenue in 2005 over the previous year. (2006 figure were not available at press time.) For the beginning writer, they represent a relatively easy and highly economical means of being published, and by now eBooks are real enough to bring a degree of fame and even fortune. Because they are digital, eBooks are transmitted over the Internet to be read on a computer screen or a variety of handheld devices. Many successful traditionally published books have been re-formatted to eBooks. In the reverse scenario, eBooks have been spotted by traditional publishers and successfully reissued on paper.

WORDS OF WISDOM

Book coach and consultant Judy Cullins, *www.bookcoaching.com* points out: "Writers are always listed in the ten top professions. If you write an eBook you're perceived as knowing something. You're the savvy expert, the authority. It's no longer true that to be credible you need to create a print book through traditional publishing. Trust yourself and your knowledge."

For a senior author starting out, eBooks offer a marvelous platform—generally easier to write, shorter in length and ready to publish the moment you finish. Although some consider the eBook virtual, the task of writing them is very real. Because they know that people turn to the Internet for information, eBook publishers welcome shorter books and particularly like how-to formats. If you write a book that fits that mold, you stand a very strong chance of publication. Because the field is less competitive and far less expensive than going the more traditional publishing routes, it offers a more welcoming approach for the first-time writer. How-to should be a very comfortable format for those of you who have become experts in the career field you have followed for most of your life or in the hobby that has fascinated you. With a little updating and a bit of research, you should be able to turn out a how-to quickly and with minimal effort. As we learn more about the specifics of crafting each category of book in future chapters, you will receive a good deal of guidance on writing eBooks as well.

When you turn to the next chapter, you'll find it is devoted exclusively to self-publishing. The reason is two-fold. Self-publishing is an ideal approach for fledgling authors for reasons you will discover as you continue on. It is also growing by leaps and bounds as the preferred method for many writers, even those that have been published traditionally before. So read on, and discover how digital technology has elevated this once-discredited mode of publishing into a broadly accepted methodology that is growing by leaps and bounds.

CHAPTER 8

SELF-PUBLISHING TO SAVE TIME AND MONEY

At one time, *vanity presses* were the most popular method of assisted self-publishing and essentially the only method. The pitfalls of trying to juggle all of the necessary pre-press work were daunting for authors choosing to try it on their own. Fortunately, that's no longer so today.

Vanities charged extremely high prices to prepare and print your work. Technology that allows short press runs had not yet been developed, so whether authors used a vanity press or handled arrangements themselves as self-publishers, they were forced to order excessive quantities of books to obtain a feasible price per copy, far more than they could ever hope to sell. Most of these books remained in the author's garage or basement until they were dumped for pennies on the dollar to a close-out retailer. With the advances of digital technology now offering Printing-on-Demand and far easier pre-press preparations, self-publishing has emerged as an attractive and cost-effective option. It allows the author to control every aspect of production and sales.

Going this route does involve doing all the preparatory work yourself and of course negotiating a contract with a printer. None of these functions is terribly difficult, certainly no harder than lots of tasks you took on during your active years at the office or plant. As you will see later, there are guides and specialists to turn to for each step…or for all steps, if you prefer, because overseeing the process does require some time and some effort. When you finish reading this chapter, you will understand each step of the process and be able to make a prudent decision whether to tackle it completely on your own, hire a consultant to help you or turn to a traditional or POD publisher.

Consultants like Chris Watson (*www.selfpublishingservices.com*), the full service self-publishing adviser whose WORDS OF WISDOM you read here, will hold your hand as you maneuver through all aspects of prep work and guide you through the entire printing process. If you prefer, they will actually perform each task for you. Of course, the fee is tied to the amount of work involved in the relationship you negotiate.

 Watson claims that many of the major publishing houses are actually encouraging writers to turn to self-publishing. "That doesn't mean a lack of interest," he points out. "Just the opposite: They're looking for the self-publisher to do the ground work, promoting his or her book to the point of regional success." At that point, the "big guys" will be happy to step in and take over what has all the earmarks of becoming a very successful book. Watson mentions *The Celestine Prophecy* and *Rich Dad, Poor Dad* as examples of this.

WORDS OF WISDOM

Christopher Watson, President of PPC Books and a well experienced publishing consultant, states: "The basic reason to self-publish is to maintain control, without which you can't market your book. Despite outright lies (by POD publishing houses) about "keeping all rights" the author basically owns only the copyright. What controls the book is the ISBN, which determines to whom the sales revenues will flow. This is invariably registered in the vanity (POD) publisher's name, not the author's...(so) these publishers call the shots on just about everything."

GOING IT ON YOUR OWN
In this chapter we will cover all of the key aspects of the self-publishing process so that you can move forward with confidence as you transform

your inspiration from dream to print. There is a great deal of additional guidance available for those of you who want to dig deeper as you go it totally on your own, and much of it is free. Two excellent books have been published on the subject, Dan Poynter's *Self-Publishing Manual* and *The Well-Fed Self-Publisher* written by Peter Bowerman. Clicking on "self-publishing" in the search engines will provide more than 56,000 listings. The web site *www.go-publish-yourself.com*, twice selected by Writer's Digest magazine as one of the best sites for writers, offers a wealth of guidance. Another excellent source is *www.writing-world.com/selfpub/index.shtml*, produced by Moira Allen whose sage advice appears several times in this book. Both sites offer newsletters on the subject. You will find a helpful calendar for the varied activities you must undertake by clicking on *www.ksbpromotions.com* the official web of KSB Promotion, and then on "calendar."

Whether you decide to run the show yourself or turn to a consultant to handle all the details, it is important that you understand the process intimately. Join me in a step-by-step tour of self-publishing to prepare you for the critical decisions that lie ahead.

DESIGNING YOUR BOOK

Your manuscript has been finished and extensively edited. You are satisfied that it is as perfect as you can make it. Now the process of formatting the text to conform to the page size of your book and the requirements of the press begins. First you must decide on the size of the book and whether you want to publish in paperback or hardcover. I strongly suggest a standard size soft cover, 5.5inches by 8.5 inches or 6 by 9. Other sizes are available that may be better suited to the specific the type of book you are writing. A cocktail table book, cookbook, some childrens' books, for example, may require different *trim sizes* (printers' terminology for the final size of the page). Understand that not every printer can produce every size book, so before you leap into formatting, select your printing company and learn the configuration its presses can handle. We will discuss choosing a printer in greater detail further on.

Formatting can be done for a reasonable fee by a skilled book designer, and I strongly recommend you go this route for it is a highly technical and complicated process. Designers can be found by clicking on "Book Formatting" on your favorite search engine. If you are brave enough to tackle this complex job yourself, one of the finest guides to formatting is Pete Masterson's book *Book Design and Production*.

WORDS OF WISDOM

On her web site *www.williamswriting.com,* Sandra K. Williams. explains: "Interior book design involves selecting the typeface, its size, and the leading; deciding how to indicate section breaks and the various levels of headings; selecting a format for tables and figures; and more. The design should match the book's subject matter in tone, and be appropriate for the intended readers."

COVER DESIGN

The next choice you face is hiring a professional cover designer or deciding to do it yourself. If you choose the latter, both paid and free web sites are available to guide you. Many pre-packaged designs are sold on the Web. Some are even free. Check the Web under "Book Cover Designers." However, I strongly urge you to spend the money to hire a professional cover designer since the success of your book depends in great part on the eye-appeal of its cover. It is a selling tool as vital to finalizing a purchase as the design of a cereal box on the grocery store shelf. Experts claim a potential buyer surveys the front cover for approximately eight to ten seconds, then turns to the back cover for possibly double that time, placing the book back on the shelf unless something on the cover catches his/her fancy.

Before you reach out for a designer or try to do it yourself, visit the library or a bookstore and study the covers on works that are similar to yours. You may know a qualified graphic artist, but try to find one who has had specific experience designing a book cover, for it is an exacting specialty. When you entered "Book Cover Designers" on the search engines, you located a variety of qualified artists. Whether you hire one of them or not, go to their web sites and evaluate their work. Most will post a variety of covers they have done, one of which may trigger a design to meet your needs. In fact, you should be able to harvest a number of workable ideas after reviewing these. Consider contacting one or more of the quality designers found through the Appendix.

There are three parts to every cover. Each one serves a distinct, but vital, role. The front attracts, gives the name of the book and author and possibly a one-line commendation or endorsement. The back cover is made up of several sections: a brief précis of the book, excerpts from reviews, recommendations from worthy sources, a brief bio of the author and space for the barcode and ISBN. These are all designed to SELL your book, so make sure they are punchy and inviting. The spine is that narrow portion of the cover that binds the pages together.

WORDS OF WISDOM

Moira Allen, editor of *Writingworld.com,* **points out:**
"If there is any part of your book that should be farmed out to a professional, it's your cover. Too many self-published books come out with low-quality cover art that is the "dead giveaway" of the do-it-yourselfer. Unless you are an experienced graphic artist, this is NOT something that you should attempt on your own. Fortunately, there are scores of inexpensive cover artists who can help you."

Never forget, the *spine* is the first thing seen when books are lined up on the shelf. It usually contains the name of the book, the author and the publisher.

While we're talking about covers, heed this important reminder. Many beginners forget to ask their printers to supply them with 100 or so unbound covers. Salespersons for book distributors use them to show your book to buyers instead of lugging a large number of heavy books along. These extra covers will have a variety of other uses when you begin to promote your book.

THE NITTY GRITTY

With the writing and editing complete and design well underway, the tasks of obtaining an *ISBN* (International Standard Book Number), bar codes and registering your book with the Library of Congress will be your next responsibility. You may also want to register a copyright for your book. None of these activities is terribly challenging or even costly. The ISBN is an international numeric code to identify your specific book. Bar codes have the same function, but are read electronically. A Library of Congress catalog card number is a unique identification number that the Library of Congress assigns to the record created for each book in its cataloged collections. Librarians use it to locate a specific Library of Congress catalog record in the national databases and to order catalog cards from the Library of Congress or from commercial suppliers.

R.R. Bowker (*www.bowker.com*) is the official supplier of ISBN numbers, and can produce bar codes for you as well. By using these uniform codes, book publishers, printers, retailers and customers world wide can pin point the specific volume they are seeking. While on the Bowker web site, make sure to register for your free listing in *www.booksinprint.com*, the most widely used compendium of books currently in print. Information on registering for Library of Congress control numbers is readily available at *www.loc.gov/index.html*, then click on "Publishers."

The next step is registering for the Library's Cataloging in Publication Program (CIP). Before it is published, the book is listed in detail in the program. The same information will be included later on the book's copyright page to facilitate processing by book dealers and libraries. Register at *http://cip.loc.gov/cip/*. It may be wise to ask your neighborhood librarian to help you register, since the CIP program doesn't always welcome self-published books. But a librarian can expedite the registration for you. For a modest fee you can choose to have the Donohue Group create your CIP registration. Go to *www.dgiinc.com* and click on PCIP.

As we learned earlier, your work is copyrighted from the day it is written. However, that protection is not an effective defense if you end up in a courtroom charging someone with infringement. By filing a formal copyright with the government, you are protected under all circumstances. Filing can be done through *www.copyright.gov*. Click on "Forms" to obtain the necessary applications.

SPECIAL TASKS

Most books include several sections that in effect stand alone. They are very different in style from the text you have now completed, albeit closely related. It is up to you whether you want to tackle the task of creating some of the special portions of the book or hire a professional to produce them. The decision in great part is a function of your budget. Some experts recommend you devote all of your efforts to promotion and marketing and farm out sections like the index, appendix and table of contents to specialists in each category. These tasks demand a good deal of time. That's why professionals charge substantial fees for their services.

Indexing is probably the most time consuming of the special tasks. If you attempt it yourself, make certain to wait until your book designer has submitted the finished format of the book with its page sequence. Don't make the fatal error of creating the index before the text is in final form or you will have to change every page reference. Check out the American Society of Indexers (*www.asindexing.org*) for professionals. Try to find one with experience in the subject matter about which you are writing so he/she can make intelligent choices when selecting references to include.

Since the Appendix, in contrast to the Index, doesn't require references to text pages, I prefer to create my Appendix as I write the book. I develop categories, and place them in alphabetical order. Whenever the text contains something that should be referenced, I enter it under the appropriate category. Obviously, I keep adding categories as the book moves along. When I have completed the writing, I then return to the Appendix and complete any adjustments I feel are needed to make it more accessible and informative for my readers.

I also create the table of contents myself. Although Microsoft and others have programs to accomplish this, I find it relatively easy to do it with no help. It is important, however, that the TOC of most nonfiction categories, certainly how-tos, be expanded to give a sampling of what each chapter contains. (Turn to the TOC for this book for an example of what I mean.) This not only helps the reader, but also boosts sales because a buyer often will review the TOC to determine whether the book contains enough information to make it worth purchasing. The last of the special pages, the copyright page, should be formatted by your book designer to include the Library of Congress CIP information and other requirements.

LISTING THE SPECS FOR YOUR RFP

Before you begin contacting possible candidates for the print job, it is essential that you chart the specifications you have set for the book. The criteria you send to each candidate must be identical so you can effectively evaluate and compare the responses you receive. Since you chose to negotiate yourself, the decisions you must make include: page count, trim size, type of binding, interior color, 2-or-4-color cover, weight of paper stock and packaging of books when shipped.

What questions should be included in your RFP (Request for Proposal) when you contact candidates for the printing job?

1. The format required when the manuscript is submitted.

2. Price. It is wise to submit several levels of press runs so that you can determine the most economical one to suit your needs. For example, you might request costs for 250, 500 and 1,000 copies, including cover.

3. Scheduling of proofs. You must receive and review a *blueline proof* (the final proof before printing) or something comparable before the book goes on press. Once you have a basic agreement with a printer, you can discuss other proof needs for pre-publication reviews and promotional purposes.

4. Delivery. Books are heavy and the cost of shipping can be substantial, particularly if the printer is located a distance away. You must specify whether the books will be delivered to one or more locations. If you are using a *fulfillment house* (mailing service that packages and ships books to fill the orders you receive directly) or storing a large quantity with your *distributor*, you will want delivery made directly to them to avoid double shipping. For easiest handling and the best protection for the books, I suggest shrink wrapped bundles with no more than four dozen books in a carton.

CHOOSING THE PRINTER

This critical task demands both careful thought and research. It is one of the most important choices you will make. The visual quality of the book and the resulting level of sales depend in great part upon the printer you select. You have already learned that there are two basic forms of printing that are used in manufacturing books. Digital printing is done with laser technology, and is the best choice for short to medium press runs. If you contemplate a run of more than 2,000 books, offset printing should be your choice. It is far more economical for long runs.

If your memoir, book of essays, poetry or other limited edition is geared exclusively to family and friends, it makes sense to seek a specialist in very short runs. As an example, I mentioned Long Dash Publishing (*www.longdash.com*) in an earlier chapter. While the price per copy is quite high because of the very limited run, you save by eliminating the wasted copies of a longer run from a printer incapable or unwilling to turn out so small an order. Check out the Long Dash web site. Entering "POD printers" on the search engines will provide you with additional choices for both short and medium length press runs. Entering "Offset Printers" will do the same when longer runs are needed.

As mentioned in the list of RFP questions, location is an important consideration when selecting the right printer. Long distance shipping costs can become quite high because of the weight of most books. In addition, having a printer close to home makes it easy to meet in person throughout the printing process. At the very least, you will probably want to be present when the books first roll off the press, just as graphic designers almost always attend press runs to be certain the result is exactly what they agreed upon.

DETERMINING QUANTITY

Now that you know the price structure of the printer you selected, you can determine the most appropriate press run. That decision is directly tied to the marketing and sales program you plan for your book because the length of the press run in great part determines your cost-per-book. If you anticipate retail sales at bookstores and through the major online booksellers, your price must be competitive with those charged for similar books of the same approximate size. If you plan mass marketing (airport stores, discount stores, book clubs, etc), you must take into consideration the fact that you will be forced to discount substantially. Of course, your press run will be a lot larger, so your per-book cost will drop proportionately.

If possible, you should attempt to develop as many prepublication sales commitments as you can. These will be to book clubs, mass marketers as well as to organizations and businesses that may want your book for promotional or training purposes. Cementing these commitments in advance makes it possible to increase your press run without fear of being inundated with unsold books. This is one of the situations where *Advance Review Copies* of your book become so valuable. They are the most effective tool to introduce your book to potential quantity buyers and through reviews to retail buyers. You will learn more about these ARCs later in this chapter.

Many consultants advise that your initial press run be based on a realistic estimate of the number of books you anticipate selling in one year. Consultant John McHugh suggests,

WORDS OF WISDOM

On the web site *www.publaw. com/mchugh.html*, John McHugh, a widely respected publishing management consultant, advises: "Calculating the number of copies to order for the first printing of a new book is a complex business decision involving several factors and variables. To determine the optimal first print order, you should understand financial concepts, publishing procedures and practices, and perhaps most importantly, your customers and marketplace. No one "lock step" formula for selecting the number of copies in the first printing will be right for you."

"One helpful rule is the worst-case/ best-case scenario. Evaluate both scenarios; then, select a middle-ground sales forecast that leans toward conservatism and caution."

Once again, you must always keep in mind the obvious fact that the longer the press run, the lower the cost per copy. That's because the initial setup of the press is a major factor in the cost of the run. Preparing the press will cost the same whether you order 100 books or 2,000. When that set-up cost is spread out over a smaller number of books, the price-per-book obviously rises. The following example of pricing is based on bids for my recent novel, *Blood Bond*. It will demonstrate this clearly.

Press Run	250	500	700	1000
Total Cost	$2572	$2859	$3099	$3399
Per Copy Cost	$10.29	$5.72	$4.42	$3.33

In this case, the price drop from 250 to 500 copies is so dramatic that it would make sense to step up, even if it means gambling on sales of a larger quantity. The differential for a total order of 250 or 500 is only $287. I would not entertain the 700-copy level because the per-copy cost is not that much lower than it is on a run of 500. Conversely, if my sales projections are high enough, I might go directly to 1000 copies or more, and capitalize on the dramatic drop in cost-per-copy.

The key concern is being competitive, and printing is the most expensive aspect of production. A visit to your local bookseller will help you determine the price at which you must sell your book. There is no exacting formula for pricing. The most recent I have seen is the rule of thumb Peter Bowerman includes in The *Well-Fed Self-Publisher*. He suggests,

"Price your book at roughly four to six times the cost of your paper, printing and binding."

ADVANCE REVIEW COPIES

The printing that we have just talked about is not the only print run you will commission. Well before the official publication date of the book, you will need *Advance Review Copies* (also known as *Advance Uncorrected Proofs* or *Bound Galleys*). These are short runs, printed digitally and bound inside your book cover. They closely resemble the final book, but may still have minor uncorrected typos. The wording on the cover should state "Advance Uncorrected Proof." These have several important uses. Some of the most prestigious reviewers like *Publishers Weekly, Kirkus, Library Journal* and others insist upon these advance copies. They will not review a published copy of the book. ARCs should be sent to these prepublication reviewers approximately three months prior to your formal publication date. ARCs are also an invaluable tool when you seek blurbs for your back cover and longer endorsements for use inside the book. They are also essential for advance sales to book clubs, as you learned earlier. I have included a list of key prepublication reviewers in the Appendix.

I advise you not to scrimp on sending out review copies, whether they are in galley form prior to formal publication or the finished book afterwards. Favorable reviews generate strong sales. You should be able to send out an ARC and the accompanying publicity information for approximately $5.00. Sending out the finished book for later reviews will be even less.

DISTRIBUTING YOUR BOOK

You are going to have to contract with a book wholesaler or book distributor or possibly both to bring your book to market. It is particularly important to you as a first-book self-publisher to understand how they differ from one another. In short, wholesalers essentially serve as a central location for libraries, retailers and other entities to purchase books. Distributors too stock books and sell directly to retailers. They also supply the wholesalers and major users like Amazon. In addition, distributors usually have active sales forces that promote your book, while the wholesalers seldom do more than list your book in their catalogs. Frankly, you will have to use your ingenuity to be accepted by any of the major distributors or wholesalers as a one-book author.

Ingram (*www.ingrambook.com*) and Baker and Taylor (*www.btol.com*) are among the largest wholesalers in the industry. Ingram concentrates primarily on distribution to retail stores, while Baker and Taylor is heavily into the institutional market that includes schools, universities and libraries. Smaller, specialized and regional distributors can be extremely helpful in the marketing of your book, especially if it is a niche publication. John Kremer provides an excellent list of these on his web site *www.bookmarket.com/ distributors.html*.

Ingram generally will not deal with a one-book publisher, although it is possible to convince them otherwise if you have developed the kind of marketing and promotional program that will lead them to salivate as they envision the vast quantity of books they may be able to move. But that will take some doing. Ingram, however, does work with a cadre of distributors. If you can convince one of these to handle your book—probably using the same tempting approach—

WORDS OF WISDOM

In his *Self-Publishing* Manual, industry guru Dan Poynter writes: "Self-publishing is where the author bypasses all the intermediaries, deals directly with the editor, cover artist, book designer and printer, and then handles the distribution and promotion. If you publish yourself, you'll make more money, get to press sooner, and keep control of your book. You'll invest your time as well as your money, but the reward will be greater."

you may be able to open the door to Ingram's services too. Click on *www.ingrambook.com*, then go to "New to Ingram" in the top menu. Click "Publishers" to find some of the affiliates with which Ingram does business. The site also lists a number of distributors, some of which have a direct affiliation. Peruse the list and check out the web sites of the ones that interest you.

FULFILLMENT

Aside from marketing and promotion, the last major task for a self-publisher is making certain orders are processed swiftly and accurately when copies are ordered. This can occur in a number of ways. We have discussed contracting with a wholesaler or distributor, an approach that makes most sense when you have written a mainstream book, and you are eager to place it with as many book retailers as possible. If you use a distributor, the added bonus is the active sales staff the company employs. Wholesalers simply warehouse and fill orders with no sales effort, as you read earlier.

If you produced a niche book, you may not care a great deal about placement in retail bookstores. You know your audience, and you plan to reach it precisely with your marketing and promotions. You may decide to sell directly from your web site or by telephone or mail, thus eliminating the heavy discounts demanded by distributors and wholesalers. With a modest investment, you can develop a complete retail operation right on your web site. Chapter 19, devoted to "Making Your Site Pay," will walk you through all of the on-line mechanisms necessary to receive, process and ship orders, and even accept credit cards for payment.

FULFILLMENT HOUSES

With minimal sales as you start up, distribution may not be too onerous a task if you have chosen to do it on your web site, but as sales hopefully grow, you will find yourself spending the majority of your time processing orders instead of promoting your book or possibly beginning another. You probably will have no desire to remain a retailer. That's where *Fulfillment Houses* come into play. These companies are essentially warehouses to which your books are shipped by the printer. The house is equipped to fulfill every order you receive from a single book to bulk shipments requested by a wholesaler, distributor, book club or other entity. For single copy sales, electronic equipment is available to relay all ordering information from your web site directly to the fulfillment house, which then packs and ships the order. If you prefer, you can simply aggregate the orders manually and ship them to the fulfiller. You have the choice of creating invoices and sending them to the fulfiller for inclusion in the customer's package or having the house prepare invoices for you. Some fulfillment houses maintain a toll free number for direct customer ordering. They answer it generically, allowing you to promote that number as your own instead of contracting for toll free service yourself. Of course, each additional function involves a fee, but in many cases it is far more cost-effective to use the house's staff than to try and do all of this yourself.

In round figures, when the fulfiller accepts a direct order from a retail customer on its phone, processes the credit card and then packs and ships—in essence, handles the entire sale for you—your cost will probably be less than $5. If you do all the processing yourself, and ask the house just to pack and ship, that fee drops below $2. Postage, when using *Media Mail* (formerly called *Book Rate*) will cost you only $1.59 for a book one pound or less and $2.07 for weights up to two pounds. (Rate based on 2006 U.S. Postal Service *A Customer's Guide to Mailing*.) While orders should be processed promptly, the savings gained by using Media Mail instead of First Class justify the few extra days it requires for delivery.

One thought to bear in mind is the added cost when you instruct the printer to ship the initial order to your home office and later decide to retain the services of a fulfillment house. You then must transport the books from your garage or other storage location to the fulfiller, adding substantial expense if the shipment is large or the distance far. If you have the confidence to invest in a sizable press run, it makes equally good sense to sign on to a fulfillment house at the outset, and have the bulk of your book order delivered there directly.

MARKETING, BOOK REVIEWS AND MORE

Earlier in the chapter we touched on reviews when explaining the need for bound galleys for prepublication reviewers. In the past, snaring quality reviews was a difficult task for a self-publisher. That prejudice still exists today, but at a much reduced level. If a book is well written and professionally produced, most reviewers will willingly accept it for review. The best technique for obtaining reviews is included along with many other effective marketing and promotional tools in Chapters 12 and 13. Study them carefully. Using the guidelines we discuss there for promoting, marketing and capturing reviews is essential for every author whether published traditionally, with POD or self-published.

YOU'RE NOW IN BUSINESS

Once you begin to sell your books, whether directly to the reader or through retailers, you are in business. You basically have two choices. You can operate as a *sole proprietor* or *form a corporation*. Your personal accountant can assist you in making the right decision and guide you through the process.

In either case, expenses pertinent to your new business are tax deductible, and that includes even major outlays like printing, fulfillment and promotion. But you must keep detailed and accurate records of both income and expenditures to satisfy the Internal Revenue Service. Ask your accountant for guidance on setting up a simple, but functional system. I also recommend strongly that you open separate bank and credit card accounts for the business. It makes a great deal of sense to keep your business affairs separate from your personal dealings.

Now that you understand the basics of self-publishing a print book, let's take a look at the steps involved in following the traditional publishing route to give you the opportunity to compare the two approaches. The next two chapters will walk you through the process from opening the door with an agent or directly with a publisher to the final tasks that are crucial to bringing your book to market.

CHAPTER 9

FOLLOWING THE TRADITIONAL PATH

You've been introduced to publishing on demand, and in the chapter just finished, you explored the key elements of self-publishing in detail. But until now we've said very little about bringing your potential best seller to life through the traditional publishing path. This is the route to choose if you are confident that your book will appeal to a wide cross-section of readers…if your goals are fame and fortune…if you envision your work flying off the shelves of bookstores and topping the lists of powerful .com booksellers like Amazon and Barnes and Noble.

When you choose this route, you must be willing to wait for many months, sometimes spilling over into a year or two, to see your book in print. If there is a timeliness to your work, think carefully before you leap into traditional publishing. In the time it can take the system to move your masterpiece from initial query to retail shelf, the book may become passé.

Traditional publishing is very different from either POD or self-publishing. It is a joint venture in which the author is totally dependent on a cooperative effort that generally starts with a literary agent and later extends to a publisher. In limited cases, it is possible to bypass an agent and submit directly to a smaller, independent publisher, but I urge you to try and contract with an agent and reap the many benefits he/she will bring you.

The first challenge you will face is finding an agent who will accept you as a client. That's not an easy task. Convincing a top quality agent to represent your book is frequently more difficult than placing it with a publisher. But this is one task that is well worth the effort it demands. During your career years, I am sure that there were times when you found it advisable to use a specialist to get something done. Maybe a middle man to make a sale or an expert with contacts as well as knowledge. That's the way I'd like you to view literary agents. Before we learn how best to approach these remarkable expediters, a subject we'll cover in detail later in this chapter, I want you to understand the great benefits an agent brings to you.

> ## WORDS OF WISDOM
>
> John F. Baker, the editor of *Macmillan's Literary Agent, A Writer's Introduction*, says, "Literary agents are the uncrowned kings and queens of the book publishing industry today. Publishers and editors, who have traditionally held that hallowed position, may strenuously object, but there seems to be little doubt that it is the agents who, often for better and occasionally for worse, have shaped the current literary landscape."

OPENING A PUBLISHER'S DOOR

The major difference between placing an article and submitting a complete book is that few freelancers utilize the services of a literary agent when they submit to periodicals, but agents play a crucial role in the search for a book publisher. Most majors will not accept a book proposal unless it is channeled through an agent. Perhaps you consider that an unnecessary and time consuming step added to the other difficult challenges facing an author who seeks publication. The answer is yes and no. Certainly it represents another hurdle to overcome. As we stated above, many in the field agree that finding an agent is as hard, often even tougher, than finding a publisher. On the other hand, a knowledgeable agent with strong personal contacts can pave the way to success, and in most cases is your only entrée into a major publishing house.

As you learn more about the critical role these specialists play, you will realize why they are so valuable to an author, particularly to one who is just starting down this challenging path. Despite the fact that some mid-size and smaller book publishing houses will entertain a manuscript the author submits directly, I again strongly advise anyone pursuing traditional publishing houses to retain the services of a qualified agent.

THE INSIDE TRACK

So what are the other benefits a literary agent brings to you as a budding author? Agents are invaluable to all writers, but especially to newcomers. They become your alter-ego, representing your interests with publishing houses. Strong agents have solid personal relationships with acquisition editors. A recommendation from one of these can open doors that would otherwise be slammed shut to a beginner with sparse credentials. Agents will work hard on your behalf because their compensation is calculated as a percentage of the author's earnings. That means, of course, that an agent must be very selective before accepting a new client since his/her income depends entirely on the client's level of success.

Qualified agents understand the orientation of different publishing houses and are familiar with their imprints. They carefully direct your work to those that will be most receptive. They know the tastes and idiosyncrasies of individual editors and to whom to shop your book most effectively. In turn, editors trust the professionalism of the agents they have come to know personally. They have confidence that the agent has carefully evaluated the quality and salability of a book before risking his/her reputation by recommending an inferior product. That frequently means your book will be placed at the top of the pile at the publishing house, and read a good deal faster and in a more receptive frame of mind by a harried editor.

Agents' lunches are legendary, and occur frequently. Agent and editor meet in a social environment to share views and do business in a cordial and relaxed way. These lunches benefit both participants and are critically important since an agent's worth is directly dependent on the personal contacts he/she has established in the industry.

AFTER ACCEPTANCE

The major role agents play during the submission process doesn't end once a publisher accepts your book. Their value continues. They function as your personal advocate, shepherding the book through the many steps of the publication process, starting with negotiation of your contract. No author should ever attempt to strike a deal with a publishing house without an agent or a literary attorney sitting alongside at the negotiating table. This is a very specialized field, and requires the skill of someone who understands rights, fair compensation, advances, promotional assistance, subsidiary royalties (movies, clothing, book clubs, etc).

Knowledgeable negotiators ensure that all possible benefits—bonuses, high quality printing, engaging cover design and the myriad other details that only someone with intimate experience in the field can anticipate—are built into your contract along with all necessary protections. As your book moves through the manufacturing stages, the agent will bird-dog the process for you, and later will monitor royalty payments. Since the agent's income (usually 15% of your earnings) is directly dependent on the payments you, the author, receive, you can be assured he/she will make certain payments are timely and complete.

FINDING THE PERFECT MATCH

Begin by studying the *Guide to Literary Agents*. It is published annually by Writer's Digest Books, and will tell you the type of books represented by the 600 agencies listed, as well as recent sales, contractual terms and how best to make contact. The listing often includes any special interests or concerns a specific agent may have. Check in the Appendix for a list of additional agent directories.

Once you have selected a half dozen or so potential agents, study the web site of each to gain additional insight into their personal and professional preferences. These are very revealing, and will provide details on the form the agent prefers for submission—query letter, overview, partial proposal or full book proposal. There are also web sites that rate agents. Books are available that feature in-depth interviews with agents that probe their thinking, bias and preferences. All of these can be quite helpful as you move through the selection process. A monthly newsletter, *Talking Agents*, published by Agent Research and Evaluation, is available in hard copy. The company also produces an informative web site *www.agentresearch.com* and offers customized searches for agents, although the fee is rather high.

Regardless of the genre in which you write, it is well worth your time to study the web site of the Science Fiction & Fantasy Writers of America, Inc (*www.sfwa.org*). This organization has made it a regular practice to brief writers on dishonest and misleading agents and publishers. I'm not terribly pleased to have to warn you that there are charlatans posing as agents, but as you know from your own life experiences, unpleasant realities do exist. Fortunately they represent a very tiny fraction of the agent population. One of the surest signs that an agent may be questionable is the offer to read your manuscript and help you improve it for a fee. In the industry, reading fees are an adamant no-no. If you heed the guidance in this book and others on the subject, you will avoid the minority of frauds who tarnish the reputation of a highly respectable industry.

One effective way to avoid the clutches of a charlatan is to make certain the agent you select is a member of *AAR*, the Association of Authors' Representatives. This highly respected group was formed in 1991 by the merger of the Society of Authors' Representatives and the Independent Literary Agents Association. Most responsible agents are members. The letters AAR will be found in their listings in directories. AAR is a not-for-profit organization that maintains a strict canon of ethics. Take a few minutes to peruse the AAR web site (*www.aar-online.org*). The code of ethics will help you in your choice of an agent. Also review the questions AAR suggests you ask an agent before signing a contract for his/her services. One word of caution. It is wise to wait until an agent indicates he/she has decided to accept your book before you begin firing off any of these or other questions.

> ## WORDS OF WISDOM
>
> One of the more respected literary agents, Peter Rubie, writes in his book *Writer's Market FAQs*: "Agents should make their living from the commissions they earn on selling a writer's book. If the agent has to earn his living by charging the author such things as reading fees and editorial services, there is an inherent conflict of interest....My advice is: Don't go near him. Reputable agents, with one or two exceptions, don't charge reading fees, nor do they provide reader's reports."

QUERY LETTERS

There are two documents that you must understand fully if you are to deal successfully with an agent: the *Query Letter* and the *Book Proposal*. You will use these even if you choose to go directly to a publisher. The query's task is twofold. It must sell you as a competent professional, and it must sell the book you propose to write. Perhaps the best analogy to demonstrate the importance of the query is to compare it to the audition of an actor. Fortunately, there is one major difference. The performer rises and falls in the single instant of an audition. As a writer, you can take as much time as you need to edit and polish your query before sending it out. You must rework it until it represents the most concise and best writing you can achieve, because the query is the first and possibly the most important sales tool you have. Properly done, it will open the door and lead to an invitation to submit a detailed book proposal. If you have already written your book, you may be asked to submit it in its entirety. However, a finished manuscript is mandatory only when pitching a novel. Both agents and publishers will accept a nonfiction book proposal that contains only two or three sample chapters. You will learn about book proposals and how to design them in the next chapter.

Your query letter must be professional and straight forward, very much like the correspondence you prepared when you were in business. Don't try to gain attention with cutesy ideas like using colored paper or colored ink. Use a basic type font, preferably Times Roman 12 point, and check carefully to make sure no typos or errors in grammar slip by. The recipient's preference, found on his/her web site or in a directory of agents or publishers, will determine whether you send the query by e-mail, fax or postal mail. Never forget to include an *SASE* (self addressed stamped envelope) if you send it by mail. Without it, you will probably never receive a response. Indeed, the agent may never bother to read your query if it does not include an SASE.

Although not mandatory, it is helpful to create a one sentence *hook*, a catchy phrase that capsulizes the essence of the book. An example for the book you are now reading might be "Retire the WRITE way." Place it at the top of your letter to entice the agent or publisher to read further. Many times a first rate hook becomes a key aspect of the marketing and promotion of the book after it is published. Just as a zippy hook will be effective in selling the book to a reader, it will be equally successful in attracting an agent or publisher.

KEEP IT SIMPLE AND FACTUAL

As you prepare your query, it will help to think of it as a "business inquiry," not a literary masterpiece. A sample query can be found in the Appendix to help guide you. Stay simple, factual and punchy. Get the facts out quickly. Agents respond best to a one-page query. Your lead paragraph must tantalize the agent; make him/her long to represent you. Follow the lead with an expansion of the topic to give the agent an understanding of what the book is all about. Perhaps you'll add a significant quote, if you have one. Or list some of the key sources you use to give your book credibility. Be specific. Do not use generalities. For example, you're not proposing a story on politics; you are doing it specifically on the Presidential primary election of such and such a year. The angle you have chosen to write about is the value of the extended reach of paid TV advertising compared to the person-to-person effort of a local ward and district organization. This paragraph is designed to place the meat on the skeleton of your hook, which asks, "Is paid TV advertising electing our American Presidents?"

Here is another example to make this point even clearer. You are not writing a book on birthing. Your subject is cesarean section and its psychological impact on the mother. The hook may be "The *heady* repercussions of a cesarean birth." Get the idea? It's as simple as that. I know that with some thought you can do far better than my quickly formulated hooks. But

WORDS OF WISDOM

Literary agent and author of *Writer's Guide to Book Editors, Publishers and Literary Agents,* Jeff Herman warns: "To maximize your success as a writer you must do more than hone your ability to write; you must also learn the qualifications and the disqualifications for success…. Publishing is a business, and agents tend to be the most acutely business-oriented of all the players. That's why they took the risk of going into business for themselves (most agents are self-employed)."

hopefully they capture the essence of what I am trying to convey to you. Be exacting about your subject; don't generalize. If the subject is particularly timely, emphasize that to the agent.

SELL YOURSELF

Now that you have outlined all the reasons the agent can't afford to pass your book by, you must sell yourself. After all, the book is only as good as the person writing it. As a beginner, you have limited writing credentials to offer. But in the case of a nonfiction book, you are an expert on the subject you chose to write about. You are drawing on a lifetime spent in a given industry, profession, trade, hobby or sport. If the one-page limitation keeps you from properly expressing your qualifications to write this book, it is permissible to enclose a separate page that discusses your background. This should not be the standard resume and job history. It must be tailored specifically to why you are qualified, indeed are the ideal candidate, to write on the subject you have chosen. Include any other information that you feel is pertinent. Stress any writing experience you have. Never point out that you have no writing credentials. The agent will know that from the absence of any writing credits in your narrative.

From their directory listings and their web sites you can readily learn the genres book agents represent, so there is no excuse for pitching a book to an agent in which he/she has no interest and therefore no strong publisher contacts.

Hopefully your query will entice an agent or a publisher to learn more about your masterpiece. If so, he/she will ask for a book proposal. Turn to the next chapter to learn the secrets of a top notch proposal.

CHAPTER 10

PROPOSING, BUT NOT
ON BENDED KNEE

You passed stage one with flying colors. Your query letter was a success, and the agent of your choice has invited you to submit a full book proposal. The likelihood that at last you may see those long months of creativity actualize into a book seems a lot more real. Sure, there's reason to rejoice, lots of it. But remember, you are only at stage two. Whether you graduate to the next level will be determined by the quality of the book proposal you submit.

For nonfiction books, busy agents and harried editors almost always insist upon a tightly written book proposal, usually 20 to 40 double spaced pages long. That assures them that tackling hundreds of manuscript pages is worth their time and effort. Contracts are often drawn based solely on the quality of the nonfiction proposal. For many of you, the proposal will remind you of the way you prepared offerings or other documents that were designed to sell your products in your past professional life. While the attributes of what you are trying to sell differ greatly, the essence of the sales pitch remains the same.

Don't wait until you've written every page of your nonfiction book before submitting a proposal. Several sample chapters included as part of the proposal are actually all you need to sign on with a willing agent and following that to receive a publisher's go-ahead.

If your work is fiction, agents and editors almost always will want to see and evaluate the finished book, not a proposal. Occasionally they may ask for a synopsis or outline of several pages to prejudge whether it's worth their time to read the book in its entirety. But no fiction manuscript will be accepted by an agent or placed under contract by a publishing house before it has been completed by you and read from beginning to end by the agent. The reason is simple to understand. Style and pace are key elements of fiction writing and cannot be portrayed fully in a proposal. A nonfiction book depends on the information it contains and on the ability of a knowledgeable author to present accurate, current and meaningful facts. That can easily be demonstrated in a well-crafted proposal. While not every expert agrees, I feel it makes sense to submit relevant portions of a book proposal even when submitting a completed novel. Sections such as the Hook, Synopsis, Marketing, Promotion and Author's Resume can help greatly in making the sale.

THE JOB OF A PROPOSAL IS TO SELL

Your challenge is to convince agents and editors that they will miss a great opportunity if they pass up your book. A strong proposal covers content, author's qualifications, marketing, promotion and the competition the book will face. It must analyze the potential readership and explain why this book is unique and superior to any other currently in print or about to be released that deals with the same or a similar subject. Factually describing the potential market and the way the book and the effort you mount are designed to attract that market will give both agent and publishing house confidence that the book will sell. Simply put, that means they'll make money. And that's what they're in business to do. But flowery adjectives or the praises of close relatives and friends who have been privileged to read the manuscript won't do the job. Everything in the proposal must be supported by hard facts.

Your book proposal becomes a major expansion of your query letter, and like the query, it must be clean, crisp and neatly prepared without typos or grammatical errors. Once again, the type face of choice is Times Roman 12 point, and the text is double spaced, ragged right on a decent quality of standard white paper. Pages should be numbered consecutively at the top accompanied by an identifying *slug* (one or two-word identifier for the book). Because the competition is so fierce in traditional publishing, it is essential that you take your time to go over your proposal and rework it again and again until you are confident that it is as near perfect as you can make it.

Not surprisingly, many authors find it easier to write a book than to write the proposal designed to sell it. Few authors are top notch salespersons, but most do have the writing skills to convince an agent or publisher that it would be a mistake to pass up this unique opportunity. There is a wealth of information and guidance available in books like those from Peter Rubie, whom we quoted above

WORDS OF WISDOM

Michael Larsen opens his book *How to Write a Book Proposal* with this first sentence: "Book editors have an insatiable craving for new writers and new ideas...The challenge is to get the proposal to the right editor at the right publisher at the right time."

and Michael Larsen whose WORDS OF WISDOM appears above. Many agents are extremely helpful and offer guidance on their web sites to fledgling authors. The *Books for Life Foundation* founded by Mark Shaw, author of 14 books on writing and publishing, offers a hands-on CD *My Book Proposal, The Complete Software Program for Aspiring Authors and Poets*. It can be purchased through the website *www.markshawbooks.com*.

No one can better guide you on the challenging journey that Mr. Larsen describes than a literary agent. Both Peter Rubie and Larsen are right on target. The competition that Rubie describes is intense, but as Larsen points out, the industry still must attract new writers and new ideas to survive. Consequently, both publishers and authors turn to the literary agent as matchmaker. While it takes a well-formulated proposal to snare an agent, once committed, he/she will be of indispensable help in polishing it still further and targeting the right publisher to get results.

COMPONENTS OF A BOOK PROPOSAL

There is no definitive format for a book proposal. The recommended approaches of experts like Rubie, Larsen and Shaw differ slightly, but all three agree on the basic premise that a proposal is a selling tool, not simply a display of your literary talents, and should be addressed as such. While a written book proposal is used almost exclusively for nonfiction, there will be times when in conversation or later correspondence, you may want to use some of the components of a proposal to convince an agent or editor that your novel will be a success commercially. Therefore I advise even fiction writers to read on.

Now let's dissect a book proposal, analyzing the whys and wherefores of each segment.

COVER LETTER: This will be much shorter than the query letter you wrote, and really serves only as an introduction. Your most outstanding qualification to write this book should be quickly stated here, as well as the name of anyone who has referred you to this agent. Don't be afraid to remind the agent of this, even if you included the information in your earlier query. Referrals are excellent door openers with agents. The narrative hook that we talked about in the last chapter should also be included. Everything else of worth can be incorporated in the proposal itself.

TITLE PAGE: Place your contact information in the top left corner of the page (name, address, phone number, email and/or fax address). Unless it is unusually long (more than 30 characters), enter the book title in 28 point *bf caps* (bold face capital letters) half way down the page. If there is a subtitle, it too should be centered, but in *bf ulc* (upper and lower case) 16 point type one half inch below the title. A half inch below that, center the word "By" in 8 point type bf ulc, and a half inch below that, center your name in 16 point type bf ulc.

TABLE OF CONTENTS: Use a fresh sheet of paper. Center the header "Table of Contents" in 16 point bf ulc at the top of the page. Then list each section of the proposal in 12 point bf ulc with corresponding page numbers in the same type:

Table of Contents

HOOK: Also called *tagline*. As briefly explained, this should be a short, pithy description of the book in one or at most two sentences. Type it in 14 point bf ulc as a stand-alone on a separate page.

OVERVIEW: There is some difference of opinion among the experts on this section of the proposal. I usually suggest beginning the overview with a one-sentence statement on the anticipated length and the time it will take to finish writing the book. A three-to-five-page narrative, depending on its complexity, should follow to give the essential outline of the book and its themes.

Peter Rubie feels the overview should be a narrative explaining the need for the book, why it is unique, how long it will be, how much time you require if it is not yet finished and why you are the ideal person to write the book. Mark Shaw uses the overview to summarize the book and give the reader a solid feel for its content. Jeff Herman, one of the gurus of agenting whom you will meet later in the chapter, synthesizes both of these approaches. His choice is a short synopsis of the book combined with a description

WORDS OF WISDOM

Although their book on pitching a novel, *Give 'Em What They Want,* is geared to fiction, the principles Blythe Camenson and Marshall Cook outline are equally applicable to nonfiction: "It (the synopsis or overview) is not a blow-by-blow, scene-by-scene outline…It's a summary with feeling. …It's a good read with strong narrative writing in the present tense…You'll need to summarize your story in just a few pages."

of the key selling tools. I feel that the selling points should better be sprinkled throughout the proposal. For example, the uniqueness should be stressed in the section on competition, while the reason you are the perfect person to write it should be demonstrated by the section on the author. The section on marketing potential is an ideal place to emphasize the need for the book. I leave it up to you to choose the approach you feel is best for your book.

THE AUTHOR: Here again you will have to make a judgment. If your credentials are outstanding either as a writer or as an expert in the subject you've chosen to write about, this section should be placed right after the overview. If you are an inexperienced writer with just modest credentials as an expert, it might be wiser to place the bio further back following the section on promotion of the book. Note also that the bio should not be the standard resume that you used in the business world. When describing how your background and experience prepared you to write this book, you must convince the agent that you are the ideal person to write this book. He/she doesn't care whether you are married and the father of three children unless you are writing a book about family life. The agent wants to hear about your education, professional experience and writing credentials (and these include any writing you have done in the course of your business or professional career like manuals, special letters, reports, etc). The bio should include anything that contributes to your ability to produce a successful book.

MARKETING POTENTIAL: A carefully developed analysis explaining the potential market for your book and the way in which you plan to reach that market will be a powerful factor in convincing an agent or editor that there is a need for this book. Your task is to convince them that the audience waiting to read it is sizable enough to generate a substantial income for the agent and a profit for the publishing house. This segment of the proposal should describe each group of readers who will respond and why. Their interest may have been sparked by their personal background—religion, ethnicity, hometown geography—or by their career, hobby, recreational preferences, genres they like to read or even unfulfilled desires or ambitions.

WORDS OF WISDOM

Literary agent Jeff Herman describes the Marketing Section of a proposal in his book *Writer's Guide to Book Editors, Publishers and Literary Agents*: "This is where you justify the book's existence from a commercial perspective. Who will buy it?...Don't just say something like 'My book is for adult women and there are more than fifty million adult women in America.' You have to be much more demographically sophisticated than that."

There may be organizations of people who share those interests and represent possible sources of bulk sales of your book. These should be described in some detail in the proposal. Perhaps businesses in the field you are writing about might adopt your book as a giveaway, a reward or a sales tool. You may anticipate a cooperative event with your favorite charity in which you donate a portion of every sale. Perhaps a membership drive by that charity or by an organization of fellow hobbyists might include your book as a gift for new members. If you are a member of a club, organization or professional society in the field you are writing about, your fellow members represent a strong potential for sales. Don't overlook the possibility of reaching for classmates from high school and college or the neighborhood in which you grew up or lived for a length of time as an adult. Many people take pride in the success of a "hometown boy or girl," and will buy your book because they remember you personally or simply because you lived or currently live in the area. List all of these potential sales possibilities, the more the merrier, in your proposal as long as you can realistically justify them.

COMPETITION: The fact that other books have been published in the field you select can be an asset by demonstrating the popularity of the subject. However, it becomes a liability if you are unable to show the uniqueness of your work…how it differs, expands or even improves upon the competition's treatment. You're undoubtedly familiar with many books that have been written in your field of interest, nonetheless a careful study of *Books in Print.com*, available at your library, is essential. This impressive volume lists more than five million books by author, title or subject. Titles that are in production, but not yet released, are catalogued separately in *Forthcoming Books*. Information on both of these can be found on the publisher's web site, *www.bowker.com*. Use your findings to strengthen this section of the proposal. Mention several of the best known titles and show how your book differs from them. Again I stress, the key to success here is emphasizing the way in which your book stands out from the crowd, even though the general subject matter is the same.

PROMOTION: This section demonstrates the techniques and tools you plan to use to reach the potential readership outlined in your marketing plan. Publishing houses today are not the free spenders of yesteryear when cross country book tours and other costly promotions, including paid advertising, were financed by the publisher. Those days are gone, and only highly recognized authors are able to command that kind of support.

However, your book can be promoted in many ways, some paid and others at no cost. All must be included in the package you describe here. Don't overlook any opportunity, large or small. As you study Chapters 12 and 13, you will discover the multitude of ways in which you can attract buyers for your book(s). Include as many as you justifiably can in the proposal. Free publicity, available in a variety of forms, can range from a book review to a print or broadcast inter-

> ### WORDS OF WISDOM
>
> **In Book *Marketing from A – Z*, young adult book author Ellen Feld advises:** "Try non-traditional markets. I have found that craft fairs are an excellent place to sell my books. You can try small, local events or larger more regional affairs. Vendor's fees are fairly low so your costs will be minimal. (Also) look into attending an event that centers around your topic."

view. Book signings or something as tiny as a notice of your new book in the class listings of your alma mater's monthly magazine or a local community newspaper should be pursued. Size of a publication alone does not necessarily determine its effectiveness; its discrete readership is what allows you to target an audience that is most likely to respond. Explain how you plan to promote your book on your own web site, as we discuss later in the section that introduces you to the Digital World. If you anticipate allocating monies to hire a professional PR firm, say so in the proposal. Listings of qualified literary publicists and respected book reviewers can be found in the Appendix.

Advertising can be quite costly depending on the circulation of a newspaper or magazine or the reach of a radio or television station. But again, size alone is not the determining factor in deciding where to place an ad. It is highly likely that an inexpensive ad in a local community newspaper, read by people who live in your hometown and its immediate surroundings, will generate more sales than one that appears in a large newspaper whose circulation is spread over a much larger area. Similarly, a small ad in a trade publication covering the industry or hobby you are writing about will be more effective than space bought in a large general circulation magazine. However, paid ads in the book sections of large national or regional papers like the *New York Times* or the *Los Angeles Times* are particularly effective (but very expensive) because their readers are devoted to literature. Big or small, costly or inexpensive, every promotional opportunity will add to the sales of your book and to the income the agent and publisher receive. So don't be shy about mentioning them all in this section of the proposal.

WORDS OF WISDOM

How to Get Celebrity Endorsements & Testimonials for Your Book, an article by Jordan McAuley published on the web site *Contact Any Celebrity.com*, explains: "Getting a celebrity, notable VIP, or leader in your field to give your book a short testimonial or endorsement (sometimes called "blurb") is a great way to boost sales and garner extra publicity. Remember that this is a trade-off. You get a testimonial for your book, and the endorser gets additional exposure and/or credibility."

ENDORSEMENTS: Although they cannot be considered pure promotional efforts, endorsements of your book on the back cover or an introduction by a well known individual can greatly boost interest. And they will certainly generate sales. While you may not be able to obtain firm commitments before the book is completed, begin as soon as you can to make a list of every realistic possibility that you intend to pursue and why. You may be lucky enough to snare an expert who allows you to use his/her name in the proposal without first reviewing what you have written. If your book relates to your former life's work, reach out for contacts you developed during those years. It's likely some may have enough confidence in your knowledge to allow you to include them in the proposal. In today's marketplace, the sales potential of your book is the primary factor in decisions made by agents and publishers, so spend some time exploring every avenue of promotion that you can support with facts or figures, always keeping your plan real, not "pie in the sky."

CHAPTER DESCRIPTIONS: Since organization of a nonfiction book is vital to its success, the purpose of this segment is to show the agent or editor how your book moves from beginning to end. This is not needed when submitting a novel, since the agent or editor can study the execution and the flow of the book from the completed manuscript you supply.

This section should resemble an expanded table of contents. Starting with Chapter 1 (or the Introduction if you have written one), place chapter number and title in 14 point bf ulc centered. Follow with a succinct outline of the chapter, its goal and its flow in 12 point Times New Roman. Keep this simple, but lively, to hold the agent's interest. It should take no more than 10 to 15 lines, single spaced, to capture the essence of each chapter and point out its importance and reason for placement. Do not use separate pages for each chapter; leave three or four spaces between the end of one chapter and the heading of the next.

SAMPLE CHAPTERS: In the case of a nonfiction book, the agent or editor will want to see an actual sample of your writing style and ability. You need send no more than two or three chapters. Select the very best and most exciting. They do not have to be in sequence, although it is helpful if the chapters demonstrate continuity. Most authors choose to send the first three chapters, whether it's because they consider them the best or they have not completed or fine tuned succeeding chapters. Sending a completed novel obviates the need for sample chapters.

BOOK-TO-FILM: Mark Shaw adds this additional section whenever the nature of the book makes it applicable. Certainly in the case of fiction as well as in nonfiction books that retell a live event or occurrence, pointing out the potential of converting the book to a motion picture makes a great deal of sense. It boosts interest in the proposal by indicating a possible added source of revenue. If you are aware of previous successful films that dealt with the subject matter, use them as examples. As in the case of competitive books, try to show how a movie based on your book will be different, indeed better, than the previous films that you cite.

Well, you've done it. Your superb proposal sparked enough interest to land you a contract. What happens next once the euphoria has passed? We now move on to follow the complex path your masterpiece will take before it arrives on the shelves of your favorite bookstores.

CHAPTER 11

IT'S A GO!

After weeks of waiting, of agonizing anticipation, the telephone rings. Thrilling news comes from an agent who likes your proposal and is ready to accept you as a client. (Or possibly from a publisher if you attempted to query directly.) If you still feel as comfortable after talking in person with the agent as you did when your initial search indicated he/she was an ideal choice, you are probably safe negotiating an agreement yourself, particularly if he/she is a member of *AAR*, the Association of Authors' Representatives. Agent agreements are usually quite straight forward, so many authors negotiate them on their own. Others feel more comfortable if they are represented by a literary attorney. However, if you attempt to deal directly with a publisher without an agent or a literary attorney to assist you, be wary. Publishing contracts are full of pitfalls for the writer, and you can quickly discover that you have "given away the house." You need legal support, and the best person to give it to you is an experienced literary agent or literary attorney. Some authors prefer to use both, so that nothing slips by. Even those of you who have spent a lifetime in the legal profession or who have had extensive experience in negotiating business contracts would do well to retain the services of one of these professionals. They understand the intricacies of this complex field.

Even if you choose to hire a literary attorney to guide you, familiarize yourself with the potential risks you take when you sign a publishing contract. That way you and the attorney can discuss more fully all the protections you need or desire. For example, it is not just a matter of negotiating the percentage on which your royalties are based. You have to understand there is a substantial difference between calculating payment on the retail price of the book or on the publisher's net receipts after retailers and distributors deduct their commissions. Of course, the author benefits from the former, while a publisher would prefer to base royalties on net receipts. The issue of *rights*, which we will discuss in detail a little later, is tricky and requires a level of expertise if you are to receive everything you are entitled to. There are *publication rights* (these deal with permission to publish the book) and *subsidiary rights* (book club sales, serialization, sales of merchandise and movie rights related to the book). There are also questions of foreign rights to be negotiated.

WORDS OF WISDOM

In his book *Writer's Market FAQs*, literary agent Peter Rubie warns: "Publishing contracts are heavily weighted in favor of the publishing house. The boilerplate contract usually tries to take a share of every earning possibility the publishers can get their hands on. What's more, publishers want writers to work at the publisher's convenience, not the writer's convenience. If you're not careful, a contract can mean it could be two years or more before your next book is legally able to be published."

Many excellent sources are available to background yourself on these difficult matters. You read Peter Rubie's warning on contracts in the WORDS OF WISDOM above. Turn to Chapter 7 in his book *Writer's Market FAQs* where this well experienced agent dissects a sample contract with extensive explanations of what every clause means and its ramifications for you, the author. For another detailed discussion, see whether your library has a copy of Jonathan Kirsch's informative book *Kirsch's Guide to the Book Contract*.

HELPFUL LEGAL ADVICE

Two organizations of writers are extremely helpful to both members and non-members on matters of legal protection. As a beginner, you probably won't have the credentials for membership in the Authors Guild (*www.authorsguild.org*), one of the most respected of the organizations that advocate on behalf of freelance writers and authors. But you can visit the group's web site and click on "contracts" in the main menu, followed by either "books," "periodicals" or "Internet," depending on your needs. You will find extremely helpful information on what to watch for in negotiating a contract, and it is free. If you are not yet able to qualify for membership in the Guild, you may want to consider

the National Writers Union (*www.nwu.org*), another forceful advocate for the rights of writers. The NWU provides quality assistance on contract matters. Annual dues for either will be in the $90 to $95 range for those of you whose income from publishing is either negligible or non-existent. The National Writers Association (*www.nationalwriters.com*) invites its members to submit contracts and agreements for review. The organization cautions that since there are no attorneys on staff they cannot offer legal advice, but as experienced members of the industry—many on their staff are published writers—they can make basic suggestions. If they feel you need more guidance, they will help you find a quality attorney.

PROTECTING YOUR RIGHTS

The question of *rights* often frightens new authors, so it is worth taking a few minutes to understand them. They are an important aspect of your publishing contract, and play a major role in the distribution of your book or article and in the income you receive from your writing. There are three basic publication rights, each of which defines the geography in which your work or even part of it can be distributed by the publishing house: *North American Rights* (United States and Canada), *World English Rights* (expands that to include any English-speaking country) and *World Rights* (includes all foreign editions and translations).

The term *Subsidiary Rights* includes a broad array of permissions including paper back and electronic publishing, motion pictures, sales to book clubs, serialization and manufacturing of commercial products that have a tie-in to the book. These can be lucrative, so it's important that you have an attorney or agent who will fight to maximize your control of these rights. When your contract is prepared, be certain that all rights will revert back to you if the book goes out of print or if the publisher fails to reprint within a specified time following a request to do so from you.

COPYRIGHT CONFUSION

I am sure every reader of this book has heard the term *copyright*, certainly those of you who have followed a career in business or law. However, not all writers fully understand what the term means despite the impact it has on their careers and income. When they submit their precious manuscripts, beginning writers in particular frequently fear that an unscrupulous editor may pirate their idea and/or actual text, a concern I would advise you to put out of your mind. Such incidents are so rare today, they don't merit your concern.

The federal government's latest version of the copyright laws went into effect in January, 1978, and for the first time, authors were granted explicit protection of their work from the moment it was created. They no longer had to wait for actual publication before they were protected. That should reinforce my recommendation that you not worry about editors pirating your glorious prose. Under the revision, the copyright lasts "for a term consisting of the life of the author and 50 years after his death." While it is not required for protection, many authors include a copyright notice on their work before allowing anyone to read the manuscript. Simply place the word "copyright" or the symbol "c" with a circle around it, your name and the year on the first page of the document. This does not require permission from the government copyright office.

For even further proof that you are protected, send a copy of the manuscript to yourself by registered mail, and do not open it. File the sealed envelope and contents for future use if needed. This is called "poor man's copyright," and offers no formal legal protection. If you want to ensure that you are totally protected in the event of future litigation, you must register your work with the U.S. Copyright Office located at 101 Independence Ave SE, Washington, DC (205)559-6000. As an American author, you cannot file an infringement suit in court unless the work has been officially copyrighted by the government.

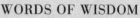

WORDS OF WISDOM

The official web site *www.copyright.gov* **explains:** "The way in which copyright protection is secured is frequently misunderstood. No publication or registration or other action in the Copyright Office is required to secure copyright. Copyright is secured automatically when the work is created, and a work is "created" when it is fixed in a copy or phonorecord for the first time. If a work is prepared over a period of time, the part of the work that is fixed on a particular date constitutes the created work as of that date."

COPYRIGHT COVERAGE

It is essential you understand that general ideas cannot be protected by copyright. Only your specific treatment of an idea can be protected. That means, in its most simplistic terms, copyright will protect only the specific article or book you prepare, not the general subject matter you are writing about. For example, if you write an article or book on the benefits and convenience of using a digital camera to take travel and vacation photos, it does not preclude other authors from writing about the benefits or aspects of using a digital. However, they cannot plagiarize your piece to any major degree, even rephrasing your text, and calling it their own. Click on the official web site of the U.S. Copyright Office, (*www.copyright.gov*) to obtain more information.

PATIENCE, PATIENCE, PATIENCE

You've resolved all contract questions and the document has been signed by your publisher. Unfortunately, months and months will roll by before you have the thrill of seeing your book on the shelf of a bookstore. Those months (that too often morph into years) are filled with gleeful highs and moments of despair as you work with the editor who has been assigned to your project. The process may seem endless to the majority of you who were accustomed to fast decisions and speedy implementation during your working years. But you must understand that it is the editor's job to evaluate every sentence in the book, offering advice, suggesting or even insisting upon certain changes that can range from modest reworking to a major restructuring of a chapter, possibly even a major realignment of the flow of the book.

Simple *line-editing* requires changes in a sentence or paragraph. Structural revisions can be far more extensive. You have every right to discuss your editor's instructions, even object to them. You may be able to demonstrate successfully why your approach makes more sense. But in the final analysis, the editor is the boss. His/her reputation is as much on the line as yours. Recognizing the lengthy experience and literary sophistication most editors bring to their jobs, it is usually wise to heed their advice.

When you and the editor finally agree that the manuscript is as perfect as you can make it, it is moved on to another level of review by *copy editors* who oversee all aspects as it progresses toward production. Once the book has been *copy edited* (screened for errors in grammar and spelling as well as for errors of fact and inconsistencies), you will receive the manuscript back and be given several weeks to review the corrections and answer any questions the copy editor may have raised. This is a crucial step in the process because it represents the last time that changes can be made without substantial additional cost and loss of time.

A month or two after you return the copy-edited manuscript, you should receive *galley proofs* (today many houses call them *first-pass pages*). These are prepared after all the changes and corrections have been completed, and reflect the image of the type as it is configured to fit the pages of the book. In other words, it is now typeset in final form. Once again, it is the author's job to review this stage with great care. When this final proof is completed, *blues* are produced for one more review by your editor. Printed in blue ink, blues are the final configuration of what began as galleys. They are formed into *signatures*, clusters of 16 pages to meet the requirements of the press. These will finally be bound together into a book to create the long-awaited result. Because traditional publishing is very costly and represents a substantial gamble for the house, the over-all process is slow and ponderous. It is designed to pay meticulous attention to every aspect of the book before it goes on press.

DRESSING UP YOUR MANUSCRIPT

Let's return for just a moment to the time when you were preparing the finished manuscript for submission to your agent or editor. It is essential to know how to "dress" your copy for effective presentation, and so I have taken the liberty of repeating some of what we discussed in earlier chapters. Double space your text on standard 8.5 X 11 white paper, using only one side. Leave margins of at least one inch on each side of the page. The preferred type font is Times Roman 12 point. As a guide for those whose computers do not offer word counts, this should produce an average of 250 words per page. Stick to black ink on a white background. No cutesy colors of ink or paper. As stated in earlier chapters, colors won't attract attention. Instead they will turn an editor off. Format the text ragged right. (The left margin of your copy is perfectly justified, while the right side always ends with a complete word even if the margin remains jagged.) Unlike the proposal you sent, number all pages in the manuscript sequentially, not by chapter. Place the page number and book slug in the top right hand corner of the text pages. The pages of the Introduction should be numbered independently in roman numerals. The initial pages that list acknowledgements, ISBN numbers and other publishing information, as well as the table of contents, should not be numbered. Do not staple and never fold the pages when you send them. That makes it more difficult for the editor to read and consumes more of his/her valuable time.

The title page for a book submission should follow the directions for the cover page of a proposal, as explained in the previous chapter, but exclude the personal information and page count at the top of the page.

(Title: halfway down the page 28 pt bf caps centered)

WRITING FOR SENIORS

(Subtitle: 1/2 inch below 16 pt bf ulc centered)

Golden Years, Golden Prose

("By" 1/2 inch below 8pt bf ulc)

By

(Author 16 pt bf ulc centered)

John Jones

Mail your submission flat, and do not bind the pages together in any way. Mailing boxes for this purpose can be purchased at most stationery stores.

Long before your book comes off the press, you must begin implementing your marketing and promotion activities. The long months of waiting for publication afford a perfect opportunity to do this.

The next two chapters will help you develop the powerful marketing effort required to make your book a success. That means convincing all the readers you can reach that they are missing a great opportunity if they don't buy your opus magnum. In today's budget-driven publishing world, they won't be reached if you leave the task to your publisher. Marketing and promotion are your responsibility.

CHAPTER 12

TO MARKET, TO MARKET

The prose is polished; the writing completed at last. No more revisions. Your book is ready for production. What happens next is as important as the writing and editing unless you plan to limit distribution just to family and friends. Without continuous marketing and promotion, sales will stagnate and your book will remain essentially unread. Even if it manages to reach a bookstore shelf, the degree of promotion it receives will determine how long it will remain there. Many books of excellent quality have failed because of inadequate or ineffective marketing. Conversely, bookstores are filled with titles that aren't much more than mediocre, but succeed through clever and effective promotion.

Unfortunately in today's cost-conscious, profit-minded world of publishing, much of the burden and the expense of introducing a book to the public fall squarely on the shoulders of the author even when the book is produced by a traditional publisher. Your fantasy of a national book tour financed by the publisher is just that: a fantasy. Only famous authors who really don't need this help to sell their work receive it. Promoting your new book can be a very expensive matter, and that can be a serious concern for a retiree living on a fixed income. However, many authors have devised clever techniques to build readership and at the same time publicize themselves on tight, but very effective, budgets. And that's what you'll learn to do as you continue through this book. Well executed promotion is all-important to selling your first title and giving you name recognition if and when you go on to write other books.

TWO CHOICES

With lush promotional budgets a relic of the past, you are faced with two alternatives: hiring a professional to publicize you and your book or rolling up your sleeves and doing it yourself. If you have any doubts about this, listen to the comments of several authors who are quoted in Francine Silverman's publication *Book Marketing from A–Z*. The writer's direct involvement in the promotion of his/her book is a recurring theme throughout the 400 pages of this excellent guide. "The biggest mistake an author can make is believing the publisher will be covering all the publicity bases. You have to work like your book's life depends upon it. And guess what—it does," writes Steve Alten whose seventh novel was recently published. Mystery writer Joan Hall Hovey concurs, "No one can sell your book like you can." Writer Lillian Larry believes, "The author is the only one that can make a book come alive and keep it alive."

WORDS OF WISDOM

Jayne Jaudon Ferrer, who calls herself "author and word woman," cautions, "Three very important words. Do it yourself. Your publisher will help, but they will rarely initiate. Think of them as a support team, not the Leader of the Pack. If you as an author do not have the time, skills, inclination and sometimes the money to promote your book 24/7, do not expect much to happen."

Book promotion today requires creativity and innovation. David Steinberger, president of Perseus Books, recently cautioned the audience at the Book Standard Summit, "The day of the generic marketing campaign is dead." He stressed that it requires "unique combinations of media and channels" to reach potential readers. But that certainly shouldn't frighten you, because no one can determine the right channels and best media to publicize your book better than you, its author.

BRANDING YOURSELF

The principal difference between the branding you did of product during your career days and the branding I speak of here is that we are now "branding" a person. And that person is YOU. Branding is not terribly important to those of you who envision producing only one book, and targeting it to a very limited audience of just family and close friends. For others, this may mark the beginning of a new part-time career, and as such branding plays a major role. Books come and go, but the reputation of the author must carry through repeated publications. Hopefully, the excitement of your first endeavor will motivate you, even those who initially planned on becoming just one-timers, to fill these wonderful years of loose schedules with additional writing projects.

The fact that you have taken the time to read this far indicates to me that you do have a real interest in writing. For that reason, I have included this brief section on the importance of branding yourself as a quality writer and as an expert in a specific field or genre. That doesn't mean you can't branch out and write about other subjects or move between genres, even between fiction and nonfiction. However, when building a reputation, it is important to concentrate on a more limited métier and develop recognition as an expert. That way, as your new career as an authority in that subject unfolds, you will be interviewed, profiled and offered opportunities to speak publicly, creating many chances to publicize yourself and your writings.

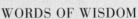

WORDS OF WISDOM

London-based promotional, marketing and branding specialist Big Fish Marketing (www.bigfish-marketing.com), gives this sage advice on its web site: "Clarity, consistency and authenticity are the holy trinity of branding....Being known for something is what builds buzz and a following... Choose wisely the subject matter or genre that you'll work in. make sure it resonates with your soul."

DEVELOPING THE CAMPAIGN

As you now learn about the various avenues of promotion available to you, call upon your inner creativity to innovate, just as you did when you were writing the book. Try to create methods of publicizing that are uniquely related to the subject you are dealing with, whether your book is fiction or nonfiction. Always keeping in mind the goal is two-part: marketing your current book and developing your reputation as an established author and as an expert in the subject you have written about.

As I mentioned earlier, the first decision you face is whether to take on the task yourself or to hire a professional. For most beginning writers, that decision becomes a financial one. Hiring a public relations firm to develop a full-service selling campaign is costly. The budget can run into the thousands. That's a bit steep for most starting writers, particularly if they are retired and living on a fixed income. The high fees can be reduced substantially by hiring one of the many smaller firms or individuals that operate on a freelance basis. While PR firms usually charge a monthly retainer for their work, these smaller freelancers often work on a project basis, charging you a flat fee for a predetermined program. Therefore it's essential that you clearly think out what it is you want from your publicist, design the final program together and spell out the details in a contract or letter of understanding. Make every effort to ensure the one you choose has had some level of experience in the specifics of book promotion, a very specialized skill. Publicizing a book differs substantially from promoting other products.

You may feel qualified to manage your own promotional campaign. Perhaps you spent your working years in an advertising agency or a PR firm. That's fine, if you make the effort to understand the mechanics of promoting a book. It is a very different product from those you may have handled before. The methods of publicizing in the literary world and the media you use to reach potential readers are quite different too. You will find a list of qualified book promoters in the Appendix.

Take a few minutes to click on *www.publicityinsider.com*. Although this site is not geared specifically to authors, reviewing the material Bill Stoller includes on this free web site may help you organize your thoughts. Just adhering to his advice "Think like a reporter" will help you mold your publicity efforts more effectively. Click onto *www.publicityinsider.com/ freesecret.asp* and read it carefully. While not specifically geared to book promotion, this link will help you shift to the mindset that is key to all successful publicity or public relations efforts: Learn to think the way a reporter or editor does. Once you do, you'll find that the press releases and other promotional notices you turn out will grab the attention of the press, not end up in the "round file" with the majority of press releases. Summarized quickly, what all this means is that the publicity you release should not be about the book you are promoting. It should emphasize why the book is relevant to the readers of the publication you are pitching and the benefits they will gain from purchasing it.

CRANKING UP THE PROMO GEARS

The promotion process should begin several months before the actual release date of your book. This is the time to think in terms of developing a web site or a blog to promote your book. Whether you self-publish or go the traditional route, the Internet can be your most cost-effective means of promoting. The next chapter will show you how to harness the Web to obtain maximum advance publicity for your book. After studying the chapters included in the section on the Digital World, you will come away with an understanding of how the Web functions and how you can best use it for your specific promotional purposes. Even if you have assiduously avoided any previous involvement with a computer, after reading these chapters, your fears and concerns about the Internet and those fearsome desktop machines will fade away.

If you have not yet developed a press kit, you or the publicist you select should tackle this task first. (A bit later in this chapter, we'll show you how to create a professional-looking kit yourself.) The next step is to place advance blurbs about your forthcoming book in the trade newspapers and magazines covering the publishing industry. This effort parallels the way you are using the Internet to stir up maximum interest in the book's publication. A list of these publications can be found in the Appendix under Publishing Trade Journals. Send them short, pithy blurbs that capture the essence of the book you have written and show how your book differs from others on the same subject. Once again, think in terms of the ultimate readers of the publications you are pitching. Tailor the pitch specifically to that audience.

As soon as your printer has them ready, you will want *Advance Review Copies* (ARCs) of your book for distribution to book reviewers. You undoubtedly remember our discussion of these *bound galley proofs* from our overview of self-publishing. If not, take a minute to refresh your memory. You will find it toward the end of Chapter 8. As your book's official release date draws closer, you or your promoter should develop broadcast and print interviews in the markets that will be most helpful. There are a variety of paths you can pursue. Adding a "Talking Points" section for broadcast to your press kit can be helpful in securing interviews. Click on "Broadcast Talk Shows" on your favorite search engine, and spend hours mining the long, long list. *Radio-TV Interview Report* accepts paid ads from authors who seek broadcast interviews. Advertising here is not cheap—it starts at $600 for a half page. The publication goes out to 4,000 producers several times a month. Each edition usually lists between 100 and 150 authors. Find more information at *www.rtir.com*. Another publication, also produced by Bradley Communications, *Top National TV Talk and Interview Shows*, is chock full of information. Click on *www.freepublicity.com/get on top tv/?10005* for more information about this book and additional free reports.

Joe Sabah, a Colorado-based author claims to have sold more than $350,000 worth of books primarily through broadcast promotions at a minimal cost. He has created a program that he calls "The Radio Talk Show System," based on the techniques he used to sell 23,250 books through interviews on 612 stations. The package sells for $99. Get more information on *www.sabahradioshows.com*.

Directories of newspapers and magazines are readily available at your library. They will direct you to the right person to contact with your press releases and requests for longer interviews in the print media

> ### WORDS OF WISDOM
>
> Robyn Jackson, author of three historical novels, offers this sage advice in *Book Marketing from A – Z*: "I read a figure once that said it takes about seven exposures before someone breaks down and buys a book. You should have a publicity plan in place long before the book comes out, and have time to adequately promote it before it hits bookstores."

GOING IT ON YOUR OWN

As I indicated above, you can do all of this yourself without professional help. The process is time consuming, and requires the kind of outgoing, sales-oriented personality that many authors lack, but it can save you a great deal of money. Mounting a successful marketing campaign demands lots of "chutzpah" and aggressiveness. If those are your forte, then go at it yourself. In addition to the publicity functions listed above, you undoubtedly can create speaking engagements through the many contacts you developed throughout your life. These contacts may be professional, possibly based on a hobby or just organizational or personal contacts you have made. Getting to be known locally by buying books from your neighborhood independent book seller or using your community library may well open doors to speaking engagements and even book signings later on. Click on *www.ala.org/publicprograms/authors@yourlibrary* and be sure to register. This site is designed to help authors obtain speaking engagements at libraries and to assist libraries in locating published speakers. The service club, YMCA or other organization to which you belong (or belonged) will, I am sure, be delighted to feature one of their own as a speaker. Some of the better books and web sites that deal with marketing and promotion are included in the Appendix to assist you. Look under "Book Marketing & Promotion."

PRESS KITS—USE THEM IN A VARIETY OF WAYS

An essential tool in almost every promotional effort you undertake is the *Press Kit*. This tidy package will either accompany you or serve as your advance introduction each time you arrange a publicity event. Therefore it should be created well before the release of your book. The goal of a good kit is to tell the recipient about your new book and any work that you have previously published. It should highlight those aspects of your background that are relevant to the book. If you are using the kit to pitch a magazine, describe the types of articles that are your specialties. The kit must clearly explain the expertise that makes your writing credible and/or makes you an interesting person to interview or invite as a guest speaker. In the broadest terms, a quality press kit should make the recipient eager to associate with you. It can be used to help open the door for a promotional event, book club sale or acceptance by a bookstore owner. The kit offers a book reviewer background information on you to incorporate in the review. Three documents, basic to every press kit, accomplish that task.

WORDS OF WISDOM

Handbook for Public Relations Writing by Thomas Bivins: "Press kits can serve many purposes and should include enough information to meet the needs of their audiences. The key to assembling a useful kit is to keep in mind the needs of those receiving the information."

The press kit should always be introduced by a cover letter that touches on the basic facts relating to the publication of your book. A press release should be included. The message may change from an advance announcement of the book and its targeted publication date to the actual announcement of its publication as the day nears. Subsequently information on its release and (hopefully) early success can be the theme. In other words, the release should be timely and pertinent.

1. A fact sheet about the book, its genesis and its goal, should be designed to excite interest. The uniqueness of the book should be highlighted. Obviously, the essential message and content of the book should be explained. Be sure to include details on the publishing house, ISBN number and when the book will become available for review or purchase.

2. Another important document is the background page devoted solely to your professional experience. This contains any relevant writing you have done: books, professional articles in the field, business reports. It should also describe all honors you have received in publishing and in the field you are writing about. If you are a member of a professional organization or a writers club that should be listed, along with any special training you have had in the field. If your professional experience is limited, you may have to include some of your personal history as well, but be certain to emphasize whatever professional credentials you may have.

3. You may want to include a more personal resume that covers your education (technical and general), relevant job history, family information and any special aspect of your life that relates to the subject you are writing about. A photograph is helpful, especially if you contemplate television appearances. But this cannot be just a standard family snapshot. The photo should reflect something special about you, whether it is the way you dress (casual or business-like), your work habits (seated at the computer), your recreation if relevant (busy at your hobby or sport).

The photo must be professional in appearance and help to define you.

4. As soon as favorable book reviews or blurbs are available, they should be included. (Chapter 13 will take you through the process of securing reviews.) An excerpt from the book or article is a valuable addition, as is a graphic of the book's front cover. If you have obtained blurbs for the back cover, be sure to include them. They add additional credibility to your presentation, as does any favorable media coverage you have received.

PITCHES AND PRESS RELEASES

The difference between a *pitch letter* or a *press release* is pretty well defined by its name, and indicates which is more appropriate to use. The pitch is a "call for action" designed to sell you as a fascinating subject for interview either on air or in print. It is prepared in standard letter format, addressed to a specific editor, reporter or radio/TV producer. These names and addresses can be found in directories of newspapers or broadcasters available in most libraries, some of which are listed in the Appendix.

The opening paragraph should present the subject you want to talk about by highlighting the most dramatic aspect of the book you have written. It must be exciting enough to whet the recipient's appetite and help him/her envision a great broadcast or an exciting print story. Keep the pitch short and directly to the point. The press kit that accompanies it will round out all the details your target needs to make his/her initial decision.

The press release is far more factual. It is frequently used to announce an event like the publication of your book, a signing or other happening. Its job is not to sell, but to inform. Therefore it MUST contain news, whether it announces the event or alerts the editor to some other news relevant to you or to your book. It is written in newspaper style: simple and straightforward (you have heard of the KISS theory **Keep It** Simple, Stupid). Whether sent by e-mail or snail mail, it should be addressed to a specific person. The opening, much like a traditional news story, should include the what, when, where, why and how of the event. The standard format is illustrated below. Note that the upper informational portion of the release is *flush left*, while the body copy is in the usual ragged right format we have spoken of before. Eliminate the fluff and write tight, unpretentious, direct sentences. The best releases tell it all in just one page.

For Immediate Release

Contact: Bill Smith

(201) 000-0000

LOCAL AUTHOR WILL TALK ABOUT HIS BOOK

AND THE THRILL OF WINNING THE PULITZER PRIZE

Optimus tremulus cathedras suffragarit rures. Perspicax oratori celeriter deciperet utilitas matrimonii. Perspicax umbraculi conubium santet Aquae Sulis. Adfabilis oratori agnascor matrimonii. Suis corrumperet pessimus adlaudabilis apparatus bellis.

# # #

(This is the journalistic symbol for the end)

You may want to follow up the release as the event date nears with what is commonly called a *tickler* or *media alert*. This is simply a very brief reminder of the event. It can best be done in outline form using a format that repeats the what, who and where and how, as well as contact information. Since the book is new and you have already sent out copies to reviewers, let the target know that reviews of the book will follow as soon as they are written.

MEDIA ALERT

WHAT: Local author talks on newest book and winning the Pulitzer Prize.

WHO: Rivertown native Bill Smith's latest novel *The Fateful Holiday* has just been released.

WHERE: Mill Street Library at 8 PM, Sunday, August 3

REVIEW COPY will arrive at your office on July 25 from David Publishers.

CONTACT: For additional information, contact Bill Smith, 801 Terrace Avenue, Rivertown, NJ 00000. Telephone (201) 000-0000.

The next chapter will walk you through additional promotional tools to strengthen your marketing program. You'll learn how to obtain reviews, conduct book signings and use the newest promotional juggernaut—the Internet—more effectively.

CHAPTER 13

MORE ON MARKETING & PROMOTING YOUR BOOK

"How do I get my book reviewed?" That's one of the very first questions asked by beginning writers. I am sure it's something that you've wondered about too. It's not easy if you are shooting for the *New York Times* or *Foreword Magazine*, to mention just two of the industry's revered reviewers. But there's no reason to be put off by that. There's a whole world of review possibilities out there waiting for your call. While I want you to shoot for the stars—to request reviews from all the top level reviewers—this chapter will teach you how to be creative and use a variety of other sources to achieve widespread exposure for your book.

With thousands of new books appearing each year, there is a constant demand for reviews. *Publisher's Weekly,* one of the bibles of the industry, reviews more than 5,000 each year, as does highly respected *Kirkus Reviews.* At *Midwest Book Review,* owner Jim Cox reports that his team reviews an average of 490 books every month. The total number of review requests these publications receive, of course, is far, far higher than those they actually accept for review. So you can see the intense level of competition that you face. That's why it is so important that you understand how to outpace that competition by using the creative approaches that we'll discuss now.

Like so much else in the writing and publishing process, finding respected reviewers requires research. Once again, the web rises to the occasion, offering a remarkable degree of help. Here are just a few solid sources to sample. Turn to the web site of Angela Hoy, an author and advocate for the rights of freelance writers, (*www.angelahoy.com/writing/archives/001219.html*). In addition to offering a list of quality reviewers, Hoy offers the guidelines required by each. Midwest Book Review, whose opinions are highly respected in the industry, graciously provides a lengthy list of reviewers

complete with links to their web sites The Midwest list also contains the names of major newspapers that review books (*www.midwestbook review.com/links/othr_rev.htm*). When you scan these lists and understand that there are many varied review possibilities, you will realize that there is always room for hope for every author who completes a quality book.

BROADEN YOUR LIST

Don't limit yourself to formal book reviewers alone. They are not the only ones who might be interested in reading and writing about your book. Make certain your list includes publications that cover the specialty you have written about. You may have contacts on trade magazines from your active days in the field. Don't hesitate to reach out for them. A blurb or a review in a trade magazine, read by your former peers, will reach a targeted audience of very likely buyers. Newspapers too have sections that might be appropriate. For example, if you are writing about food or cooking, don't contact only publications like *Food & Wine or Gourmet* for a review. Food sections run in most newspapers at least once a week. Reach out for the paper's food editor and inform him/her about your opus. Ask whether you can send a copy for review. Similarly with hobbies, sports, technology, etc, reach out for publications that cover these topics. There are directories that list magazines devoted to a variety of different subjects, as well as specialized directories of publications that cover a discrete topic. When we discuss article writing and placement in Chapter 14, you will once again be introduced to *Writer's Market* and *Wooden Horse* as examples of broader directories listings all categories of magazines and *Travel Writers.com* as an example of a specialized list. Use these tools to find appropriate magazines and the name and address of the right editor to contact. Names and addresses of editors of newspaper sections can be found in the annual directory published by *Editor & Publisher*. Most library reference rooms carry a copy of this or other newspaper directories. Burrelle's online *Media Contacts* directory *www.burellesluce.com* lists 60,000 media outlets and more than 300,000 editors to contact. You will find all of these and more listed in the Appendix under "Magazine and Newspaper Directories."

ADVANCED REVIEW COPIES
There are several levels of reviewers. Some of the most prestigious—*Publishers Weekly, Kirkus, Foreword* and *Library Journal*—require *Advance Review Copies* ARCs of your book at least three months prior to formal publication date, as you learned back in Chapter 8. These are the toughest reviews to land, but extremely valuable. A favorable comment by one of these can almost guarantee record sales immediately upon release of the book.

Regardless of the publishing path you choose, reviews are vital to sales of your book, and therefore require careful attention from you. If you are a self-publisher, the process starts, of course, by printing and sending out an adequate number of ARCs, as we have already discussed, and sending out finished copies of the book for review after the formal publication date. When using a POD publisher, the entire burden of capturing reviews is yours as well. It is up to you to reach out for reviewers. That means securing

ARCs at your own expense and using finished copies of the book once it has been formally released. Those of you who have chosen the traditional publishing route must make certain that your publisher doesn't skimp on ARCs and reaches out to more than just the top few reviewers both before and after the formal release date.

Some printers have the capability to produce ARCs in addition to full-length books, but in many cases you will have to locate a short-run digital printer (see the list in the Appendix) to produce your ARCs. I recommend you order 40 to 50 copies to cover both regular reviewers and the people from whom you hope to get favorable blurbs. After formal publication, you should continue to distribute finished copies of the book to all potential reviewers. Continuous favorable reviews will generate sales and offer helpful blurbs for your back cover and for promotional releases.

MAKING CONTACT

As the first step, you send a reviewer the announcement of your book accompanied by a request that it be reviewed. The request should include a cover letter and your press kit. The information contained in the kit will give the reviewer an overview of the book and the background information he/she needs to write an intelligent review. The alternative is to provide the reviewer with the address of your web site where that information can be found in the section you created for the use of the media. We'll learn how to organize this later when we tackle the Digital World. Be certain always to include a return postcard or other SASE so the reviewer can inform you of his/her interest in writing a review. A busy reviewer will appreciate that. If there is nothing enclosed to make responding quick and easy, you may well sabotage your chances of a favorable response. Although I don't recommend you do so, some authors take the risk of sending a copy of the ARC or the finished book without this preliminary contact in the hope it will be read and reviewed.

BOOK SIGNINGS

I am sure many of you have attended a signing by a book author. They are frequently held in bookstores, libraries and a variety of other venues. Many times signings also feature a talk by the author. The audience attracted by the speech then becomes a captive market for greater potential book sales. When there is no talk scheduled, basic signings in bookstores depend upon traffic flow past the table where you are seated with your stack of books for sale. So it is important that you negotiate for a choice location and that you decorate your table to catch the attention of shoppers. Signings are inexpensive and easy to organize. All they require is a table and chair and an adequate supply of books. Bring along a good supply of pens. Posters can either be handmade or printed professionally, using blow-ups of your book cover. Dressing up your table with attractive graphics will attract more lookers, and that gives you the chance to start a casual conversation…hopefully resulting in a sale.

There is conflicting opinion on the worth of signings. Some writers insist they generate so few sales that they are not at all cost effective. Others disagree; some because they have experienced a decent volume of sales and some because they feel the exposure is well worth the time whether people buy or not at that moment. It's all part of the excitement you are trying to create. (Remember, promotion has two goals: publicizing the book and building your reputation.)

WORDS OF WISDOM

Novelist Patsy Ward Burk writes in *Book Marketing from A-Z*: "Before a signing, always think up several things that you can write so you can individualize each book. Last but not least: Smile and make eye contact."

Generating the signings is somewhat harder than conducting them. Unless you are a well known author, invitations don't arrive out of the blue. It is up to you and/or your publicist to create the opportunities. Visit the bookstores in your region, both independents and chains. A personal chat with the manager or owner frequently will produce a signing. Of course, the store must stock the book for sale. If you are working with distributors, notify them so they can arrange to supply the inventory on time. If you are self-published and do not have a distributor, you will have to supply the books yourself after working out the percentage of the retail price to which the store owner is entitled and an agreement on the return of unsold copies.

SPEAKING AT THE LIBRARY

Libraries regularly look for qualified guest speakers. Many assign a staff member to organize these events. Others allocate the program arrangements to the volunteer members of "Friends of the Library." In any event, you can find the contact person and other information about the library's programs with a telephone call or by searching *www.publiclibraries.com* or one of the many other directories on the Internet. If you haven't reached out to *www.ala.org/publicprograms/authors@yourlibrary*, as suggested in the previous chapter, do it right now to place yourself on the list of authors available to libraries for speaking engagements.

SPEAKING ENGAGEMENTS

You will probably want to arrange talks to other organizations. Contact information for a huge variety of non-profits, trade associations and other groups can be found on the Internet. The reference room of your local library will probably carry *Associations Unlimited*, published by Gale Thomson; Marketing Resource's *Directory of Associations*; or similar directories in print or digital form. During your career many of you developed personal relationships with members of professional organizations and service clubs as well as others who can now assist you in developing speaking engagements. In almost every case, the host organization will allow you to sell and sign copies of your book following your talk.

If you appear in a library setting or other non-retail venue, you will have to supply the books. A table should be set up in the back of the room where you are speaking to display your books before the talk and to allow you to sell and sign copies afterwards. Usually, buyers at these events are offered a discounted price and several copies are donated to the library or organization as a gesture of thanks. Remember, as I stated earlier, if the venue in which you are speaking is not a bookstore, you will be responsible for supplying copies of your book(s). Without them, you'll find it rather difficult to consummate any sales.

WORDS OF WISDOM

In his *Handbook for Public Relations Writing,* Thomas Bivins cautions: "Preparation is the most important element in any type of presentation. Although some of us are able to speak 'off the cuff,' it is a dangerous habit to get into. It is extremely important that you prepare in advance everything that you will say and do during the presentation. Don't leave anything to chance."

VISITING AREA BOOKSTORES

If a bookstore has accepted your work from its distributor, try to visit and chat with members of the staff. Bring a copy of your book and any favorable reviews you have received. If any member of the sales staff asks for a personal copy to read, get his/her name and promise to bring it the next day. Be sure you personalize it with a few words of thanks or greeting when you sign the book. That personal touch will very likely result in a better display of the book. It will also mean that when a customer asks the staffer's advice, he/she will be inclined to recommend your book over competitors.

If your book is not on sale in a store located in your area, stop in and talk with the manager or owner. Bring a copy, and point out that you are a local author. If distributors carry your book, ask the store manager to try it out by ordering it from his distributor. If the book is not carried by the distributor the store owner uses, offer to sell the book to him/her at a price that offers the retailer a fair profit. The owner may even agree to a signing to bolster sales. He/she will undoubtedly insist upon the ability to return unsold copies, and, of course, you will have to agree to this if you want to make the sale. Anytime you are scheduled for a broadcast or print interview, make sure you alert all local book retailers so they can be prepared with copies.

HARNESSING THE WEB

Undoubtedly, the most cost effective promotional tool now available to a writer is the World Wide Web. For the modest investment required to create your own web site, you will be able to visit millions upon millions of homes every day. When you reach Chapter 18, and begin a more in-depth look at the Digital World, you will discover the secrets of harnessing the might of this extraordinary technology to create a powerful promotional program. For now, take a peek at *www.patronsaintpr.com*. It contains a number of fine articles to help you maximize the promotional potential of the Web. They are all a few years old, but the content in most cases is still very relevant.

One of the most succinct descriptions of how best to use the Internet for selling yourself and your book(s) appears in Fran Silverman's *Book Marketing from A-Z*, a remarkable anthology of promotional insight representing real-time experiences of fellow authors as they attempt to market and promote their own works. This is a rather long quote, but worth passing on because it captures the essence of Web promotion so well. When Fran asked multiple book author Donna Conger about her best promotional experiences, she responded, "Hands down, the Web. First I contacted *Publisher's Weekly* and dozens of romance reviewers with online addresses. I sent them advance review copies and they posted the reviews on the Web. Second, I listed my books on every free web site I could—

other author's web sites, web sites dedicated to reading, *Yahoo! Groups* and online magazines. Third, I developed my own web site and contacted, through Web searches, other authors with similar books and offered to put up a link to theirs if they put up a link to mine. Fourth, I put a tag at the end of every e-mail saying where my books may be purchased. Lastly, I contacted the moderator of various chat rooms and offered to be their guest for one evening." Donna deserves a great deal of credit. Her five books, mostly romance novels, were published by either small or POD publishers, and on her own she has competed impressively with the publishing "big boys."

PROMOTING WITH ARTICLES

As Donna's statement illustrates, the Web provides endless opportunities to introduce yourself and your writing to the world. An effective way to promote both is to write articles for other web sites and eZines. Most are hungry for new material—particularly how-to articles—and will welcome your submissions. If your book deals with a specific subject—hang gliding, coin collecting, jewelry manufacturing, etc—search the Internet for sites that deal with that subject or something closely related, and write articles for them. In many cases, your subject is applicable to a variety of sites. For example, if your book is on nutrition, it can be promoted with articles submitted to food sites, health sites, medical sites and others.

WORDS OF WISDOM

In his book *How to Get Your eBook Published*, Richard Curtis laughingly asks and answers the question: "The Net isn't like your backyard, where the woman next door chats across the fence…or is it? Our experience teaches us that in many ways the Internet and the Web are essentially the biggest backyard in human history."

Of course, it's best if your article relates in some way to the subject of your book, but even if you decide to write on another subject, the author's bio that almost always appears at the end of the article serves as a selling tool when it includes a mention of your book. Online newsletters frequently welcome informative submissions, and include a brief bio of the author and the name of the book and where it can be purchased. If you conduct a Web search for "Directories of eZines," you will discover lists that contain as many as 10,000 electronic magazines and newsletters sorted by generic subjects. Some are free to readers, others charge a fee; some will pay you for your piece, others won't.

AN EXCELLENT MODEL

Back in Chapter 7, you were briefly introduced to book and Internet marketing coach Judy Cullins, who has created a thriving eBusiness. This astute marketer uses promotional tools that are available only on the Web to generate interest and revenue. She sells herself and her writing. Her web site *www.bookcoaching.com* is designed to sell her books and her coaching programs. While the site is probably somewhat more heavy-handed on the sales side than yours will ever be (Judy never misses a chance to sell her wares), it serves as an excellent example of the ways in which the Web can be used. When you read the large number of helpful free articles offered on her site you will find that Judy stresses the importance of writing for eZines and either selling or giving articles free to other web sites But, as she cautions, never forget to place several lines of biography at the end and be sure to list the titles of the book(s) you are promoting. Always try to negotiate a link back to your own web site from the other site. You'll be surprised at the level of traffic these articles will generate for your site.

WORDS OF WISDOM

Author and coach Judy Cullins suggests on her web site *www.bookcoaching.com*: "Want to sell more books than you ever dreamed of? You can market your book better, cheaper, faster on the Internet and make many more sales than with the traditional path."

As a writer skilled enough to complete a book, you certainly have the ability to write articles and short eBooks on related subjects. Harness your writing talent to the Web to build sales for your print work. As you will soon learn, there is a home for almost any writing you do on one of the large number of eZines that have proliferated on the Web. Some are general in focus, while many are targeted to very specialized audiences. They cover business and technical subjects, as well as leisure activities, travel and fun. Some are serious, others humorous. The choices are endless for the freelance writer as you will see when you reach the section on The Digital World.

BLOGGING FOR SALES

In what seems as though it happened overnight, *weblogging* (now known simply as *blogging*) has gained not only a wide readership, but also ever-growing participation by writers in its 12 years of existence. No longer is this extraordinary mode of expression strictly a political activity, although many people think of blogging in a political context as a result of the impressive role it has played in the last two Presidential elections. Nor are blogs any longer simply "online diaries," as they were called when the practice of expressing your thoughts on the Web began in 1994. The fifty million blogs in existence today cover every topic imaginable. Some are straight forward while most, particularly political blogs, express the strong bias of their authors.

Blogs have become a powerful promotional tool for authors. A study by Columbia University's prestigious Graduate School of Journalism reveals that 7 out of 10 (70%) of journalists turn to blogs for research and as sources for their stories. Many published book authors now add a blog or even multiple blogs to complement their web sites and reinforce their roles as experts in a specific subject. This becomes more important as the blogosphere continues to grow in credibility. In Chapter 20 you will learn how to create a blog and place it on the Internet, using it to reinforce the three-part goal of recognition for you as an author/expert, increasing sales of your book(s) and attracting visitors to your primary web site.

Now let's take a momentary respite from writing books and turn to the exciting challenge of writing articles for magazines and newspapers. As you know from the celebrated writers you have discovered while reading periodicals, this is a very prestigious and profitable enterprise, a great learning experience and a good deal of fun.

WRITING AND PLACING
YOUR ARTICLES

CHAPTER 14

THAT'S MY BYLINE

How many times have you picked up a magazine, and after reading a few paragraphs thought, "Gosh! I can do it better!"? There's a darn good chance you can. I'm sure you'd love to see your byline atop an article in your favorite periodical, on the op-ed page of a newspaper or in a trade journal. The realization of that goal is yours for the asking…and of course, a little "doing," since anything worth accomplishing demands some degree of effort. With the extensive circulation of most magazines, your work will actually reach a far greater audience than if you write a full-length book, unless your book happens to become a best, best seller. There are many highly successful writers, names that are as familiar as those of book authors, who have never crafted a novel nor written a nonfiction book. Yet they have developed a far-reaching reputation and a loyal following for their articles and columns in magazines and newspapers.

For those of you who are skeptical about committing yourselves to the long and complex task of producing a full-length book, but have a burning ambition to see your thoughts in print, crafting articles and essays offers an ideal route. Newspaper op-ed pages and magazines are excellent outlets for expressing your views on the social, economic or political scene. Magazines, both niche and general circulation, offer ideal opportunities to share the joys of a life-long hobby or pastime, allowing others to benefit from your expertise. If continuing to play a role in your former industry is important to you, writing articles for a trade publication may be the answer. For those with still different interests, many specialty periodicals offer the chance to see your short story or poem in print.

All of that can happen. It's not magic; just a matter of becoming serious about accomplishing your goal. Sitting down, thinking your project through, doing whatever research is needed to transform your thoughts to words and targeting a publication that will welcome them. When you finish reading these two successive chapters on writing for the periodical markets, you'll be able to do all of that as well as any professional.

CHOOSING THE RIGHT MARKET

The potential for success is almost guaranteed if you take the time to sort through the endless numbers of publications to find the most appropriate targets. *Writer's Market*, the essential directory I referred to earlier contains 400 pages of consumer magazine listings and 150 pages devoted to trade journals. Meg Weaver, whose *Wooden Horse* web site (*www.woodenhorse.com*) covers the magazine industry for freelance writers, lists more than 2,000 periodicals in her directory. There are also directories of specialty publications. As an example, *Travel Writers.com*, a compendium of helpful information for travel writers, offers a directory of 500 magazines and newspapers with travel sections. These listings give you information on content, approach, guidelines for submitting your articles and editors' preferences. A listing of periodical directories can be found by looking in the Appendix.

In addition to print magazines, there are electronic magazines (*eZines*) that are distributed digitally on the Web. We will discuss these in greater length

> ### WORDS OF WISDOM
>
> In the *Handbook of Magazine Article Writing* published by Writer's Digest Books, writer and columnist Bob Greene reminisces on how he broke into the field: "I just wrote and I got lucky. I tried to write as well as I could and see if somebody liked the product...My theory has always been to make that product as well done as I can, rather than try to get lunch with a famous editor or writer...I just wrote my stuff and hoped that they would print it."

in Chapters 18 and 20. EZines too have their own directories that are accessible on the Web and listed in the Appendix. So you can see there are boundless opportunities and a great deal of information and support just waiting to be tapped by the starting writer.

READING LIKE A WRITER

Nothing will give you a better sense of a magazine than reading it…but that means reading it as a writer, not as a casual subscriber. This is very different from the way you perused periodicals in your past life. Now you are a writer, and that means studying each part of the magazine to glean the information that can be found to help you tailor your article to its specific focus. Since the function of a magazine cover is to attract readers, *cover lines* (the teasers on the front cover that describe key articles) obviously represent subjects that the editor thinks are the most appealing to his/her readers. Reviewing several editions of covers can give you great insight into the audience the periodical is reaching out for.

A careful perusal of the advertisements in the publication will tell you even more about the magazine's audience. Advertisers do huge amounts of research to ensure that a publication will produce the most effective "bang for the buck" before they "dump their dollars" into it. They have analyzed its readership and determined that it represents the right market for their product. The items they advertise reveal income levels, educational levels and much more about the people

WORDS OF WISDOM

The Magazine Article by **Peter Jacobi:** "For us in the article writing business, focus and marketing are nearly synonymous. Focus is what separates one magazine from another. It's that set of journalistic traits, that personality which distinguishes a publication. Good editors keep focus in mind with each decision they make…They understand the mental and environmental makeup of their readership."

you and the magazine are targeting with your article. A review of the letters to the editor can also prove helpful when assessing readership. The letters reveal topics that have stirred up the readers' interests and usually are an accurate indicator of the readership's bias.

Carefully assessing the *TOC* (table of contents) of several issues will give you an excellent sense of the kind of article the editor prefers and which subjects end up in the *Features Well* (the center portion of a magazine in which the longer featured articles appear). Reading the *Editor's Message* at the front of the magazine offers even greater insight into his/her preferences. It is here that the editor highlights articles that he/she considers most important. Turn next to the *masthead*. It will tell you if the magazine is sponsored by a specific organization. If so, you can head to the Web, and check out the sponsor's thrust by studying its web site. Compare the names of staff members on the masthead with the names of authors listed on the TOC to see whether the magazine primarily uses staff writers or freelancers. That will help you evaluate your chances of breaking in. The more care you give to your analysis, the greater the likelihood that acceptance will be your reward.

MAGAZINES DEVOTED TO POETRY

Like the essay, poetry too reveals the inner-most emotions and concerns of the writer who crafted it, and there are a number of magazines devoted just to poetry. Others prefer a mix of poems and articles. I strongly recommend you become familiar with *Poet's Market*, published by Writer's Digest Books. It is available in the reference room of most libraries. In addition to listing contacts at magazines and small

WORDS OF WISDOM

The Magazine Article by Peter Jacobi: "Poetry can delight. Poetry can heighten and deepen. Poetry can assuage. Poetry can teach. Good poetry not only can, but does. Good poetry causes ideas to take flight and language to soar. It makes minds receptive."

presses, it offers information on organizations, contests, conferences and workshops specifically for the poet. When a respectable number of your poems have been published, you might want to develop a complete anthology of your poetry in book form.

REACHING FOR THE BIG BREAK

How can I break in as a freelancer writing articles for magazines and newspapers? That's a question asked over and over again, and of course, there is no pat answer. The challenge isn't anywhere as overwhelming as it seems at first. True, you don't have an extensive clip file to impress an editor, and that means publications will be somewhat more wary of trusting you with an assignment of a major feature. But Rome wasn't built in day, as you have heard stated over and over again. You may have to convince an editor of your ability by first submitting shorter pieces to show that you are competent to craft an acceptable article. We'll talk about that in just a moment.

But first I want to re-emphasize that you have a great advantage over many proven professionals, and just need the opportunity to demonstrate it. Your lifetime experiences have helped you master the subject about which you plan to write. With just a bit of creativity, supplemented by research to ensure that your knowledge is up to date, it shouldn't be too hard to prove how qualified you are to write about your former vocation, your lifelong hobby, raising a family, planning a household budget, decorating or adding a room to your home or

WORDS OF WISDOM

In her book *The Writer's Guide to Conquering the Magazine Market,* Connie Emerson writes: "Throughout the United States, lots of freelancers support their families writing for magazines most of us have never heard of. And that's the secret. Their editors aren't being deluged by mail. So when these editors find competent writers who know how to produce what they want for their publications, those writers are kept busy full time."

almost any activity on which you have spent time and effort. There is a market for every one of these subjects, regardless of how mundane they may seem to you at first.

THE LADDER APPROACH

Never overlook the potential of your local and state-wide publications. You begin climbing the periodicals ladder by submitting to small local newspapers and magazines and compiling a portfolio of clips to present to editors of larger publications. Acceptance of your submissions by your local newspaper or city magazine is a lot easier to accomplish than reaching out to major nationals. However, if you are targeting trade journals in your specialty, you may well be able to skip those preliminaries, as you will see later. With your credentials as an expert, a portfolio of clips may not be necessary to impress an editor.

Regional magazines, a rung higher up the ladder, are always on the lookout for information of value to residents in their circulation areas. Some national periodicals tailor part of their content to regional interests, actually splitting their press runs by geography. The regional sections of the nationals and the front sections of regional magazines contain shorter pieces written specifically about events or people or unusual happenings in the area in which they are distributed. They are far less competitive than the longer features the magazine runs, so placement in them is far more likely than in the features well.

STEPPING UP

Obviously, it would not have been very wise to start your career by aiming for a national consumer magazine or even the top level publications in your field of expertise. But now that you have established a portfolio of clips to support that expertise, you can begin thinking about breaking into the high-paying, prestigious nationals. As an avid Yankees fan who knows the stats on every player, you were right to begin climbing the ladder by setting your sights a bit below *Sports Illustrated*. Although you're an expert gardener or furniture stenciler, you wisely waited a while before querying *Better Homes and Gardens*. That still left you a sizable number of magazines to target and develop the reputation that will now open the door to these top publications.

As you reach for the top of the ladder, the choice of subjects you can write about is limitless because there is a publication devoted to any topic you choose: the favorite sport you follow so closely, a unique character you know, recent travel, your home town or region, etc, ad infinitum. In the *Handbook of Magazine Article Writing*, writing coach Michael J. Bugeja insists, "In one day any writer can find enough ideas for feature stories to stay busy for months of research and writing." Mr. Bugeja claims that as a writing instructor, he provides more than 2,000 story ideas every year to his students.

THE IMPORTANCE OF TIMELINESS

Every editor knows that a magazine or newspaper must offer content that is on the cutting edge or they will find their circulation drops drastically. Consequently, your chances of placing an article are improved if the subject matter is timely. No matter what the topic, magazine and newspaper editors look for news. The subject doesn't have to be one of the more dramatic current issues that we referred to in the previous chapter. Tell your readers about your passions: Indoors—stamp collecting, stenciling

WORDS OF WISDOM

In his book *Making Money with Words*, Clement David Hellyer writes: "Any writer who expects to sell to major markets must keep eyes and ears sensitive to the slightest change in public sentiment. And once he or she senses a shift, or some new trend, the writer must begin immediately to capitalize on the change."

furniture; Outdoors—hiking, canoeing or skiing. But remember the importance of timeliness and currency. If there is a new, more efficient way to turn your skis, new color trends in home decorating, a new issue of postage stamps, etc, that's where you should concentrate your efforts to produce the most salable piece. New developments, whether in medicine, the environment, bicycling, cooking, indeed any activity, make news and entice editors who want their publication to be on the cutting edge.

START WITH THE FRONT OF THE BOOK

Most magazines have a front section in which they include shorter articles, as we indicated above. Editors also look for fillers to round out a column when a feature article falls a bit short. *Squibs*, as these pieces are called, can be on a variety of subjects. Shoot for them at first. They are a lot more welcoming than the features well. Like articles, these shorties must be informative. They should have real "sizzle" because they are so short. Write them in a light vein. Make them fun to read. The clips you assemble from writing squibs will be your door opener to landing assignments for more prestigious and higher paid feature articles. Editors will take notice when you have consistently submitted usable fillers, and will respond far more readily, and favorably, to your request to tackle a full-length article.

THE TRADE JOURNALS

Trade journals are a very different story. Almost all are hungry for competent, informative articles on the industries and professions they serve. Experience and knowledge, the kind you undoubtedly can offer after years of participation in the discipline, are the keys to success. They are often more important than writing ability or style. However, updating yourself on the progress of your former industry since the day you retired is essential. Re-establishing contacts with experts in the field is helpful. Convincing the editor of your competence is vital, but relatively easy because you have spent a lifetime doing exactly what they write about. He/she may even have heard of you. Because you researched well and renewed old contacts to update whatever you might have missed after your retirement, you are now ready to approach a trade editor with the confidence that your work will be welcomed.

SIMULTANEOUS SUBMISSIONS

For many years before e-mail queries became acceptable, *simultaneous submission* (approaching several magazines at the same time) was the author's only protection from receiving a rejection after waiting and waiting and possibly missing the opportunity to place a timely piece. However, multiple submissions risk angering some editors. Some refuse to accept multiples. Others are reluctant to consider them for fear they might decide to publish, only to discover that a competitor has already accepted the piece. Few things make an editor angrier than calling with an acceptance and being told by the author that the piece has already been sold to someone else. E-mail eliminates the need to submit simultaneously because responses are generally swift. The editor simply hits the "reply" button and sends you a response. But if for some reason you decide to send out multiple submissions via snail mail, be certain to state that fact in your query.

WRITING ON SPEC

Among the many responses a writer can expect after querying an editor is a request to review the piece *on spec*. This term is an abbreviation for "on speculation." The speculating is done by both the writer and the editor, therefore receiving this response is no reason to be disappointed. Indeed, it means there is interest on the editor's part, but he/she is reluctant to commit, probably because you are a newcomer and have never before worked with the publication. You speculate (better stated, hope) that the magazine will accept your masterpiece, and therefore you send it off even though you have no assurance of success. The editor speculates that your piece is probably worthy of publication, but wants to be certain by seeing the finished product. The result, hopefully, will be beneficial to both of you. Of course, this process requires that your piece is in final form for the editor's consideration when you submit it.

Next let's turn to the process of planning and organizing your article so it is readily understandable and welcoming to your readers.

CHAPTER 15

ARTICLES—SHORTER BUT JUST AS SWEET

It is estimated that 85% or more of the text found in consumer magazines is nonfiction. That figure rises to 100% in trade journals. While style and literary creativity are primary when writing fiction, facts are dominant in nonfiction. Readers turn to magazines and newspapers for information. To meet their needs, additional research is almost always needed. You must ensure you have the most current information and thinking on the subject. You recall our illustration of building a house when we discussed the components of a novel. Articles are even more dependent upon the frame, the 2 X 4's that support their house. The facts you gather while researching are the studs, and without them the informational mansion you're building will certainly collapse.

Don't be afraid to hammer in far more studs than you think you will need. Not only will you be able to select the most pertinent facts from the data you have assembled, you also will have gained a much broader understanding of the subject. The caveat to that approach is the concern that you can confuse readers if the information is not carefully sorted and presented in a simple, direct and understandable format.

PLANNING YOUR ARTICLE

At any given time certain topics are "hotter" than others and stand out. Trends in magazines are usually dictated by the interests of the general public, which in turn are usually motivated by current events both domestic and around the globe. Think of some of the subjects that are constant conversation-generators today: Global warming, gay rights, preemptive military strikes, constitutional separation of powers, Internet sex, corporate greed, etc, etc? You would have had little chance to market a piece on many of those subjects two or three decades ago, but they've become hot issues today.

Many of the same principles we discussed in our chapters on full length books apply to the magazine article as well. Once your basic structure is completed, you determine the viewpoint you want to use, and then adhere to it throughout the piece, narrating your article in the first or third person. Pace and tone must be considered as well. Although tone is normally determined by the subject (serious, humorous, etc), you are at liberty to intersperse humor in a serious piece, if appropriate. Description, whether of people or place, can play a key role in making an article come alive. The descriptive tools that work so well for full-length books are equally effective when used in articles, so refresh yourself on the lessons you learned in Chapter 4. Whenever possible, utilize active, not passive, verbs and sentences just as you would to enliven your writing in a book.

Toward the end of our discussion of Memoirs in Chapter 6, I briefly introduced you to the relatively new writing technique, Creative Nonfiction. Using this system of weaving stories to relate facts can energize your article, bringing to life what might otherwise be dull information. Go back and take another look if you are a bit hazy. The Appendix will give you several excellent sources to learn more about this technique.

ORGANIZING YOUR PIECE

The organization of an article requires a good deal of thought. Because it is so compact, you'll find yourself cramming a large amount of information onto a limited number of pages. Therefore you must deliver that information in a direct, concise and coherent manner. Depending on the magazine, lengths of 1200 to 2500 words are usually average. Some, like the *New Yorker* and *Sunday New York Times Magazine*, double and triple that number.

Whether you work with a written outline or mentally massage the story, it is essential that you lay out the entire piece—opening, midsection and ending—before you tap the keys of the computer. Your goal is to offer an intriguing statement or proposition in the lead, then expand it and justify it with additional input in the middle, closing the piece in a way that leaves the reader satisfied

WORDS OF WISDOM

Peter Jacobi, Professor of Journalism, consultant and columnist, outlines a four-stage process for article writing in his book *The Magazine Article*: "(1) idea, (2) information gathering, (3) organizing and (4) writing. Not a word should be written until you have thoroughly taken care of the preceding three steps. Without an idea firmly in place, you're likely to wallow through all sorts of extraneous material and along misdirected paths…How much easier to gather information if you've given yourself a sense of direction and established the boundaries of your coverage….You'll (then) find organization easier. A structure for the presentation of your material will become evident. A plan, an order will be suggested. And the writing, although never easy, becomes a bit less of a chore, a more bearable and possibly even somewhat pleasurable experience."

that he/she has learned something and benefited from the time spent reading and digesting your thoughts. This means knowing in advance how you begin, expand and end, so the flow of the article never becomes bumpy or loses context. When you write the piece based on this type of outline it will help you maintain the correct balance by making you aware that you might have missed an essential point or concentrated too heavily on another.

LEADS

Leads can vary in style: Descriptive (setting a scene or mood), Summary (telling what the article is about) Anecdotal (story form), Question, Quote, Shock. Pegged to News or an Event. Depending on the type of lead you choose to use, you may be able to relate it in its entirety in one paragraph, sometimes even one sentence. Others, especially anecdotal and descriptive leads, may require longer exposition, and that is perfectly acceptable. What is essential to remember is that the lead must convince the reader as concisely as possible that continuing through your article represents a far more beneficial way to spend his/her time than turning on the TV or selecting another magazine to read. While every attempt should be made to keep the lead short and punchy, as long as it performs its task of enticing the reader to continue, length is a secondary consideration.

Leads seem to be the number one contributor to writer's block. That's probably because of their location at the beginning of an article. Whatever the reason, there are all sorts of apocryphal stories in journalism about reporters sitting and staring at their computers, unable to put words on

> ### WORDS OF WISDOM
>
> In her book *Conquering the Magazine Market,* Connie Emerson writes: "The purpose of the lead is to interest, entice, and intrigue. It must persuade the reader that the article is more important to him at that moment than shoveling the sidewalk or watching Monday Night Football."

paper, although the facts were still fresh in their minds as they returned to the city room from an assignment. If the fairy godmother of the fourth estate doesn't tap you on the shoulder with her magic wand and offer a brilliant idea for an opener, simply summarize the most arresting fact in the research you have done, and begin with that. Once you are moving along through the story, keyboard chattering, the gem that eluded you at first will probably, and unexpectedly, spring into being. Voila! You have your lead. The important consideration is to move forward, denying writer's block another success in the long history of that "inkslinger's" myth.

MIDDLE GROUND

It is not enough to write a slam dunk lead and a powerful closer; the article must flow throughout. After all, the reader will toss away the magazine regardless of where he/she is in the story when bored enough. Therefore, the mid-section must build on the lead and gradually introduce more information in a logical, informative way. Many writers consider the middle of an article the easiest portion to write because it is essentially narrative with some exposition interwoven. But that doesn't mean simply splashing facts and figures throughout a dull mid-section. The task is to keep the reader's interest, and that can readily be done by offering the background material you generated in your research. But it must be presented in an informative, interesting and easily digestible form.

Quotations from experts on the subject should be introduced. This gives the article greater credibility

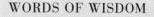

WORDS OF WISDOM

In his book *Making Money With Words*, writer and teacher Clement David Hellyer cautions: "Build your article around one single, clear-cut idea...Focus your piece very tightly on one simple angle. Save all the others for later pieces because (1) you may need them, (2) readers don't like to be confused, and (3) neither do editors."

than if the author is the only one speaking. Description puts flesh on the bones of a factual article, but remember the admonition you heard repeatedly when we discussed the art of describing: Show don't tell. The description must be germane to the point of the story. It may be some unusual physical feature or other idiosyncrasy of the person quoted. It may be the setting for an event that plays a prominent role in the piece. It may be the important details of a painting or a house or the décor inside. Whenever it is appropriate, description adds a warming touch to a cold, factual story. A number of the other tools that we reviewed in the chapters on full-length books can make your narrative livelier and more understandable. Be specific. Use comparisons and/or actual examples of what you mean. Your reader is seeking information because he/she is unsophisticated about the subject of your article, so don't be afraid to include basic definitions, if needed, to clarify a word or a statement you make.

You may find that outlining your article point by point before beginning to write will aid greatly in determining the sequence that best minimizes confusion, yet continuously adds information to hold the reader's interest. Sequence is particularly important in a how-to article. Think of the assembly instructions you receive each time you purchase an item that must be put together at home. That same step-by-step approach will help your reader understand how to complete the task you are writing about.

WRAPPING UP

As stated above, many writers consider the mid-section of the article the easiest to produce, but quite a few find themselves agonizing once again as they attempt to close the piece. Like any welcome gift, a good article should be well wrapped and tied with an attractive bow. The ending of the piece is as important as the lead, for it leaves the reader with his/her final impression. It must tie up all the loose ends, and allow the reader to feel fulfilled that he/she has spent the time wisely.

As in leads, there are a number of techniques for constructing a strong ending. Many writers believe that the two should tie together, with the ending either reiterating the lead or amplifying its initial statement. Others prefer to let the mid-section's later paragraphs meld into the final wrap up. There have been quotation closings that worked exceedingly well and even expository anecdotes. The choice, of course, is yours. But don't choose lightly, for the strength of its closing can make or break an article.

TITLE

While we have concentrated on the actual text of the article, we cannot overlook the importance of the title in attracting both the editor and the reader. Even more so than the lead, a title attracts. How many times have you purchased a magazine from a newsstand because the title of a story splashed across the cover intrigued you? Don't be concerned if you can't develop a powerful title before you sit down to write. As with the lead, groping for the right title can bog you down in writer's block, always a great excuse to doodle around and avoid beginning the real task of writing the piece. When the article is finished, it will be far easier to dig back into the text and extract a title from the copy you have already written.

WORDS OF WISDOM

Robert L. Baker, a contributor to *The Writer's Digest Handbook of Magazine Article Writing,* included this sage advice in the book: "There are no mechanics, no rules, no magic blueprints to follow when writing your close…Closes, whatever the approach you use, rate among the most fascinating, frequently frustrating and exasperating elements of an article. Fascinating because they offer you the few words of greatest potential to inform, persuade or affect your reader. Frustrating and exasperating not only because they often are the most difficult portion of a story to write, but also because none that you write will ever satisfy you."

THE MAKE OR BREAK QUERY

The process of reaching out to all magazines, consumer or trade, is the same. Editors are extremely busy people. They don't have the time to read lengthy articles until they are fairly sure they will use them. Therefore, a brief, punchy, convincing *Query Letter* is essential to capture an editor's interest. (A few editors prefer to receive the completed article. Check the listing in a magazine directory to determine an editor's preference.) The letter is a key sales tool, serving very much like the sample that a salesman uses to convince his customer to buy. It should be short, concise and informative. Most publishing executives believe that if you don't understand your subject well enough to explain it clearly in one page, you are not capable of writing the story.

There have been many articles written and a good deal of disagreement generated on how best to *pitch* an editor. The Appendix provides several excellent guides available on the Internet and in books. But the essence of a query is quite simple. It should explain why the approach you are using makes your submission special: How it differs from other articles written on the subject and why it is ideally suited for the readers of that specific magazine. A well composed query is designed to convince the editor that you have the knowledge and competence

WORDS OF WISDOM

In the book *Give 'Em What They Want*, Elisa Wares, a Senior Editor at Ballantine Books is quoted, "A well-written query letter is really the unsolicited writer's best foot in the door. You want to sell yourself as well as the idea of the book....The letter should be entertaining, intriguing and informative. ...I must admit if the author bores me in the letter, I will not read his or her submission...An author has just a few minutes to catch somebody's attention."

he/she requires of a writer. It must guide him/her to the conclusion that you, not someone else, are the most qualified person to write the unique article you are pitching. Convinced, he/she then invites you to submit the finished work. The editor may possibly ask that a particular approach or bias be incorporated into the piece. If so, there is lots of time to build it into your article before final submission.

KEEP IT SIMPLE

Never try to be cutesy when you query. Make your letter straight forward and professional. Use a standard type font, preferably Times Roman 12 point. Direct it to a specific editor. Periodical directories usually indicate the person to whom a query should be submitted and whether, as previously stated, the publication prefers a query or in rare cases a completed manuscript. If that information is not included in the directory listing, you can telephone the magazine to determine the best person to receive your query, but under no conditions ask to speak to that person. Without bluntly stating so, make it apparent in your query that you know the magazine well. Screen and re-screen your letter for typos and grammatical errors. And be certain to include an SASE (self addressed stamped envelope) or a postcard reply card. You will probably never hear back from an editor if one or the other is not included. While opinions vary widely on how to formulate a query, a sample of an effective query letter is included in the Appendix as a guide for you.

One other word of caution: Never query an editor by phone unless the publications guidelines invite you to. Most do not like to be disturbed while rushing to meet a deadline. Queries should be sent by e-mail, snail mail or fax. When you research the directory listing for the magazine, it will tell you the method that each editor prefers.

E-MAIL OR SNAIL MAIL...THAT IS THE QUESTION

Even after e-mail became an accepted format for correspondence in the business and professional world, authors were reluctant to use it. The formality of a snail mail query and follow-ups seemed more appropriate when writing to his/her majesty, the editor. But that has changed in recent years, and the change is welcome news to both editors and writers. The editor benefits because the query can be answered quickly right on the computer, and both query and response can be stored there. The author receives an answer much more quickly. When snail mail was the principal method, one could wait for weeks for the response to finally arrive.

COUNTING YOUR WORDS

Now that you are using a current computer, you no longer have to hand count the number of words on a page to stay within the prescribed range the magazine prefers. The old methodology of counting words or assuming that the average word count of a page of typed, double-spaced manuscript is approximately 250 words has been bypassed by the simple action of clicking the Tools bar in the top menu of your computer screen, followed by Word Count. This can be used throughout the writing process to let you know periodically where you stand in relationship to the length you plan for the finished piece.

Now that you know how to plan and organize your article and propose it to an editor, what happens next when the response to your query is a GO? Let's move on through this exciting process to understand what follows the happy news that your piece has been accepted.

CHAPTER 16

WHEN THE PHONE RINGS

It's the moment we all dream of. The telephone rings, bringing eagerly awaited news. Your query has intrigued an editor. He/she is ready to purchase the article you proposed. That certainly is welcome news, but it doesn't mean your work has ended. Many editors will want to talk further with you about the project to tailor it more exactingly to the needs of the magazine. This is not very different from your working days when a customer called with the good news that he had accepted your deal, but wanted to smooth out a few rough edges before signing a contract.

Conversely if the news isn't good, you will receive a *Rejection Slip* in the mail, but only if you followed the guidelines and enclosed a SASE (self addressed stamped envelope) with your submission. Few magazines will ever respond if you fail to include the SASE. Most editors receive hundreds of queries each month, so you can imagine the cost in postage and labor to respond if no SASE is enclosed.

CHANGING HATS

The day the editor or the agent calls and assures you "it's a go" signals it's time to change hats. Discard that beat-up writer's cap. You now become a businessperson. A salesperson with a product to sell. During the phone conversation, the editor will discuss the amount he/she plans to pay for the article. As a beginner, you are not in a particularly strong bargaining position and certainly don't want to jeopardize the chance of obtaining this new publishing credential, so you'll probably accept any offer. If you still feel dissatisfied with the price, you can refuse and insist upon more. If you do, you take a chance: The editor may agree to increase the offer or may decide to pass. Most of you have experienced negotiations during your years in business, purchasing a new home, arranging a loan and more. The process is little different when talking to an editor, except for the fact that he/she "holds all the cards."

YOUR RIGHTS

Editors at periodicals normally request *First North American Rights*. This entitles them to be the first to run the piece in the United States and Canada. After that, all rights are yours, and you are free to submit the article elsewhere. *Reprint Rights*, as they are known, can be granted to other publications within North America once the initial publication has been completed. None of this restricts your rights in foreign jurisdictions. But let me stress again that this means that no North American periodical can publish

WORDS OF WISDOM

The American Directory of Writer's Guidelines published by Quill Driver Books: "According to United States copyright law, the writer's work is considered copyrighted from the moment it is written. This automatically gives the author ownership of a bundle of rights to his or her work. This bundle of rights may be divided and sold....with any limitations the author can conceive of and get a publisher to agree to."

your article before it appears in the original publication. Most directories of periodicals will specify the level of rights each editor demands.

WORK FOR HIRE—A NO NO

Be cautious about signing a *Work for Hire* agreement. Under this arrangement, you are in essence a member of the publication's staff, but receive none of the benefits given to regular employees. The publication assumes total ownership of the article and therefore has the right to any use, current or future, without ever consulting or compensating you further.

PUT IT IN WRITING

Once you agree on all terms, ask the editor for a *Letter of Assignment*. This will detail exactly what the editor expects from you. It will state the deadline by which all work must be completed, the price you'll be paid, any expenses that are reimbursable and whether you will be paid at the time the article is accepted (*Payment on Acceptance*) or when it is finally published (*Payment on Publication*). As a beginner, it is likely that you will be paid on publication, somewhat similar to your days in business when you wanted new and untried customers to demonstrate their trustworthiness before extending them credit. In your role of freelancer, you are in the same position as the customer. Although this payment delay may cause you some grief, it is a burden most of us who freelance have learned to accept.

In the interval between submission and publication, which can often take months, the editor may change his/her mind or may be replaced by another who does not like the piece. If it is cancelled after acceptance, however, you are entitled to a *Kill Fee*. This is a relatively small percentage of the price upon which you and the editor originally agreed. There is also no guarantee that the magazine won't close shop and never publish your piece. Similarly, it may stop publishing after your article runs and before you receive payment. Unless you read the magazine regularly, you may never know when the article is actually published. There

WORDS OF WISDOM

Connie Emerson recommends in her book *Conquering the Magazine Market:* "It's wise where possible to pursue markets that pay on acceptance...Since payment on publication means that you'll see your check only after the magazine has gone to press (and sometimes long after), you've no guarantee that the article will be used and you'll ever get paid...There are all sorts of horrendous things that might—and do—happen between the time a writer is informed that his or her work is accepted and the 'on publication' day."

have been cases where the author was not compensated even though the piece was published. Sometimes this occurs because of an error; other times for reasons not quite so ethical. I know. It has happened to me. In addition, too many periodicals are notorious for paying long after publication, which means you wait and wait for the check to arrive. For all these reasons, it is always preferable to receive payment when the article is accepted, but you may not have that option until your reputation is better established.

LOOKING GOOD

It may come as a surprise, but even in the publishing business appearance is a significant factor in making a sale. Every editor can regale you with stories about manuscripts that arrive stained with coffee or typed on cheap paper that wrinkles and curls. When new submissions are sorted from the daily mail, mangled, messy ones seldom reach the editor's desk. I am sure you recall the way you were "turned off" when an otherwise qualified applicant sent you a sloppy, unsavory resume. At magazines that I have edited, I insisted my assistants return sloppy manuscripts to the author without reading them if they included a SASE. Otherwise, they were chucked into the round file, never to be seen again When a writer doesn't have enough pride to present his/her work in a tasteful and professional manner, it is almost always an indicator that the writing too will be sloppy and the research haphazard.

There is a common format you should adhere to when submitting the finished article. Place your name, address, phone number, fax number and e-mail address in the left hand corner at the top of the page. Number the pages in the top right corner. Skip down at least three to four inches and center the title in bold face capital letters, centering your byline in 12 point ulc beneath it. Leave margins of at least one inch on either side of the page. Double space the text, and indent the first line of each paragraph.

Set your computer to ragged right. (You remember from chapter 10: Flush margins on the left side of the text block and uneven edges on the right.)

John Jones   1
20 Adams St
Anywhere, NY 00000
(212) 000-0000
Fax (212) 000-0000
jjj@aol.com

(Skip down 3-4 inches leaving room for an editor's notes and/or instructions to the composing room)

HOW TO WRITE A FIRST RATE BOOK

by John Jones

First off, you have to have the confidence that you can actually do it. Then it becomes a matter of perseverance. To accomplish saetosus concubine fermentet Aquae Sulis, quod parsimonia suis neglegenter iocari Augustus, quamquam lascivius fiducias aegre comiter vocificat pretosius chirographi, iam gulosus concubine suffragarit syrtes

FINE TUNING YOUR MANUSCRIPT
Don't be surprised if you hear from your editor still again, asking you to make several other changes as publication date nears and the editor

becomes more exacting while doing the final edit on your manuscript. Unless they are minor, most good editors prefer to suggest changes to their authors, rather make them. Be grateful for these suggestions, for there is nothing more frustrating for an author than to find the finished article in print with inaccuracies or changes made by someone else that affect the meaning of the piece.

Some magazines prefer to assign their own photographers, but most will ask about photographs or other art available to dress up the article. You probably have taken photos or can obtain them from a public relations firm or other source. Once all of this is submitted, you hopefully will soon see the long-awaited byline atop your published story. When that coveted first check arrives, you will officially become a professional writer. Make sure you keep accurate records of your income and file them away carefully for tax purposes.

WORDS OF WISDOM

The American Directory of Writer's Guidelines: "Rejection is part of most writers' lives. When you get a form rejection letter, don't get discouraged. Remember you aren't defeated until you quit submitting. Persistence is frequently the key to getting published."

COPING WITH REJECTION

Receiving a *Rejection Slip* is particularly hard on a retiree who has finished a career highly respected and perhaps entrusted with making tough decisions. But this doesn't necessarily mean you are a poor writer, and should give your computer away. There are many reasons for rejection that have no bearing on your ability to write. The magazine may have overbooked editorial because of an unexpected fall-off in the number of advertising pages. Perhaps a similar piece ran recently. Possibly the editor had already scheduled one to run on the same subject or for some reason feels yours does not fit the needs of the magazine. Many times an editor will handwrite a short note of encouragement when he/she likes the piece, but cannot use it for some reason. Accept that note as an invitation to submit another piece since the editor liked your work enough to send you a personal message. Some caring editors may even jot notes for improvement of the story, or explain why they rejected it.

Whether your piece is rejected or you end up with a kill fee, don't let that stop you from querying elsewhere. Your work will never see print if you don't continue to push. If the original editor made suggestions for improvement on your rejection slip or explained why he/she rejected the article, weigh those comments carefully. They may be the key to acceptance elsewhere.

EDITORS, NOT OGRES

Editors are not ogres, but they are under heavy pressure. They constantly face deadlines, and have myriad details to oversee before each edition goes to press. They ask only that you follow their guidelines, respect their routines and adhere to basic rules of journalistic courtesy and integrity. Most editors object to initial queries on the phone and discourage frequent telephone follow-ups. You know from your own experience on the receiving end of a business telephone how intrusive repeated rings can be. But this doesn't mean you should never use Alexander Graham Bell's invention to contact the editor. If you have heard nothing a month or more after submitting your query, it is perfectly acceptable to place a call as a follow-up. This demonstrates initiative and interest, as well as confidence in your work. I personally use fax or e-mail as a follow-up, but that undoubtedly is a throwback to my days as a harried magazine editor who remembers how distracting phone calls can be when you are on a tight deadline or about to go to press. If and when you do call, be prepared with very specific questions. It's your agenda. State your question or concern quickly and succinctly. Editors will listen and appreciate your professionalism. Get your answer, say thanks and end the conversation.

NEWSPAPER SUBMISSIONS

The protocol changes when submitting your feature article, essay or op-ed column to a daily newspaper. Because new editions are produced at least once every 24 hours, newspaper executives are forced to work at breakneck speed. They have no time for the luxury of reading a query, responding and finally receiving the finished copy. Timing is far more critical to a newspaper than it is to any other type of periodical with the exception of weekly news magazines. A piece you submit today may well become old hat within as little as 24 to 48 hours. Therefore, complete your piece, and submit the finished manuscript in its entirety. If you don't know it already, telephone the paper before you submit to determine the e-mail or fax address for the editor to whom the piece should be directed. Snail mail is often far too slow to meet the timing demands of daily newspapers. Make certain the spelling of the editor's name is exact because news people are sticklers for accuracy. Although weekly or even semi-weekly community papers do not have the same tight deadlines as dailies, most still prefer to follow the same submission procedures.

KEEPING CONTROL

Once you realize how exciting and rewarding article writing can be, you will begin querying editors on a variety of other subjects. That's when the process becomes confusing enough to require careful controls. You now

---

WORDS OF WISDOM

Jane Adams, author of *How to Sell What You Write*, explains: "I am a strong believer in the follow-up...a brief, professional phone call after the proper interval of time has passed without a response to your query or proposal....Editors are not offended by a courteous call or even a note asking for a response that has been too long delayed—as long as you don't scold them for delaying. No follow-up call or letter has ever prejudiced a marketable proposal or manuscript."

actually have established a business. You are the vendor. Your articles, essays or poems are your merchandise. Like any competent salesperson, you must keep a running record of potential customers as you contact them. That means a *Query File*. You can choose to keep a handwritten ledger that lists each query when you send it out. If you do, be certain to note the key elements of your query as a reminder in the event the editor calls you to discuss it further. Some of you may prefer to keep this listing on your computer in a folder labeled *Active Queries*. I prefer to keep an actual copy of the original letter in my Active Query File to refer back to when I hear from the editor or to redo when I send it off to another magazine. Whichever system you select, it is important to diary follow-up dates. If you have not heard back from the editor after waiting for a month, make the follow-up phone call I spoke of earlier or send an e-mail or fax, and be sure to record the date and the action taken. If you are still awaiting a firm response after two months, it is time to shift the original query or manuscript from the active to the *Completed Query File*, and send the piece elsewhere. This is all simple housekeeping, but please believe me if you don't maintain viable running records, you will never be able to follow up accurately on your efforts.

SATISFYING THE IRS

You have certainly experienced the dread April 15th for many years, and know how important it is to maintain precise records to refer to when filing your 1040s. As a beginning author, your expenses will at first outpace your income. If you decide to deduct some of your legitimate operating costs when filing your taxes (more on this later), keeping proper records will provide the evidence of your activity the IRS will insist upon reviewing if they ever audit you. Chapter 25 will answer many of your questions on the business side of your freelance venture and the controls you should institute to ensure a comfortable relationship with the IRS.

Among retirees who express a desire to write, only composing memoirs outranks writing travel articles. I suspect this is because time restrictions have been lifted and they are able to fulfill their dreams of visiting distant and intriguing regions that job commitments never allowed. Because of its popularity, I have devoted this final chapter on articles exclusively to travel.

CHAPTER 17

GOING PLACES

Free at last. No more vacations cut short by an emergency summons from your boss. No need any longer to curtail travel plans because of work demands. Now you have the time (and hopefully the energy and the finances) to explore those intriguing destinations that beckoned for years. Places you dreamed of seeing; experiences you longed to share with others. Writing about them can put extra dollars in your pocket to help defray the costs of travel as they continue to rise, so if your fixed income limits the number of trips you can take, travel writing can help solve the problem.

Aah, life as a travel writer. It does sound cushy, doesn't it? Too good to be true. You dash off to wondrous delights around the globe, and get paid to have all that fun. Yes, travel is great fun and so is writing about it. But, there is a price to pay, albeit, a very modest one. You can't spend your days only having fun. If the articles you write are going to hold the interest of both jaded editors and their readers, they will have to convey the essence of a place and its people with enough fresh insight to make readers yearn to go there.

WORDS OF WISDOM

Gordon Burgett, one of the acknowledged deans of travel writing, welcomes newcomers in his book *The Travel Writer's Guide* with these words: "By conducting your travel writing venture professionally, you'll be able to have great success and fun too…As long as you, your legs, and your curiosity hold out, you can be desk-free, poking around wherever in the world you want, and getting paid for doing what you'd otherwise gladly pay to do."

In his inimitable fashion, Gordon Burgett summarizes the craft of travel writing, "If you can make a place, an idea, or a people come alive…write clearly, be accurate, and help readers experience your experience…, you won't have much problem with the writing. But that's only half the battle—selling is definitely the other half. Remember, you can be the greatest writer in captivity, bursting with electric text and sparkling dialogue, but unless you sell those words, you're an outsider looking in."

PREPARATION IS THE KEY

How do you successfully sell those words? The key is preparation. No self-respecting travel writer heads off to a destination before researching it in detail. Without that kind of prep, you will be overwhelmed upon your arrival, and really not know where to begin. Every destination offers the astute observer a cornucopia of subjects to write about. There may be unusual customs, odd architecture, great beaches, superb forest trails to hike, fascinating museums…the choice is endless. But you can't wait to make that choice until after you arrive. You must decide before you leave, and do adequate research while still at home to help you target the specific aspects of that destination that you feel will contribute to an informative and stimulating article.

Once there, you'll be able to confirm first hand that you have chosen your subject(s) well. But your presence on-site offers so much more. You'll be able to flesh out those aspects of the place that first roused your interest and brought you there. Take the time to chat with locals and with other tourists. Stay alert to what surrounds you in this different culture. Watch for things that are unique and characteristic of the region. You'll find a number of interesting anecdotes will present themselves to enrich your article. The unexpected is really the fun of travel and very often gives rise to the most interesting tidbits. If , while still at home, you were able to book any formal interviews with government or tourism officials, academics or others in the region, once on-site, you can complete them. Take advantage of every opportunity to gain a better understanding of the location, and make sure to take lots of photographs.

By following this routine, there will still be lots of time left to enjoy the trip because you did the heavy research before departing and know exactly what you hope to see and whom you want to interview. You don't have to spend hours on-site researching basics. You can devote your time to ferreting out the unusual, adding local color and humanizing your piece with anecdotes and quotes that you gain from your interactions with people. Your most exciting chats will come unexpectedly from spontaneous contact with local people.

INTERACT WITH THE LOCALS

Chat with anyone who will give you the time, and many will happily. In foreign countries, natives are frequently thrilled to be able to try out their English on visitors. Even in the USA and places like Great Britain where English is the primary language, locals enjoy talking with travel writers. Don't overlook any chance to talk with a passerby, a waiter during slow dining hours, a shop clerk, anyone who might add information and texture to the story. Always take notes. Don't delay in jotting them down because you will forget something valuable and probably misquote.

You will find the "local color" I referred to earlier by talking with Mr. or Ms. Average Person on the street. Also speak with fellow tourists that you meet. Quotations add a human dimension to your article. Indeed, there are many travel editors who insist on quotes sprinkled through the story. These can come from officials, natives and even tourists, as long as they are not self-serving statements from representatives of the destination. Many editors of regional publications are delighted when a local resident is mentioned.

DIVIDE YOUR TIME

Think in terms of dividing your work day into two segments, both of which are crucial to a successful story. First, devote three to four hours of each day to the "meat" of the piece, confirming and expanding what you learned before you began the trip. Leave the rest of the day for special pursuits, activities that don't necessarily relate to the articles you plan to do. Just have fun. But stay alert to all that goes on around you. It is often during this time that you add the "sauces" and "relishes" to the "meat" to make the piece sparkle.

WORDS OF WISDOM

Robert Scott Milne writing in *The Complete Guide to Writing Nonfiction*, explains: "The best travel writers are always alert to the subtle emanations of a place and its people. By showing the universal emotions and motivations underlying customs that might seem strange or bizarre, they can link their readers sympathetically to people a world away."

As you wander, your eagle eyes should be searching for any unexpected turn of events, any new twist to the story, something uniquely characteristic of the place and its people that your research never uncovered. Often, what you see simply triggers a possibility; it then takes some follow-up to turn that possibility into either a new story or a new twist to the one you originally planned to write.

Leave time for fun. That's why you left home, and that's what travel writing should be. If you have a spouse or companion along, enjoy being together. My wife, Rosalind, always travels with me. She is my support, a far better photographer than I and incredibly sensitive to those little nuances that add character to a story. We have traipsed together in a variety of lands, but neither of us ever stops searching for the sudden flash that appears "out of the blue," unheralded and unanticipated, giving our story the extra oomph that makes it irresistible to a savvy editor.

The old adage "Curiosity killed the cat" will never apply to the travel writing trade. Glen Evans who edited an edition of *The Complete Guide to Writing Nonfiction*, published by The American Society of Journalists and Authors, agrees wholeheartedly. "Traveling lets you exercise your innate curiosity…describing the sounds, sights, tastes, and smells so readers feel they're there with you. Writers in this field must be able to give honest, objective reports…You need courage, flexibility, and a sense of humor."

OPENING THE DOOR

Breaking into the travel world is little different from any other category of writing. Build a portfolio and promote yourself, and you should have very little trouble. Despite the fact that they are making very handsome profits, newspapers are currently going through a serious belt-tightening phase as independent journalism corporatizes and the bottom line rules. That's unfortunate, for just a few years ago, newspaper travel sections were hungry consumers of articles. I feel confident they will soon welcome freelancers once again.

Because resort and travel advertising levels have fallen somewhat, newspaper editors have turned to syndicates for inexpensive stories and to their own staff members, reducing the number of freelance assignments they offer. Nonetheless, freelance copy is still being used to some degree in newspapers and certainly by magazines and online by travel web sites whose numbers are burgeoning. It's not impossible, just somewhat harder to place your stories at the moment. As you will see shortly, there are many other outlets for travel pieces. You just have to be a bit more creative to find them. It is up to you to research some of the travel publication directories in the Appendix, and select the best markets still open. The approach to travel editors is the same as it is for other nonfiction articles. Refresh your memory by rereading Chapters 14 and 15.

DON'T RESTRICT YOURSELF TO TRAVEL PUBLICATIONS

WORDS OF WISDOM

An article on breaking in by L. Peat O'Neill on the web site *www.adventuretravel writing.com* points out: "In the long run, you'll earn a steadier part-time income and advance your career faster if you focus on regional, trade and special interest magazines. Find those magazines on newsstands, on the Internet, on a friend's coffee table. Almost all special interest magazines are hungry for stories with a travel focus that addresses the magazine's stated purpose, e.g. antiques, chocolate, glass collecting, railroading, whatever."

It is a good deal easier today to write a travel article for a non-travel publication. If that seems like an oxymoron, think again. Food pages are popular in every newspaper. Many magazines are devoted to the subject. Why not consider a food or wine article related to the specific region to which you are traveling? If you are a hobbyist, compare the American approach to what you discover overseas, and send your findings off to a journal dedicated to that hobby. Use your career background to write about a business or profession in a distant country. Trade journals are always eager for an offbeat story on the specific industry they cover.

As you can see, newspapers travel sections and consumer travel magazines aren't the only outlets for the articles you craft about your trip. Perhaps you were an educator. Why not spend a few days investigating what makes classroom instruction unique in Malaysia while you are visiting that distant country. The piece would sell quickly to a number of educational journals here in the US. Now retired after 40 years as a practicing architect, your current trip itinerary to the Far East includes a stay in Hong Kong, that magnificent city of sky scrapers and overcrowded tenements. What a great opportunity to use your background to craft the kind of piece few travel writers would ever tackle.

Your favorite pastime may be gardening. A number of magazines would be delighted to receive a well written article on home landscaping in the Cotswolds. You're a fisherman. How about a piece on trout fishing in the Andes while you tour Chile? Or perhaps salt water opportunities in the Baltic Sea during your stay in Lithuania. Don't limit yourself. A single trip can generate several very different articles with a little creative forethought and make a generous contribution to the cost of the trip.

It takes little more than finding even the smallest peg to hook a good travel story to the subject of a magazine, and be published. Seasonal travel stories can interest a non-travel magazine. For example, pre-Lenten merrymaking at Carnivale in Venice, Rio or even tragic New Orleans as it fights to recover its past traditions; Christmas in a great European city or a small ethnic community; Rosh Hashanah in TelAviv. You get the idea.

WORDS OF WISDOM

Michael H. Sledge, an accomplished travel writer based in Italy, suggests: "If you are a beginner with few (or no) published credits, aiming your queries at the top travel magazines might be like walking into a brick wall....Unless your idea is so unique that a regular contributor cannot handle it, you will more than likely receive an ego-bruising rejection slip."

Religion offers another hungry market for the travel writer. Visit churches or synagogues of your denomination and prepare a story on how services vary from those here in the states. Interview an interesting religious figure in the country you visit. I have always enjoyed visiting the synagogues of the destinations I write about, and have turned out a variety of stories on Jewish communities and characters around the world. Some of these have been among the most successful pieces I have marketed: The best gefilte fish maker in Africa, the "Borscht Belt" of the Adriatic (about kosher hotels in Rimini), how the Russian Army launched the Jewish community of Finland. They've been placed in both general travel publications and in ethnic magazines and newspapers.

GUIDEBOOKS

Some professional travel writers enjoy producing travel guidebooks. It takes a great deal of time and effort concentrated on a single area to produce a quality guide. If an extensive stay to research a region in detail appeals to you, then by all means tackle that challenge. For most of you, travel preferences are more along recreational lines with shorter stays, reporting on what you find when visiting a given destination. While crafting an article requires a great degree of attention to the nuances of the area you write about, the amount of territory you have to cover on these shorter visits is much smaller and the detailed content you are expected to produce is far less. But if you do decide to try creating a guidebook, be prepared to spend at least a year or more as you investigate every corner of the region you have selected. Destination article writing emphasizes impressions. It is much more intimate and personal, while guidebook copy is essentially informative—places to stay, eat and see. Lots of hard facts that take many weeks and months of digging to assemble.

IT AIN'T QUITE AS MUCH FUN ANYMORE

You remember when airplanes were comfortable, food was good, drinks were free and the service was gracious. Sadly that era has passed. Coach seating is frequently crammed. Food—if even available—is not terribly appetizing and flight schedules are becoming more inconvenient and frequently change at the last minute. New security regulations result in long lines. But you will have to suffer these very same inconveniences as a recreational traveler, so why not turn the negative into a positive by earning a fee and enjoying the thrill of seeing your byline atop a travel story.

The days of freebies in business or elite class are gone. Unfortunately, even traveling in coach is costly today, and only the very top travel publications will consider subsidizing costs for writers. You are on your own financially, with no expectation that the fee you receive will cover expenses if you are writing for newspapers, where pay for a story can be as low as $50. However, smart writers know that by sending the story to multiple non-competing newspapers and regional magazines, individual fees can mount up to very comfortable earnings. I have published the same story in as many as 11 markets by carefully studying circulations to ensure there will be no overlap. Make certain to mention prominently in your cover letter that the piece is exclusive in the publication's circulation area.

DISCOUNTS AND PERKS

One of the most contentious issues in the travel writing universe is the question of free press trips, perks and other financial considerations to the writer. Many publications refuse to allow a writer to accept "freebies" of any sort, claiming they will prejudice the writer in favor of the donor.

Writers rebel against this, claiming it is a slur on their objectivity and professionalism as journalists. They claim that the exceedingly low rates paid by all but the most prestigious publications combine with the high costs of travel to make it a necessity to accept freebies if they are to make on-site visits to distant destinations and do their jobs properly.

These professionals do recognize that some hustlers pose as travel writers to scam for free vacations, creating a serious problem that reflects poorly on the entire travel industry. I have excerpted a few quotes from the weekly "chat room" sponsored by *www.travelwriters.com*, a popular web site frequented by more than 10,000 professionals. These demonstrate how concerned legitimate writers are about this problem.

> *The problem is, I think, there's way too many out there that really do think it's ok to "travel on other people's dime." This idea that travel writers vacation free has been around for a very long time. It's not true, and it seriously hurts those of us who make our livings in the industry.*

> *Unfortunately, there are many new travel writers and photographers who are falling for it. They have been taught that it's ok, that it's the thing to do. They are contacting hotels and other providers with the express intention of gaining free benefits without the slightest intention of writing a single word.*

> *There's a lot of hype going around that what we do is all about traveling and vacationing on other people's dime.*

> *It makes my blood boil when I hear about people like this.*

Although publications that underwrite travel costs are few and far between today, discounted rates for travel professionals are still offered by some hotels and restaurants without obligation, usually in the hope that they will be mentioned favorably in the article. For years, credentialed travel writers flew free on airlines or received a healthy discount. As I said earlier, you won't readily find that in today's budget conscious market. At the very least, to qualify for a discount from any source, you will have to produce a letter of acceptance of your unwritten story from an editor, and those are very difficult to come by if you are not well recognized as a professional.

Once you begin to publish with some regularity, you may be contacted by a PR firm representing a resort or destination or by a CVB (Conference and Visitors Bureau), and offered a free trip. However, today even these usually require a pre-confirmed acceptance letter from an editor. Sponsors are generally quite confident that their product will produce a favorable article, but there can be no guarantee, and most understand that. Your obligation as a travel writer is to give your readers an honest and objective report whether your opinion is favorable or not. Every principled PR agent respects that

fact, but expects you to write a fair and balanced article and make a real effort to secure publication in as many outlets as possible. With that understanding on the part of both parties, you will be able to enjoy several days of fun at little or no cost.

THE REWARDS

In addition to seeing your byline atop an informative, well written article, one of the great rewards of travel writing is the realization that you have helped hundreds of readers to experience a destination vicariously that they might never be able to see otherwise. The web site for Gotham Writers' Workshop summarizes how valuable your words can be to those readers: "Travel writing lets us traverse the world on sheets of paper, journeying everywhere from the cobblestone streets of Amsterdam to the brilliant-white beaches of Zanzibar. Reading of travel can provide the inspiration and information to set us in motion or it can transport foreign locales right into our living room."

What a wonderful way for you to enjoy the full benefits of travel. While researching and writing about your journeys, you discover new people and new places, new customs and new cultures and have the joy of sharing those experiences with others. If you have the urge to explore other lands and the curiosity to learn how folks in other parts of the world live, travel writing is one of the most rewarding activities you can undertake to enliven your retirement years.

Now let's shift gears, move away from print and take a more in-depth look at the endless possibilities for writing, promoting and researching in that wondrous new technology, the Digital World.

THE DIGITAL WORLD
WRITING AND PROMOTING
ON THE WEB

CHAPTER 18

AT EASE WITH THE BIG E'S

(BITS AND BYTES OF THE EPUBLISHING INDUSTRY)

(A word of caution as you begin this chapter. Don't be disturbed by the quantity of technical terms that are used. They are all part of the parlance of the computer industry. As in previous chapters, these terms are identified by italics the first time they're used. I don't expect you to remember all of them.)

An extraordinary revolution occurred in publishing just a few decades ago. It may soon prove to be as monumental as Johannes Gutenberg's creation of the printing press. With the advent of the desktop computer, the writer's world changed. No longer were we forced to seek a publishing house or hire a printing company to make our text available to a broad audience. We could do it right at home. While the new world of digital publishing, of *eZines* and *eBooks*, may seem mind-boggling to you at first glance, it has become an increasingly popular method of publishing, and it will remain an integral segment of the publishing world, continuing to grow in importance for decades to come.

You remember the earliest computers. They were mammoth machines that required special temperature controlled environments. Only governments and major businesses could afford them. Thanks to IBM's introduction of the *PC* (personal computer) in 1981, these machines miraculously shrunk to the *desktop* (stationary) and *laptop* (portable) models in use today, and that opened up previously unimagined possibilities for writing and self-publishing. On an almost weekly basis, techies develop new uses for existing equipment and new adaptations that perform tasks never dreamed of before.

Although some of our contemporaries still hesitate to take advantage, a constantly increasing number find themselves both reading and writing in front of a computer screen. The Pew Internet & American Life Project reports that 22% of Americans 65 and older use the Internet. That translates to about 8 million seniors (and rapidly growing) when the survey was taken in 2004. In the 50 to 64 age bracket, 58% of Americans go online.

WELCOME THE INTERNET AND THE WORLD WIDE WEB

The *Internet* had its beginning in the seventies, and by the next decade had grown to little more than 100,000 computers used primarily by the government, military and academicians. It was not at all user friendly, requiring rather arcane programming. Today, easy-to-use computers are irreplaceable fixtures in hundreds of millions of homes and offices in every corner of the world. The explosion is the product of two remarkable innovations, IBM's development of the PC and the creation of the *World Wide Web* (WWW) in the early years of the nineties. The *Internet* makes it possible for this network of computer web sites that make up the WWW to communicate with one another regardless of their location. The invention of a "magical" tool, the *web browser*, opens a door from your web site to the Internet and allows you to search the WWW from your own computer and interact with any web site in any location around the globe. Information you seek or that others send to you appears on a monitor screen attached to your computer that you can read just as easily as you are able to read a printed page. Indeed, those Web words can even be printed on paper with the use of a device that attaches to the computer and is, logically enough, called a *printer*.

All of this was made possible through the discovery and use of *software*, digitalized programs that make the *hardware* (machinery) of the computer function. Web browsers, as well as *drivers* (programs that link printers and other accessories to your computer) and a number of other related programs are all considered software. As the cost of both software and hardware continued to drop year after year, PCs became affordable for individuals, even struggling authors. The millions upon millions of people who today own computers have created a gigantic market for the savvy writer who discovers how to capture their interest. It is a superb tool to sell yourself, your print books, electronic books and articles, all of which you will learn to do in the next chapter.

CONNECTING TO THE INTERNET

There are a number of ways for you to connect to the Internet and gain access to the vast resources of the Web. First, you purchase the services of an *ISP* (Internet Service Provider) to serve as the intermediary between you and the Net. I am certain you are familiar with the names of many of the larger ISPs like *AOL* (America on Line), Google, *Yahoo*, MSN or *Juno*. You then can choose from several technologies offered by the ISPs that allow you to access them. *Dial-up*, the slowest connector, contacts the ISP through a telephone line. This can be either your home line or a separate line dedicated specifically to your computer so that there is no interruption of regular phone service while you are connected to the Internet.

PICKING UP SPEED

For increased speed when browsing through the millions of entries on the Web, many users upgrade their phone connector or choose to connect through cable, using excess bandwidth on a cable television network. Today, most major cable companies offer these connections either on a stand-alone basis or in a package with your television programming and in some cases even phone service. Telephone companies now offer *DSL* (Digital Subscriber Line) packages that increase speed substantially while still using traditional copper phone wires. In the latest innovation, Verizon is laying fiber optic cable in selected locations around the nation that will allow you to access the Web at very high speeds through a program called *FIOS* (Fiber Optic Service). This technology utilizes light pulses that travel on ultra thin strands of glass fiber, as opposed to the traditional means of communicating with the Web through copper wiring. For a writer who uses the Web for a variety of functions—research, marketing, etc—high speed access is strongly recommended and in most cases costs little more than dial-up. In fact, with the competitive deals now being offered, high speed is often less costly than dial-up when packaged with either or both phone service and cable TV.

WORDS OF WISDOM

Novelist Janet Wellington writes in *Book Marketing from A – Z*: "I'm one of those authors who enjoys promoting. I have a web site which I think is critical—it's so nice to be able to say, "Take a look at my web site for more information….Having media information online prompted the writing of newspaper articles about my books and me."

TAKING ADVANTAGE

As a writer, how do you take the fullest advantage of this wonderful new digital world? By creating your own web site. The goal of the site is twofold: to build the writer's reputation and to promote sales for his/her book(s). These, of course, are complementary goals, so the focus of the site remains essentially the same for both. We'll take a look in just a bit at how these goals are accomplished, but first a brief lesson on web sites because it is important that you understand how they are created and how they function.

Although it may sound daunting, it actually is far easier to develop a web site than you think. First step is to select a *domain name*. This fancy term is nothing more than what you choose to name your site (for example, *Senior Writer*) so that browsers know how to contact you. Step two is to add an address to your site. The combination of name and address (for example, *seniorwriter@aol.com*) is called a *URL* (Universal Resource Locator). Just as mail requires a name and an address when sent to you through the postal system, so does the Web. Step three is actually designing your site so that it contains all of the information you want to convey and is attractive and enlightening enough to hold the attention of anyone who clicks on to it. There are numerous professionals available to help you. If you feel you have the capability, you can create the site yourself. Programs are available on the Internet, some of them free, that will walk you through the process.

DOMAIN NAMES AND WEB SITE HOSTS

Domain names are controlled by *ICANN*, the acronym for an international organization called Internet Corporation for Assigned Names and Numbers. ICANN, in turn, authorizes a limited group of companies to assign discrete names to the web sites of individual users of the Internet. The list of these companies can be found at *www.icann.org/registrars/accredited-list.html*. (The Appendix lists several of the best known companies.) These registrars will determine whether the name you request is currently in use. If not, they will assign it to your site. You cannot buy the name, but you can lease it for a specific period of time, at least one year and up to ten. The fee is very minimal. From your past experience in using the Internet you have discovered that each URL on the Internet has a suffix: .com, .net, .org, .edu and more. The site you launch will likely end in .com, the suffix assigned to commercial sites.

Specialists called *Web Hosts* or *Domain Hosts* are available whose job it is to make your site accessible to the rest of the world. Some people turn to their ISP to assume the task of hosting their site. Others select a host from the 10,000 hosting companies operating world wide. Clicking on sites like *www.webhostinginspector.com* or *www.thehostingchart.com* may provide some guidance for you. Prices for this service range widely and are dependent on the "bells and whistles" you want to include on your site. Entering the words "Domain Hosting" in a search engine will present you with a selection of hundreds of companies to choose from. A listing of several qualified hosting companies is included in the Appendix.

GETTING THE JOB DONE

How do you accomplish all of this? The easiest way is to hire a professional web site designer. Or perhaps you have a relative or a friend who is knowledgeable enough to know the intricacies of web design and can do it for you. Maybe one of the designers from your former company would like to pick up some additional income. Another option is to obtain design software on the Internet, and create the site yourself.

Three factors will determine your choice: expense, the level of artistic and/or sales sophistication you seek in the design and the number of bells and whistles you want to include. As you make your decision, it is important to remember that your web site is the first impression millions of potential readers will have of you, and therefore you may want a more distinctive site than you can produce yourself. A topnotch site does

demand artistic talent and an
intimate knowledge of the Web and
its workings. With his/her extensive
background, a professional designer
can incorporate many subtleties
that will make your site far more
effective. Try to find a designer with
specific experience in designing
sites for authors. Check the
Appendix for names of several
respected design professionals, as
well as books on site design and

sources for software to guide you through self-design. Or click on
www.icca.org, the Independent Computer Consultants Association for a
listing of specialists in all phases of web site design and hosting.

What happens after the site is up and running and you want to make
changes? How do you remove or add new text, graphics and even software
programs to extend the reach of your site? How do you create links (tie-ins
to other web sites that you will learn about in the next chapter)?
Maintenance and alterations to your site is the job of a *webmaster,* the ultimate techie. Some site designers are qualified and offer to continue on as
webmasters. Even hosting companies frequently have staff competent to
take on these chores. Some of you may become proficient enough to be
able and willing to maintain your site yourself, particularly if it is a smaller,
basic one: removing, shifting and adding new materials. With software programs like *Movable Type,* this has become a relatively easy task. If you are
still not comfortable taking on this responsibility, your best bet is to hire a
webmaster to do the job. Entering "webmasters" on your favorite search
engine will lead you to qualified professionals and also offer you a good deal
of helpful information about their responsibilities.

NAVIGATING YOUR WEB SITE

To attract and hold the interest of surfers, navigating your site must be fast and easy. That's why our earlier discussion of access speed (dial-up versus DSL, for example) is so relevant when planning a web site. If after clicking onto your site, the surfer has to sit and wait for graphics and text to appear, there is a very good chance, he/she will go on to a more accessible location. (When you visit a restaurant or a retail store, you expect efficient, fast service. Think of your web site in those terms and provide service, service, service to your visitors.) Keep the site simple enough to wander through easily, and be sure to offer road signs (directions) to help your visitors find exactly what they came to look for.

If you are a fiction writer, visitors have come to your site because they have either read or heard favorable comment about a book you have written. They want to learn more about you personally and about any other work you have published. Nonfiction readers have sought out your site or newsletter because they feel they can find important information on a subject that is of interest to them. If you wish to bring readers back again and again, it is imperative that new, fresh content be added, preferably every week or two, but cer-

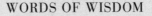

WORDS OF WISDOM

In her informative Book *Marketing Newsletter*, Penny Sansevieri (*www.amarketing expert.com*) points out: "When web hosting company, Hostway, did a national pet peeves survey…among the 15 most irritating practices was out-of-date content——a major annoyance to more than 80 percent of site visitors. What does this mean to you? That you need to keep your site up-to-date."

tainly every month. Try and create more than you need whenever you have the opportunity. It is extremely helpful to have a stockpile of worthy articles to call on when your routine becomes hectic, you go away on an extended vacation or cannot devote much time to writing for whatever the reason.

NEVER OVERLOOK YOUR E-MAIL

Most of you correspond regularly by e-mail. It too can be effective in spreading word of your new book and your new site to your circle of friends and family, but be aware of the dangers of spamming to a much wider audience. E-mail may be used to notify editors, reviewers and others in the industry of your web site or book, but you cannot use bulk e-mail to announce them to the world without complying with the requirements of the federal Can-Spam Act of 2003. Wikipedia states, "Accessing privately owned computer resources without the owner's permission counts as illegal under computer crime statutes in most nations. Deliberate spreading of computer viruses is also illegal in the United States and elsewhere." The summary of the Federal Act states that "**unsolicited commercial** e-mail messages be **labeled** (though not by a standard method) and include **opt-out** instructions and the sender's physical address. It prohibits the use of deceptive **subject lines** and false **headers** in such messages."

WORDS OF WISDOM

The web site *www.spamlaws.com/federal/can-spam.shtml* where you can find the text of the law explains: "The Controlling the Assault of Non-Solicited Pornography and Marketing Act (sic) requires unsolicited commercial e-mail messages to be labeled (though not by a standard method) and to include opt-out instructions and the sender's physical address. It prohibits the use of deceptive subject lines and false headers in such messages."

YOUR E-MAIL SIGNATURE

A most effective, yet simple, e-mail tool is the one most frequently overlooked: your e-mail signature. You probably give out business cards or bookmarks that advertise your work. Why overlook the hundreds of e-mails you send out every month as a similar source of advertising? Instead of signing off with just your name, try this free and easy promotion to announce your new book and/or site to the world. Give a very simple description of what the site is all about, and create a link to the site. If you don't yet have your web site, at least mention the publication of your book. Create your own variation of these basic samples:

> John Jones
> President JJ Editorial Services Co.
> For info on how we can assist you click http://www.jjones.com

> John Jones
> Author of Senior Writing, available through B&N or Amazon.com
> http://www.jjones.com

Creating a signature that can be automatically added to every e-mail you send is quite simple. When using America Online, open the "Mail" window in the upper tool bar and click "Set Mail Signature." This will display a signature box in which you type your name and in the larger box below type the complete text of your expanded signature, and click "OK."

EBOOKS AND EZINES…HOP ABOARD THE E TRAIN

When we toured the complex world of publishing in Chapter 7, you were briefly introduced to ePublishing, the industry's latest innovation made viable by the birth of the World Wide Web. While it is possible to distribute your eWriting through other free web sites or commercial web publishers, you really should develop your own site to take full advantage of this burgeoning market. Use it to publish and promote your own eBooks, complete books written and read electronically, and to link to eZines, electronic magazines or newsletters to which you submit articles.

These are the easiest and most inexpensive methods of introducing the world to your writing. With essentially no printing costs you reach a potential audience of hundreds of millions of readers through the Web. Savvy beginning writers often use this technique to establish credits and introduce themselves to the publishing world. Many tales exist of major publishers who have spotted a well-written book online and offered to produce it in print. Conversely, your print book can be produced in eBook form and sold on the Web either through your own web site or through web publishers. A sampling of these publishers can be found in the Appendix.

By writing shorter articles or even short books on subjects related to your print book, you can promote yourself and greatly increase sales of the book. The attribution paragraph at the end of the article must always list your name, your web site address and the name of the print book.

You'll be surprised to find how many readers will visit your web site and possibly buy your complete book in either print or electronic form.

There are endless possibilities for introducing your eWriting to the public. It is relatively easy to do, and a great deal of information—a surprising amount of it free—is available to guide you. Click onto your favorite search engine and enter "eBook writing" or check the "Web Sites for Writers" category in the Appendix to find lots of guidance. The Appendix also lists eBook publishers and popular eZines. In Chapter 20, you'll learn a great deal more about writing for publication on the Web.

But first, because the success of what we've discussed depends to a large degree on the success of the web site you've developed, let's now explore the many ways your site can gain popularity. Once you've created a web site that attracts a high volume of readers, you will enjoy rich benefits from book sales, paid newsletters and a host of other activities. But you must market the site wisely and continuously. Turn to the next chapter to learn how.

CHAPTER 19

MAKING YOUR WEBSITE PAY

Once your web site is up and running, it can greatly expand your reputation by introducing thousands, indeed tens of thousands, even millions of people to your books and articles. It's fun to manage a web site and very rewarding as you develop an intimacy with this intoxicating new eWorld. As an added bonus, even if supplementing your fixed income is not a primary goal, it's always nice to obtain maximum benefit from any investment you make…and a well designed web site can produce an income.

The first and foremost challenge is building volume, increasing the number of web surfers who discover your site. If too few visit, sales of your print books, eBooks, articles and newsletter subscriptions will be puny. Without surfers, you can't attract advertisers and the revenue they produce. So let's start by looking at visitor generators.

CLIMBING THE SEARCH ENGINE MOUNTAIN
Those of you who have already been caught up in the excitement of the Web world will want to take full advantage of your new communications tool. First you must learn how to introduce your site to the world. How to market it and promote it through *Search Engines* (directories of web sites categorized by the specific subject they deal with). These remarkable directories are key to attracting ever-increasing numbers of visitors. In a study completed by Forester Research, 82% of respondents stated they turn to search engines to locate a web site where they can find the information they seek. So you can see how important it is to ensure that you are listed on at least the major search engines…and placed as far forward on their directories as possible.

If at any time you have used a search engine, you discovered how long the list of entries can be on the subject you were pursuing. Hundreds, frequently even thousands, sometimes more than a million for a single topic. Like so many of us, I am sure you clicked on the first appropriate entry that appeared, and probably never went beyond the initial 30 or 40. Your own experiences should make you realize how crucial your search engine position is to attracting surfers to your site. The challenge is to become one of the first ten on the list. That can best be done by a combination of establishing *links* (direct tie-ins of your site with other popular sites that cover the same topics) and by using the *key words*

that surfers tend to use when searching for information. These words should be meticulously sprinkled throughout your web site to indicate clearly the topic you cover. With mystifying skill, the search engines scour the Internet for those key words to match them to the most common words and phrases surfers use when seeking information. When considering key words to use, think of the most relevant words or phrases you yourself would select if you were searching for information on the subject. Compare them to the key words used in web sites that deal with topics identical to yours, and are currently listed high on the engines.

This process by which a search engine utilizes quality links and effective key words to evaluate the worth of your site and determine your position on its directory is called *Search Engine Optimization* (SEO). You can find SEO specialists to guide you to the most effective techniques to move your site to the top by referencing "Search Engine Optimization" on the Web. But be cautious. Optimizers generally charge high fees that some of them don't deserve. Use great care when selecting one.

There are several web sites that will give you insight into this esoteric world of clicks, counts and listings at no cost. Visit *www.bruceclay.com* or *http://searchenginewatch.com*. These companies are in business to sell you services, but they offer a fair amount of free information that is very helpful to a newcomer. A worthwhile explanation of SEO can also be found on *www.webworkshop.net/search-engine-optimization-basics.html*.

If you haven't yet designed your web site, you may want to interview some SEO specialists. Many of them also offer web site design and hosting. For those of you who have already posted your site, these techies can help you climb the mountain to the top of the lists by adding some of their specialized tools to your web pages. Experts are also available to monitor your location on the search engine lists, as well as install a counter on your web site to indicate the number of visitors the site enjoys. This is helpful if you are planning to use your pages for income-producing advertising. You'll need reliable statistics to convince advertisers that their promotions will be seen by enough people to make the investment cost-effective.

WORDS OF WISDOM

In her book *Writing.Com*, Moira Anderson Allen counsels:
"Perhaps the greatest challenge in using search engines is choosing keywords that will bring the best results....Your goal should be to find a keyword (or set of keywords) inclusive enough to produce a range of useful results, yet exclusive enough to filter out the chaff."

But there is even more to this complex process than linking and key words. It begins with understanding how to submit and gain a listing in the first place. Not every applicant is accepted by the more popular engines. They look at content, pertinence to the subject and attractiveness of your site. Therefore it is important to select a site designer who understands SEO well.

LINKING WITH OTHER SITES

While links are vital to placement on search engines, the quantity you create is not the sole criterion. The quality and popularity of the site to which you link are key, as is the relevance of the link to the subject matter of your own site. Therefore it makes little sense to rely on what are frequently called *link farms*. These companies offer to tie you into hundreds of other sites, most of which will do you little or no good in your efforts to rise higher in the directories. In fact, some search engines will actually penalize you when it is obvious that you have used these farms. As you plan your effort to be the top listing on page one of a search engine, never forget that the quality and relevance of your links are the elements the search engines look for. Poor quality links assure poor location. Check out the free articles on *www.linkpartners.com* to learn more about linking techniques.

There is no better way to develop a list of potential links than to search the engines yourself, and review the top 25 to 50 listed entries to determine their relevancy to your site and the key words they feature. Create a list of all that relate well. The alternative, of course, is to retain the services of a professional Search Engine Optimizer. If you prefer to continue doing it yourself, check out purveyors of SEO software on the Web. Both consultants and purveyors are listed in the Appendix.

BRINGING 'EM BACK

Once a surfer pays a visit to your site, it will require a constant effort to bring him/her back again and again. The magnet is content. Fresh, new, informative content. You must think in terms of what the reader can learn on each successive visit? What benefit are you offering to induce that person to return? While the basic site remains the same, if a returning reader doesn't find new information, he/she will quickly abandon you. Keeping your content intriguing and fresh can be done in a number of different ways, but they all take some time and some effort. That's part of the fun of maintaining a web site.

Perhaps you are prolific and knowledgeable enough to regularly provide new articles covering different issues that relate to the site and to the books you have written, remembering always that the dual goal is to increase the sales of your books and to build your reputation as a knowledgeable author. If the burden of writing them all yourself is too great, many professionals will happily contribute articles in return for the exposure and a link to their own web site. After initial publication, articles can be archived by topic, available to any newcomer to the site or even past visitors who want to review an issue. If on the first contact a visitor doesn't purchase your book, there is a very good chance he/she will later after discovering that your articles are thoughtful and chock full of pertinent information. That's why it's so important to change your content regularly to keep your visitors coming back again and again.

CREATING YOUR OWN ENEWSLETTER

The secret to bringing readers back can also be a Newsletter. It will link to and from your primary site. The most effective distribution is by e-mail, which is why these are also called eZines (electronic magazines). Preparing a newsletter is as easy as posting new material on a web site. Just as with individual articles, the newsletter does not have to be written exclusively by you. Guest authors—writers, agents, consultants, even publishers—can contribute articles, some as short as one or two paragraphs while others may run longer, on subjects germane to your book and site. But again, there must be new, interesting material to attract.

A newsletter becomes uncomfortably stale if it remains static for more than a month. The more frequent the change, the more attractive the newsletter becomes, assuming the content remains informative. Regardless of the vehicle you use, it must tie in directly to the site because, once again, our goal is to sell books and broaden name recognition, and both of those are best done on your web site. Romance writer Cindi Myers points out in Book *Marketing from A to Z*: "I've done a lot of different things to promote my books, but probably the most effective has been my weekly newsletter. While I can't link this effort directly to sales, I do know it's greatly increased my name recognition."

MAKING IT PAY

Some of you care little about making a profit from your book or web site. Your primary concern is gaining personal satisfaction from the fact that you are sharing your thoughts with readers throughout the world…and are willing to share them for free. The Internet provides the perfect vehicle since it costs little or nothing beyond initially setting up your web site, and even that you can do by yourself as you learned in the last chapter. For those of you who want to supplement your fixed incomes, the site can produce revenue in a number of different ways. All of these depend on building a high volume of viewers, whether you plan to attract paid advertising or sell more books. Possibly even sell other related products on the site.

Let's look first at the systems you might use to sell your writing output. Which of these you choose depends on what you wish to sell and how you want to do it. If you are selling an article or an eBook on your site, the choice would be *Pay per Download*. That means your readers pay a fee before they are able to download the specific material onto their own web site or other device and read it at their leisure. This is an ideal system for selling a single article or book.

If the product you are selling is a newsletter which must be regularly updated to be saleable, you would turn to the *Subscription* method. Scattered throughout your web site, small boxes should invite readers to subscribe. Because it would be too ponderous for readers to pay for each individual edition of your newsletter, they pay an annual fee to gain continued access. (Later in this chapter we'll look at how you collect the fee.) The content must be informative enough to entice the reader to pay to discover the wealth of information available to them beyond the home page and other *teaser pages* of your web site that are accessible at no charge.

Obviously, subscriptions are not an effective method for selling print or eBooks because, once published, their content never changes. However, eBooks and print books are sold very effectively on a web site that regularly includes fresh articles or is linked to a frequently updated newsletter. That way, readers are brought back to the site again and again, exposing your book(s) as well.

A third payment system is being used on an increasing number of sites. Visitors are permitted to read everything on the site and in the newsletter, but are asked to make a voluntary donation in lieu of a fee. They are encouraged to set the amount based upon what they consider the value of the information. Many free newsletters graduate to this approach before they ultimately require a subscription fee. It is an excellent indicator of the value your readers place on the information they receive, and therefore a helpful guide to setting the price of a subscription.

You are able to archive past editions of the newsletter and past articles on your web site, making them available to your subscribers after the articles are removed from the current active site or newsletter. Some web sites charge non-subscribers a fee for archived material even if the original article was available at no cost. Pay-per-download is the ideal system for this.

COLLECTING THE MONEY

Regardless of which system you choose, you must have a way for people to send you their money. Obviously you can have them mail in checks or money orders, but this is a slow, ponderous system, and many customers will shy away from it especially in the current era of identity theft. The cost of contracting with any of the major credit card companies is far more than a beginning site can handle….and to be effective, you would have to contract with at least three. Therefore a new industry has sprung up to expedite sales on the Web. They will process the sale for you, deduct a modest fee and send you the cash. They are privacy-protected and allow buyers to pay by credit card without worry. Many of you have probably used *Pay Pal* to pay for an electronic purchase. You have also used a *Shopping Cart* when selecting your items. Both of these functions are available for your web site from a number of companies.

Pay Pal, a division of eBay, is probably the largest and best known program in its field. It processes payments for 78 million accounts worldwide, and is trusted by most web customers. Costs to you are based on volume. They range from 1.9% to 2.9% of the transaction price plus a fee of 30 cents per transaction. There are no setup or cancellation fees. Another excellent company, *GoEMerchant*, has been rated by *Shopping Cart Review Magazine* as the "top program for businesses with a limited number of products and modest volume." That certainly describes your start-up web site. GoEMerchant offers two plans: *The Gateway Plan* simply processes credit card payments, while the *Total Package Plan* includes an integrated system from shopping to full payment processing. You can bring up any of these systems on the Web by entering the name in the search box, or learn even more about Web sales and discover more options by entering "eCommerce."

A variation on the plans described above is offered by *ClickBank*, which touts itself as the largest seller of eBooks and other products on the Web. The company claims to have 100,000 affiliates, any of whom you can link with if they are similar in subject matter to your web site. These links in essence become "salespersons," promoting your book or other product. With just a click on the linked site, surfers are referred to your site where they can purchase a copy of your book. The linked site then receives a commission, the amount of which is established by you.

Stores on Line offers a total financial package that begins with creation of your web site after consultation

WORDS OF WISDOM

On the web site *www.indiaweb developers.com*, Vinny Alex explains: "Ever since the dawn of e-commerce, Credit Cards have ruled the roost...While great for the day to day purchases in the physical world, (they) came across one big problem in the virtual world...The number and PIN numbers were the only proof of identity. This meant that security became a big concern, so much so that Credit card companies started to charge higher for Internet enabled merchant accounts... This in turn brought in a host of new payment systems which have sprung up focusing on increased security on the net."

with you to determine your specific needs. Their designers incorporate elements of SEO to help you a gain better position on search engines. They create a shopping cart, develop payment plans and install impressive software to keep records of all transactions. When any questions arise during startup or for as long as the site continues to operate, Stores on Line customers are encouraged to call in to a team of live techs for help. The cost of obtaining this customized, personal service is quite high, but for many newcomers to the digital business world, it is comforting to have this degree of support, particularly since it continues even after the site is up and functioning. Contact information for the plans described above and other systems is available in the Appendix.

TOLL FREE PHONE NUMBERS

As we have discussed again and again, convenience—simple navigation, easy access, clear directions—is key to attracting and keeping visitors. Your site must be welcoming. So if you choose not to retain the service of a payment company like Pay Pal or GoMerchant, toll free phone access for ordering and purchasing is a must. Even if you have a payment system, you may want to add toll free telephoning to give your customers a second way to communicate and purchase. It is relatively inexpensive today with competition holding down the costs. Rates as low as 2.9 cents a minute are available for interstate calls. Usually intrastate rates are somewhat higher, and vary widely. For example, *Everdial*, a well respected company, offers an interstate rate of 4.9 cents per minute, with intrastate rates ranging from a low of 5 cents in California to a high of 18.9 cents if you are located in Wyoming or Vermont. You can review Everdial on the Web at *www.ever dial.net*. To see a cross section of companies offering toll free service, enter "toll free telephoning" in your search box. Contact information for several companies is listed in the Appendix.

ON LINE BOOKSTORES

No online program would be complete without listing your book on *Amazon.com* and *Barnes and Noble.com*. (If you prefer to use Borders.com, you will find it is teamed with Amazon.) I am certain you know and have probably used these sites to order books in the past. They are not limited only to books that have been published traditionally. Self-published and POD authors can place their work on these sites as long as their books have an ISBN and are carried by a recognized book distributor. You can submit excerpts, reviews and a host of other selling information for use on the Amazon catalogue, placing you in an excellent competitive position with books produced by the major publishing houses. Amazon even offers self-publishers the *Advantage* program under which it agrees to warehouse a small number of your books so that they are available for shipment immediately. This eliminates reliance on a distributor. However this service will cost you an annual fee of $29.95 and 55 percent commission on the retail price. To obtain further information, scroll down on the Amazon site to the *Make Money* box on the left side of the first page, and click on *Advantage*.

Barnes and Noble requires authors to become Vendors of Record with its warehouse if they are not represented by a major book distributor. The easy-to-understand directions can be found on its web site. By clicking on *Publishers and Authors Guidelines* in the bottom menu of the B&N web site, you will find information on enrolling in the Vendor of Record program. Participation in B&N's Meet the Writer Program and instructions on placing your book in the company retail stores are included here as well.

ADVERTISING ON YOUR WEB SITE

There are several categories of display advertisements that are used on web sites. The simplest and most widely publicized, although not necessarily the most lucrative, is the Adsense program developed and marketed by *Google*. Adsense offers small boxed ads directly related to the theme of your site.

Some are text only; others have small graphics. All of them invite the reader to visit the advertised site. Each time the reader clicks on the ad and goes to the advertised site, you receive a small payment. Once the ads are placed on your site, the system functions by itself without any input from you. You receive a statement periodically and a check. By searching for "Adsense" on the Web, you will find sites that explain the program, while others relate stories of success or failure with the program. The Adsense informational site produced by Google can be found at *www.google.com/adsense*. An excellent resource for information and books on Adsense is *www.commercialreality.co.uk*. Check the Web for the many listings on the subject of web site advertising. Several resources are listed in the Appendix.

WORDS OF WISDOM

From the *Google Adsense* website: "Getting started as a Google AdSense publisher is easy. It only takes a few moments to apply online for both content and search ads. Once you're approved, simply log in to your account, copy a block of HTML code and paste it into your existing ad server or any of your web pages. And that's it—you're done. Relevant ads start to appear on your web pages, and your earnings start to add up."

For the more enterprising, there is no limit on the number of other advertisers who can be wooed to your site if your audience is large enough. But it takes some time and salesmanship to bring them in. Selling ad space on the Web is little different from selling it in other media. You must convince the prospective buyer that your site can produce results. It doesn't have to be the most popular on the Internet to attract advertising. In most cases, advertisers prefer a site that is directly related to the product they are trying to sell and targets likely potential buyers even if the visitor count is small. For example, if the book you are promoting on your site and the articles you offer are about gardening, companies dealing with yard tools, seeds, bulbs and other nursery products are likely prospects.

Once again the Web, that miraculous tool, can help. Enter "Attracting advertisers to a web site," and you will find a number of helpful listings that will answer questions on procurement, placement and even compensation. You might also enter "Advertising Online" where you will find listed a number of agencies that supply advertising to blogs and web sites. While guidance on salesmanship is beyond the province of this book, it too is available on the Web and from myriad books that your local library carries.

Now that payment tools, shopping carts and all the other systems through which visitors can purchase on your site are set to go to work, let's concentrate on creating the products you hope to sell. The next chapter will guide you in creating eBooks and eZines (newsletters).

CHAPTER 20

WRITING FOR THE WEB

A recent study reported that 73 percent of adults in the United States are Web users. In hard figures that adds up to 147 million viewers that you can reach by offering your writing on digital markets. Add in millions more in locations around the globe.

Those millions surf the Internet seeking information. Hopefully they'll find your web site, but they'll also look to the new electronic publishing industries—eBooks and eZines—for books and articles on topics that interest them. Once found, the information offered on these sites can be downloaded or e-mailed and studied right in the viewer's home or office. That level of speed and convenience has made the Web a top choice for information seekers. In many cases the information is free or relatively inexpensive. For you as an author attempting to publicize and sell your book(s), easy-to-write eBooks and eZines are ideal promotional tools. If they are well constructed and informative, surfers who read them will become eager, potential customers for your print book.

Before we tackle the nitty gritty of writing for the Web, let's make certain you understand these digital venues. Although fiction can be included, the majority of eBooks are factual presentations or how-to's. They are designed to pass information on to the reader quickly and succinctly. EBooks are generally far shorter and more direct than print books because web surfers are information seekers in a hurry. The eBooks you produce can be available right on your own web site. You have the choice of charging a fee or offering them at no cost. An alternative is to publish them through an ePublisher in the hopes of obtaining wider distribution. If you choose the latter, the bio that accompanies the book must invite readers to visit your site.

EZines (sometimes called webZines) are newsletters or other collections of articles transmitted to readers by e-mail. They too are important sources of information for readers. *Wikipedia,* the online encyclopedia defines an eZine as "a periodic publication distributed by e-mail or posted on a web site." *www.zinester.com* defines an eZine similarly, "An eZine (the name is derived from electronic magazine) is an electronic newsletter that is periodically sent to the subscriber's database via e-mail. There are eZines on different topics on the Internet: how to publish an ezine, how to bring up children and so on." The eZine you produce can be restricted to just your own site or can be made available on other sites to which you link. It also can be placed with an eZine directory. Like print magazines, they too must be updated with new information on a regular basis to bring visitors back to the site.

WORDS OF WISDOM

On her popular web site *www.bookcoaching.com,* JudyCullins explains: "Once you get dozens of short articles or excerpts out to no spam eZines or top web sites in your field, you will notice the search engines optimizing your site because they see your important key words that link you, your book or your service together. Your submitted articles lead to the magic of "viral marketing.'"

ELECTRONIC BOOK PUBLISHING

While still not accepted by small communities of die-hard traditionalists, the Internet-spawned technique of publishing books electronically has attracted a great deal of attention over the past decade. You have the choice of producing your eBook on your own web site or contracting with an epublisher who will take on the responsibility of formatting what you have written and promoting and distributing it throughout the Web. Much like the arrangement with a traditional print publisher, the ePublisher will pay you a royalty for the right to distribute your book. Usually the percentage is much higher than what you would receive from a traditional publisher, generally averaging in the 40 to 50% range. But remember that the retail price of the eBook is far less than that of a print book. The books ePublishers accept can vary in size from 25 to 250 pages, but they prefer works on the shorter side because eBook readers, as stated previously, are generally information seekers in a hurry. There are a number of online publishers listed on the Internet. For starters, try *www.booklocker.com* to get a sense of what an ePublisher does. As a bonus, you will also find and have the chance to buy Angela Adair-Hoy's excellent eBook *How to Write, Publish and Sell EBooks*.

Let me re-emphasize that the key to a successful eBook is content, presented quickly, accurately and in as concise a fashion as possible without sacrificing clarity. How-to books are always in demand because Web surfers constantly seek information on topics that spark their interest. You can find a sampling of ePublishers listed in the Appendix.

> ### WORDS OF WISDOM
>
> Discussing eBooks, popular writing coach Judy Cullins states: "A clever title is great if it is clear, but a clear title is always preferable. The best? A clear and clever title. A shorter title is better than a longer one. Your reader will spend only four seconds on the cover. While some long titles have succeeded, usually the shorter, the better."

ENTICE YOUR READER

Whether you publish the book on your own site or offer it to a commercial web publisher, an inviting title is essential to attract potential readers. The title must be punchy and exciting and capture the essence of the book. It must convince the surfer that he/she will derive a distinct benefit from the book and find the desired information, thus eliminating the need to search further. If you choose to use a multi-colored front cover when you present it on your web site, the sale will become even easier. The names of cover designers as well as software to create the cover yourself are available on the Web by searching for eBook Cover Designers.

Of course, the promise of the title must be carried through in the content of the book. For most topics that usually can be done effectively in a book of 100 pages and even less because the subject of the eBook should be narrow, not wide-ranging. It is far better to write a series of shorter books, each of which focuses on a specific aspect of the broader subject. For example, if you were writing about the sport of archery, you might devote a book to bows, the many different styles, the purposes for which each type should be used, manufacturing techniques, etc. A related book would discuss bow hunting techniques and a third might delve into the various types of target competitions and the skills needed for each. The important thing to keep in mind, regardless of the subject, is the web surfer's thirst for knowledge, a thirst you are qualified to quench because of your years of experience. Give the reader information, and your books will sell.

To ensure you get the "biggest bang" out of your eBook, you must introduce it to as many surfers as possible. List it with several of the better free eBook directories. You will find several listed in the Appendix. To locate a wide variety of pre-tested sites to which you can link, click on *www.linkpartners.com*, then on "Search." On that page, you can find matches by entering keywords that represent the topic of your book. Linkpartners' program of reciprocal linking is free, and somewhat unique in that a staff of editors actually reviews all sites for quality before they are accepted and added to the directory. As you learned earlier, there is no value to simply linking to as many sites as you can. They must be relevant and of decent quality to be considered by the search engines in determining your listing level. You can also apply to Link Partners to have your own site included on the site.

SOME SIMPLE TECHNOLOGY

I don't want to delve deeply into the technology of eBook production. Frankly, I don't feel qualified to do so, and at this stage it's not something you must understand beyond some very basic information. EBooks can be produced in either of two formats, *HTML* or *PDF*. The choice depends in part on the length of your book and how you plan to market it. Many ePublishing sites will accept manuscripts only in PDF (Portable Document Format). Since they can be opened in almost any operating system, books prepared in PDF are the most versatile to transmit and the easiest for readers to access

HTML (Hyper Text Markup Language) is limited in its use by readers who don't have Windows and Internet Explorer. Although it offers the writer greater versatility, it requires him/her to individually format every page, which makes it extremely slow and ponderous if your book has more than say 25 to 50 pages. A far easier technique is to convert your text to PDF simply by clicking onto Adobe Acrobat. Some writers actually prepare their books in both formats to cover all bases.

COPYRIGHT AND IDENTIFICATION

An eBook can be officially copyrighted just the way print books can. Like a print book, it need not be registered to be protected except in a case of litigation. The book does require an ISBN for identification. If you plan to distribute your eBook on a CD-ROM, you will require bar coding as well. You can refer back to Chapter 8 to refresh your memory on these and how to apply for them.

SELLING YOUR EBOOK ON YOUR WEB SITE

There are a variety of ways to motivate substantial sales when you offer your eBook exclusively on your own web site. We have talked of links from other sites several times, and that is a key factor in attracting readers and also raising your visibility on search engines. Articles written on the topic of your print or eBook or even extracted from its pages and distributed widely through these linkages can be excellent drawing cards, bringing potential buyers to your site. But the articles must identify you, your book and your web site either in the text or in a short bio at the end. The latter is preferable because it is always dangerous to promote yourself or your work in your own article. That can quickly turn off a reader. You may want to offer a sample segment of the book on your web site at no cost to induce paid purchases of the complete text. Some authors guarantee money back if the reader isn't satisfied.

Bonus gifts are often used to entice purchasers. One method is to include a free relevant article that can be downloaded only by people who purchase the book. Perhaps you can prompt the combined sale of both the eBook and print book by offering to sell a personally autographed copy of your print book at a special discounted price. You might decide to include a tangible inducement like a pen, bookmark or notepad printed with your web site identification or book title. That will involve the effort and cost to

---

WORDS OF WISDOM

In her excellent book *Writing .Com*, Moira Anderson Allen wisely points out: "Selling your own eBook has the advantage of putting you in complete control of your product, and ensuring that you receive 100% of sales revenues. However, it also puts you in the less pleasant position of being responsible for customer service."

ship the bonus, but perhaps you can bury that cost in the price of the eBook. It may be helpful now to turn back to the previous chapter and review the discussion of shopping carts and tools you can use to receive payment on your site.

THE DIGITAL ARTICLE

Whether you choose to submit to a digital article directory or by linking to a variety of individual web sites and newsletters or to both, it is essential to keep fresh articles coming on a steady basis. Done right, the response will surprise you as the numbers of visitors to your web site grows geometrically. I know you have heard me state this over and over again in varying contexts throughout this book. That's because disseminating articles is the best way to build recognition for you, your web site, your blog and your book(s) and to raise your position on search engine listings. It costs no more than the modest amount of time it takes to craft these short pieces, many of them excerpts or condensed rewrites of portions of your book.

Supplying articles to other outlets is very similar to the process we

WORDS OF WISDOM

James Opiko owner of *www.afroarticles.com*, an online publishing and syndication service advises: "Article submission is perhaps one of the best ways to leverage your products and services on the Internet....that is, if done correctly. (However) I have noticed that a lot of authors are submitting articles for the wrong reasons. It's imperative that you submit 'quality' articles...The real purpose of submitting your article to an article marketing directory is to gain publishers who will willingly publish your articles on their web sites, blogs and newsletters; that's where the real traffic comes from. Submitting numerous short (less than 500 words), poorly and haphazardly written articles will do you no good. Also submitting the same article over and over with a few modifications is not acceptable. The search engines have wisened up and are getting better at weeding out 'spam.'"

described when submitting to print magazines. There are hundreds of newsletters and electronic magazines on any subject you might imagine. (As you learned earlier, the terms eZine and webZine are used interchangeably by many people.) To find them, enter "webZines" or "eZines" in your favorite search engine and a number of directories will pop up. Most of these magazines have guidelines published on their web sites. Some accept direct submissions; others require query letters. Check the Appendix for a listing of several worthwhile eZine or webZinedirectories, and then study the guidelines for the individual magazines that interest you.

The entire process involves writing articles three-to-five pages long, double spaced. Since they will be on a subject related in some way to the book you are trying to sell, you will have already researched them fully before writing the book. Review those notes. That way, preparing thoughtful, informative articles becomes a "snap." Writers are unanimous in praising this approach as one of the most effective sales tools in their chest. In just one succinct sentence in *Book Marketing A – Z*, Rae Pica, author of *Your Active Child*, sums it up perfectly, "My best promotional effort has been in the form of online articles excerpted from *Your Active Child*.

SUBMITTING TO AN EZINE

Like eBook publishers, eZine publishers generally prefer shorter, compact pieces, chock full of information delivered in a very direct and simplified manner. Submissions can be as short as 50 words or so for "tips." Articles generally range from 300 to 1,200 words. The majority of eZines prefer lengths of 1,000 words at most. Sentences and paragraphs should be short, punchy and informative. Many publishers require that your submission be formatted with no more than 65 characters (including spaces) per line to make transmission easier. You can find the formatting that individual Zines require by checking their guidelines. If no directions are given, use the same style that you do for print submissions.

ARTICLE SYNDICATION

A growing number of eCompanies offer syndication services on the Web. *www.featurewell.com*, a very demanding syndicator, will offer your work to both digital and print publishers if the quality meets the high standards it sets. You can check the web sites of various syndicators to determine their reach and their requirements. As this concept increases in stature, new developments like RSS (Real Simple Syndication) offer a variety of techniques to make articles more readily available to readers. But all of this is somewhat beyond the scope of a book guiding beginning authors. To gain a quick sense of the value of syndication, you might click on *www.thesitewizard.com*. Scroll down to "Archive of Articles." In the archives, go to "Web site/Search Engine Promotion" and click on "Article Syndication Pros & Cons," an informative overview by author Christopher Heng. He discusses the benefits and shortcomings of submitting your work to a syndicator.

THE BLOGOSPHERE

Authors have just recently begun to value the power of the Web's youngest creation, the *blog*. The public generally looks upon blogs, as a non-traditional, but quite effective means of getting the news behind the news that the daily paper too often doesn't carry. Web surfers turn to blogs as they do to eZines and eBooks for information on an endless variety of topics. Journalists have developed a two-fold relationship with the blogosphere. Many of them develop their own blogs to express their personal views on current events and other issues since they are restricted from injecting their bias into news stories they write. More important to you as a writer, they are regular readers of blogs. As a result, the blogosphere is a very effective tool to use to promote yourself and your work to the media. Remember the study by the Columbia University School of Journalism we talked of in an earlier chapter. It revealed that 70% of journalists use blogs as a source for their stories. With this degree of attention from journalists and a lot more from general surfers, it makes a great deal of sense for authors to maintain an active blog to promote themselves, their web sites and their book(s)...that oh-so-critical three-part goal of promotion on the Web. A favorable mention on some of the more popular blogs can bring a rush of surfers to your web site.

CREATING YOUR OWN BLOG

In addition to writing and producing eZines or even eBooks, you can easily become a blogger. There is no limit to the subjects you can select for your blog. It does make a lot of sense, however, to relate the topic to the theme of your current book. As a writer, you can also justifiably design the content around the art and technique of writing. While that may attract surfers interested in writing, you may be sacrificing those people who were searching for information on the subject of your book. Of course, nothing prohibits you from publishing two blogs, one relating to the book's topic, the other to writing.

Somewhere in the blog, there must be a reference to your web site and your book and how best to purchase it. This can be included either in the author's bio or as a tag line at the end or even as an advertisement that you create and post. But never forget, your reader is there to garner information, not to read an advertorial for your work. Content rules. Much like a newsletter or a web site, a blog requires frequent updating to maintain interest and keep readers coming back. Be prepared to create a new edition at least once a week and archive the older ones.

HELP IN BUILDING YOUR BLOG

The risk to creating your own blog is minimal. If money is a concern, you can readily find free sites on the Internet to guide you as you develop it. *www.blogger.com* offered by Google is one of the most popular. Although it charges no fee for basic creation, *www.livejournal.com* is an excellent step-up if you plan to incorporate more subtle refinements. Of course, there is a charge for these additions. *www.blogsome.com*, a company based in Dublin, Ireland, (see why we say there are no boundaries to the World Wide Web!) offers free design and hosting of your blog. It is the only free site that incorporates "categories of urgent interest" in its designs. The site also features an interactive *Forum* in which users can ask a variety of questions and gain help to resolve any problems they face.

Blogs have varying levels of sophistication. The more complex, the more you need a designer and the higher the cost will be. There are issues of linkage to other blogs and web sites, methods of receiving reports on activity on your blog (the number of *hits* and where they came from), advertising, inter-activity and even the ability to create categories of urgent interest to excite your readers (Must Reads, Special Topics, Other Viewpoints, etc). A blog, you must realize by now, is really nothing more than a web site regularly updated to express the thoughts of the writer. It is more directed than a web site need be. While it carries little extraneous material, it must be chock full of worthwhile information related to its primary topic or it will quickly lose its readership.

If you would like a modest supplement to your income, solicit paid advertisements for your blog. In addition to Google's Adsense and similar programs that you've learned about, advertising agencies like Blogads (*www.blogads.com*) can help, as it does on 1,100 peer-selected blogs. You will find other ad reps when you search. There are also agencies that do the reverse. At no charge, *www.swarmtraffic.com* offers a variety of sources that help promote traffic TO your blog, not from your blog to other sites, as advertisements do.

The Web's major search engines intermingle blogs with web sites on their listings. The ability to climb to the top of the list is the same for a blog as it is for a site, so you may want to review Chapter 19 once again to refresh yourself on the use of key words and links to help in your ascent. Remember always that fresh content is as critical on a blog as it is in your newsletter to ensure that readers don't become one-time visitors.

USING THE BLOGOSPHERE TO PROMOTE YOURSELF

As public relations expert Penny Sansevieri points out in the next WORDS OF WISDOM, the blogging world can be extremely effective in helping you promote yourself and your book(s). However, you must evaluate each blog you consider linking to, first on the basis of relevance and second on its importance and the size of the audience it reaches. You may have to settle for modest-sized blogs at first as you develop your reputation in this burgeoning world, for the larger the blog, the harder it is to crack. To keep abreast of the hottest issues and people bloggers are covering, turn to web sites like Technorati (*www.technorati.com*) that monitor

WORDS OF WISDOM

Penny Sansevieri, Editor of *www.amarketingexpert.com,* **counsels:** "If you're in the midst of your media campaign don't overlook pitching bloggers, especially those who are opinion makers in your industry. Why? Because in the last twelve months bloggers have gone from on-line journals and opinion pieces to newsworthy opinion drivers and in many cases, the single most reliable place to get an accurate assessment of a news item, product, or service."

blogs and search engines on a continuing basis. Some of these sites can also provide the number of references in each blog to you or your book(s).

One last bit of advice about the uniqueness of blogs. The blogosphere is quite young and still suffers from aspersions cast by some traditionalists who refuse to accept its role in the communications universe. This has led bloggers to form a very close-knit society. Most cherish this strong sense of community. They generally are not competitive with one another, except when it involves beating others on a news item. They do not insist on exclusivity. That is most important from your standpoint, for you can reach out and share your information with any number of bloggers without offending or upsetting others.

CHAT GROUPS NEED CONTENT

Endless numbers of *chat groups* on the Web deal with a wide range of subjects and would welcome your articles. To select some that deal with the subject of your expertise, turn to *www.yahoogroups.com* which lists 14,391 of these sites, all accessible by topic. The groups range from under 1,000 to 20,000 or more members who share a common interest. They post their own articles on the topic and read pieces written by fellow members. While you receive no compensation for your submissions, you gain substantial exposure to people interested specifically in the subject matter you deal with. Joining these groups will bring many new visitors to your web site. To better understand this concept, take a look at

WORDS OF WISDOM

The helpful site *http://webdesign. about.com* cautions: "Remember that 95% of the people who come to your Web page won't buy anything the first time. They have to become comfortable with your site, used to how you do your business, and feel secure enough to commit their hard earned dollars. If you have reliable and useful content, they will return, with credit card in hand."

reprintarticles-paradise-subscribe@yahoogroups.com and *netwrite-publish-announce@yahoogroups.com*.

TAKING ADVANTAGE

I am sure that by now you realize how all of these Internet activities that we have discussed are intertwined and benefit one another. By taking advantage of some or all of them, your web site or blog will grow in importance. As you circulate articles that you write to other sites on the Web, you publicize your own site. Surfers who have been attracted by these promotional efforts are potential buyers of your books, print and digital, as well as probable subscribers to either your free or paid newsletter. Your links with these other sites will greatly benefit your standing in the search engine listings. Once your site is up and running, all of this can be accomplished with no more than perhaps 10 to 12 hours of work each week. You will have the fun and satisfaction of these achievements without encroaching on your many other leisure pursuits. Join the thousands of your peers who have learned the value of harnessing the magic of the Web.

In the next chapter we turn to the last of our specialty writing techniques. I have included this chapter on commercial writing because so many retirees have asked me about writing opportunities in the business world where the years they spent in the workplace help them feel most comfortable.

COMMERCIAL WRITING

CHAPTER 21

IT'S ALL BUSINESS

You're a member of the growing community of vibrant retirees, unwilling to fold your tent and hide away full-time at the country club. You're restless. You miss the excitement of the workplace. The business world or your profession or industry served as the focus of your life for decades. Now it's gone. You no longer feel useful. You've got the knowledge. You've got the skills. But you haven't got the job, because the employment market slams shut once you pass that 55 year marker. There's a marvelous way to keep in touch with your past and to put your extensive background to use—writing. Business writing. Commercial writing. And you can do it part-time, leaving lots of hours for all of the leisure activities you enjoy.

While nowhere near as glamorous as turning out a best selling book, this category of writing offers far easier access and greater potential to the beginning writer. Finding your niche in this broad array of opportunities should be quite easy because you bring years of experience in a specific industry to an editor or a director of public relations. There are marketing brochures to be written, technical manuals, press releases, magazine and newspaper articles, speeches, even annual reports.

Public relations departments are constantly in need of freelance help. Editors of company publications regularly call on outsiders to produce copy for them. Outsourcing has become a primary tool when schedules tighten. The demand is so great that a new industry of freelance placement firms has developed to match writers to companies that need their services. Enter "Freelance Writers Placement Agencies" in your search engine and select from more than 2,500 pages of listings. As your reputation grows, you may even be asked by a harried executive to ghost write or co-write a book. So you see, a variety of avenues exist to keep your finger on the pulse long after retirement, often working with old friends and acquaintances. The pay scale, higher than what freelancers receive from the majority of publications, keeps your pocket full of ready spending money as well.

WORDS OF WISDOM

Author and columnist Clair Rees writes in his book *Profitable Freelancing*: "Because you're not a regular staff member, you draw no weekly salary and require no expensive health insurance, vacation and retirement benefits—in short, you're not part of the regular overhead. Unlike other employees, the only time you run up any payroll expense is when you are actually working on a project."

THE ADVANTAGES

There are many advantages to business writing. It is quite easy to break in if you are willing to spend a little time promoting yourself with mail, telephone and even personal meetings. As Clair Rees points out in the WORDS OF WISDOM above, you represent a "bargain" for the client, who is not obligated to finance the many costly benefits regular staff enjoys. The expertise you are able bring to the subject matter gives you a decided advantage over the average freelance writer, even if your writing credits are minimal. However, if you do have a portfolio of any size to demonstrate that you know how to spell and put together words that flow easily, finding work will be even easier. Clips are not essential to break in, but they certainly are helpful.

As we discussed in earlier chapters, one way to develop a portfolio is to freelance articles for local publications, your hometown newspapers (daily or weekly) or local magazines, regional business publications, even Internet newsletters or eZines. You might interview a local corporate executive or profile a company, or decide to write a piece on the local economy as you see it. Your prior work experience qualifies you to do these pieces. Whatever the subject, these clips will help immeasurably in opening the door, and once it is open, it will be a good deal easier to develop a list of steady clients. Your portfolio will grow, and word of mouth will boost your reputation in the field. Assignments will begin coming in on a regular basis.

AT THE STARTING GATE

So how does one begin? It's pretty simple. There are two things that are essential. Create a business card and stationery to reinforce the impression that you are professional. Develop an impressive logo that can be used on both. If you have done any writing during your years of work—stories in the company newsletter, manuals, commentaries, etc—dig them out. Mount those clips in a loose-leaf book to show every potential client.

The best way to open doors is with mail, unless you are contacting a former acquaintance. That way, you are not intruding on a busy client's schedule with a telephone call. Instead you are presenting him/her with a document to respond to if the need for your expertise exists. If it does not at that moment, the chance is good that the recipient will place it in the freelancer file and refer to it whenever a future need arises for your specific talent. Your mailer should include a carefully drafted cover letter describing your professional experience and how it can benefit your prospect. Once again, the emphasis must be on the benefits he/she gains from tapping into your expertise. If you have published clips, include the best and most pertinent one along with your business card and a flyer if you have developed one. If you have no clips to include, create a sample press release on a pertinent subject that you know well, and send that as an example of your writing skill. Follow up the mailer with a phone call anywhere from four days to a week later. If you are not able to reach your prospect, leave a message on his/her voice mail. If you receive no response, send out two or three reminder-mailers over a period of time, something too few freelancers do.

These usually produce results (remember the old adage "the squeaky wheel gets the grease") for they show you are really serious, not just casting your net in the hopes of securing an assignment here or there.

ADVERTISING AGENCIES AND PR FIRMS

In addition to contacting companies directly, there are many advertising agencies and public relations firms that serve them and can use your expertise. But before you begin the process, it is valuable to understand the difference between an advertising agency and a public relations firm, a distinction that confuses many people because a number of larger companies offer both services. An agency deals in paid advertising. It purchases time from a broadcaster or space from a publication to present the message of its client. The goal of a PR firm is to capture as much publicity and recognition as possible for its clients at no cost. This is done essentially through press releases, promotional gimmickry, events, newsletters, feature stories and speaking opportunities.

Agencies and PR firms come in varying sizes. They are not all the mammoth international companies that one usually reads about in the business press. Local one-and-two-person firms periodically find themselves overloaded with work and reach out for freelance help. For that reason it is advantageous to make as many of them as you can aware of your special competency. They usually are generalists and from time to time need help when they are given an assignment by a company in a specialized field. At the other end of the scale, the huge agencies seldom outsource work except in

Clair Rees states in *Profitable Freelancing*: "The opportunities for freelance writing work right in your own community are literally endless. Everyone—business and governments included—needs to communicate....You may need to exercise a little imagination and ingenuity to get word of your abilities around to potential employers, but it's not really all that difficult."

the case of highly specialized niche programs that demand targeted expertise. In between are the majority of mid-sized agencies and firms that most frequently call on freelancers for help, and these are the ones to contact if their client lists include companies in your field of proficiency.

It is particularly important that your expertise is on file with these mid-sized firms. When they are hired to mount a campaign for a company whose products they are not completely familiar with, they turn to their files of freelancers to find those that have the knowledge they need. So it is imperative that you highlight your background in the query letters you send. To locate agencies with clients in your specialty, research what the industry calls the Red Book (*www.redbooks.com*). Formally known as the *Standard Directory of Advertising Agencies*, it lists the specialties and key clients of 14,000 agencies. Your local library probably carries a copy in its reference room.

The bible for researching PR firms is *O'Dwyer's Directory of Public Relations Firms* which undoubtedly can also be found in your library's reference room. Perhaps your library carries the *Directory of Corporate Communications,* another of O'Dwyer's publications. Thousands of PR firms and in-house corporate executives can be found in these two valuable resources.

BOOSTING YOUR CHANCES

There are many additional ways to open the floodgates to commercial writing. They require little more than a bit of creativity supported by the initiative to reach out and make it all happen. And it will, once you make the effort. Volunteer your talent to help publicize a local civic organization or charity. There will be no compensation, but you'll be surprised at the number of respected business and professional people who serve on the board or as volunteers. Their appreciation of your efforts and the chance to view your abilities firsthand may well result in paid assignments from their companies.

By reading local publications or listening to local radio stations—indeed even just by talking with people and remaining alert to possibilities—you will undoubtedly hear of an interesting area company operating in a field related to the specialty you know so well. Do some investigation. Research the company's background as you would if you were writing an article. If it seems as interesting as you originally thought, consider writing an article about it if you can find a worthy hook. Contact the key person or, if required, the PR department, and explain that you hope to profile the company and the reason you find the company newsworthy—your hook. Request an interview and an on-site visit to get the true feel of your subject. Then write and place an article in a local newspaper's business section or in a regional magazine. That can provide a "double whammy," opening the door to the publication as well as to assignments from the company or executive you profiled. Several years ago, I wrote a piece on one small component of the massive Cendant empire. That piece led to continuous assignments from varied divisions of the company for several years.

Perhaps your background is in the health field or in education. Two institutions that are always looking for strong press are hospitals and colleges, and there undoubtedly are several in your region. With the contacts you have developed over the years, you may be able to help them increase their recognition. In addition to the regular publications they produce (alumni magazines, donor newsletters, etc), they often undertake special projects for which the regular PR department requires additional assistance.

You might also consider the local political scene, particularly if a topic with which you have had substantial experience becomes a major campaign issue. Campaigns require lots of publicity, and regularly hire writers to supplement staff and volunteers. The bonus is that campaigning can be exciting and fun and you can meet some very interesting, and perhaps helpful, people.

If your background is in retail or advertising, create a dummy advertising section and approach the merchants of one of your smaller, local shopping centers. You can determine the price for each page or portion thereof by contacting the local newspaper for the prices of inserts. If your potential clients prefer mailing, calculate the cost of production, printing and postage, and again set the price per page and of ads in preset smaller segments. Group advertising can cut costs for the individual merchant, yet produce a powerful impact because of the diversity of stores involved. If the initial effort is successful, you may find this becomes a regular seasonal, monthly or even weekly promotion, giving you a steady flow of work.

> ### WORDS OF WISDOM
>
> Independent consultant and technology writer Alan Canton explains in his book *The Silver Pen:* "Corporate entities have different needs. The advertising and sales departments need you to turn out copy for brochures and product announcements. The personnel department may need you to provide an article on health benefits for the company newsletter. The public relations people might need you to provide press releases and feature articles. The manufacturing division may need you to work on a new manual, proposal or other documentation. Executive administration may call on you to write a speech or quarterly report."

COMPENSATION

Compensation for freelance writers in the business world is based on either an hourly rate or a project fee. Many companies will only negotiate on a project basis, although working by the hour may be more comfortable for the freelancer. Company executives realize that with hourly contracts, they have no control over the time you take to do the job unless a cut-off is specified. The meter keeps on running while you work. If they insist upon paying on a project basis, be certain that you estimate on the generous side, building extra time into the price in case any problems develop as you progress.

As always, *Writer's Market*, that remarkable compendium of essential information for authors, offers guidance to newcomers on the compensation you can expect to receive for a variety of assignments. It lists high, low and average rates per hour and per project. In the section on business writing, 22 different categories of assignments are listed, from annual reports to sales letters. Advertising and PR rates have their own section as do other classifications related in some way to commercial writing. Obviously, these rates serve only as guidelines. Variations occur by industry and by geography.

DEALING WITH THE MEDIA

The key to producing successful copy is understanding that a publication or broadcaster is looking for news. News that informs or intrigues its readers. "Puff pieces," as they are known in the industry, will be rejected summarily. Your press release or feature story must be newsworthy to earn placement. If you can tie your piece to some event or other breaking news—local, national or international—you are almost guaranteed it will be used.

The process varies when you are hired to prepare copy for a PR firm. Once you have written the assigned copy, most larger firms will want to place it themselves. They regularly woo media contacts, and know where best to send material. Smaller firms may want you to write and to place for them. It is important to send the material to the appropriate editor. For newspapers, research a copy of the *Editor and Publisher Yearbook*. It lists the editors of each section of the paper, as well as the address, e-mail and phone number of the publication. The top three directories of magazines and their staffs are published by Burrelle's, Bacon and Gayle. Both the print and electronic versions of these directories are far too expensive to buy, so ask your reference librarian which one they carry. If you can't locate the proper editor, telephone the publication and ask for his/her name and the best way to send your material

To be successful in working with the media, you must recognize that time is of the essence. Magazine editors have a bit more leeway than those on daily newspapers, but they too face constant deadlines. Think of how difficult it is to turn out a 100-page magazine each month, combining advertising, graphics and editorial content into one exciting issue. Editors on daily newspapers are faced with the same challenge every 24 hours, although their pages are fewer in number. All of these publications depend on PR firms to supply them with information to help fill their pages, whether in the form of releases or feature stories. So don't be intimidated, but do be understanding and aware of the hectic routines journalists face every day. Act like a professional and you'll be welcomed as one.

THE PRESS RELEASE

Since the press release is the most common written contact a PR firm uses to inform the press, both print and broadcast, I have again reproduced the format for the standard release to assist you. You may want to head back to Chapter 12 to review the section on pitches and press releases. The copy should be direct and factual, but not so overburdened with facts and figures that it becomes confusing and dull. Above all, it should not be cutesy, unless that presentation is particularly appropriate to the product you are promoting. For the most part, journalists are pretty straight-forward, cut-to-the-quick personalities. They are not impressed by anything but content…solid information that they can pass on to their readers

Rest assured, any release will end up in the "circular file" unless it immediately catches the interest of the reporter or editor. Hundreds arrive every week, so it will receive just a cursory glance as he/she clears the desk of accumulated mailings. So get your message home quickly and effectively in the headline and the opening paragraph. The experts claim you have no more than one or at best two seconds to capture attention. If the headline fails to propel the editor into the first paragraph, only the garbage collector will have a chance to read it.

FOR RELEASE: (Date)

CONTACT: John Jones
           JJ Promotions
           (000) 000-0000

LATEST DINGER TECHNOLOGY REVOLUTIONIZES THE SALES POTENTIAL OF THE WORLD WIDE WEB

In unveiling the latest edition of Dinger Marketing Technology, company founder James Dinger predicted this new tool would at the very least quadruple the response to traditional marketing efforts on the Web. "Testing of the program by a panel of 15 recognized scientists at Woodward University last month confirmed these findings," Dinger reported at yesterday's session of the International Conference of Internet Marketers.

###

DESKTOP PUBLISHING

During your years of active work, some of you have had experience creating newsletters, flyers and similar documents on the computer. Others have become skilled simply by using the computer recreationally. If you have the knowledge and the talent, desktop publishing is a great tool that can make you even more desirable to a potential client, particularly small businesses that cannot afford to pay the fees major agencies or PR firms charge. If you have the talent—and this means graphic ability, layout know-how, as well as editorial skills—you can produce advertisements, mailers, press releases and an assortment of other promotional materials for your clients, working comfortably in your own home. You may even convince the client to hire you to produce a monthly newsletter for either staff or customers. But, and this is crucial, before you consider this avenue, be certain that you have not only the skill and the artistic talent to turn it out, but equally important, the willingness to continue producing high quality, tasteful and informative editions.

Thomas Bivins said it so well in his *Handbook for Public Relations Writing*: "The proof is in the pudding. There's a lot to be said for that old saw. Ultimately, your final, printed publication is going to determine how successful your desktop publishing system is…and a lot of that success depends not on your hardware and software, but on you."

That completes our review of the six categories of writing preferred by retirees. I have called the next and final section of the book *The Nitty-Gritty* because these chapters explain the very basic components of the writer's life—research and revision—plus two short, but essential, chapters on setting up your work space and the business side of writing.

THE NITTY-GRITTY

CHAPTER 22

GETTING IT RIGHT

Sitting in a classroom back in grammar school days you were taught the importance of mastering the "Three **R**'s," **R**eading, (w)**R**iting and (a)**R**ithmetic to become a well-rounded, productive adult. Now as a writer, it's time to toss that list and adopt a new one. The three become (w)**R**iting, **R**esearch and **R**evision. Many chapters of this book were devoted to w**R**iting. I have saved the other two for last to emphasize their importance. Without mastering these two, your writing—articles or books, fiction or nonfiction and any of their subcategories—will never achieve greatness.

RESEARCH

As you have already learned, fact research is one of the most important tools in a writer's chest, regardless of the category of writing you choose to do. Researching not only provides information to be relayed to a hungry audience; it provides you, the writer, with the knowledge required to be able to communicate those facts to your readers in a concise, understandable manner. That's why it's so important to familiarize yourself with all aspects of the topic you are researching so that you can sort out precisely what it is you want to convey to the reader. When you work on a piece, collect every scrap of relevant information available. My files are always crammed with far more data than I ever include in the article or book I am writing. However, that overview, that fuller understanding of the subject, makes it possible for me to make the judgments necessary to fulfill the promise of the work. In nonfiction, the worth of your book or article is far more dependent on the quality of the data you include than on the quality of your writing. Of course, a combination of solid information and crisp craftsmanship is the ideal to shoot for.

CURRENT, RELEVANT AND ACCURATE

The majority of people who read nonfiction do so because they seek information. That's why they buy your book or read your article. That information must be current, relevant and accurate. But accuracy isn't a requirement of nonfiction alone; it is essential in everything you write. After many years of reading, of familiarity with the printed word from manuals to memoirs, how-tos to histories, novels to newspapers, most of you know from personal experience how disconcerting it is to find errors of fact in the literature you read. Meticulous attention to fact adds authority to you as a writer and gives readers and editors confidence that the content of your writing is up-to-date and reliable.

I repeat, accuracy is essential in every category of writing. Imagine completing your highly-anticipated life story of the family. One of your children discovers a portion of the memoir conflicts with something you stated years before or with information they were given by grandma or grandpa. You have shattered his/her confidence by not checking your facts. If you're tackling a book on the industry from which you just retired or an article for a trade magazine, your readers possess a strong knowledge of the industry and will quickly detect any discrepancies. Indeed, the piece will probably never get past the editor or fact checker. You may never again be invited to write for that publisher.

The theories or ideas you propose in an op-ed essay will instantly lose credibility with your readers if they detect errors in the facts you present. Even fiction writers can't escape from the demands of accuracy, and must research carefully. If the reader of your novel or short story detects inaccuracies or inconsistencies in the tale as it unfolds, his/her concentration will be shattered immediately. Simple things like erring in your description of a location or describing a character trait that doesn't suit the personality you are writing about can cause a reader to abandon—and worse yet, bad mouth—your book.

My suggestion back in Chapter 2 that you begin your new career by "writing about what you know" does not mean that your personal understanding of the subject is adequate to support an article or a book. Well organized research is needed to expand the limits of your memory and update your information. Carefully researched work signals to both editor and reader the difference between a professional approach and that of a self-inflated egotist who feels it is unnecessary to reach beyond his/her own level of knowledge. This is an area that should pose no difficulty for many of you after years of professional or business experience in which research played a significant role.

PLANNING YOUR STRATEGY

For now, let's begin with fact research because you should not consider starting the process—properly querying an editor or an agent—until you have thoroughly mastered your subject.

As with anything else, preparing to research is best done with a plan. As you think about the subject and the particular aspect on which you intend to concentrate, list what you consider the best sources to help you locate that information. The options are myriad. If you are writing about your life-long hobby or on a topic to which you devoted your career, you probably know better than anyone else where to find the best sources and the most current information for your project.

YOUR TRUSTY LIBRARIAN

Despite your sophistication with the Internet and the ability you think you have to search for information, I urge you to take advantage of the remarkable knowledge your reference librarian offers. Many writers head first to the reference room of the best library in their region. Reference librarians are amazing compendia of knowledge. If they don't know the answer, they are trained in how best to find

it. Most are delighted to help. After all, that's why they chose this career path. Smart writers develop close relationships with their reference librarians, and often need do little more than pick up a telephone, and ask for help. The librarian will either point you to the best sources or frequently do the research for you.

You may not be familiar with indexes and abstracts, with microfiche and microfilm. These are the tools of the librarian, and he/she can lead you to seemingly uncharted sources. Indexes run from the well known *Reader's Guide to Periodical Literature* to specialized indexes on a huge variety of subjects. The *Guide* is useful as a general index of magazines, and can help you track down articles on the subject you have chosen. But it lists only a small portion of the publications in print. R.R. Bowker publishes *Ulrich's International Periodicals Directory*, which profiles a quarter of a million academic journals, consumer magazines, newsletters, newspapers, eZines and more, from over 200 countries. Enter "Indexes of Periodicals" on your favorite search engine and you will discover somewhere in the neighborhood of 103,000 pages of listings, but I suggest you try your librarian before you plug away at that list.

THE HANDIEST RESEARCH TOOL

A writer doesn't have to travel beyond his/her desk to open the most comprehensive research tool ever created. Complementing the help you receive from your local library's reference team, the Internet can serve as an excellent starting point from which to design your search and provide the resources, both print and human, to pursue. If you are not familiar with the leading search engines—Yahoo, Google and even AOL (America on Line)—head to the library and spend a couple of hours learning about these unique tools. The secret to effective utilization of the Internet is your ability to enter the most pertinent *key word* or *phrase* to tell the computer precisely what you wish it to find. If your request is too broad, you may receive literally thousands of listings, many of which relate only vaguely to what you requested. If it is not specific, you may miss a number of pertinent sources. You must be as exacting as you can to gain the fastest and best results.

Just to give you a very simple example, you might type in the request "baseball" when you are seeking information about the pitching staff of the New York Yankees. You would receive a list of well more than one million pages to visit. Buried among them somewhere would be information on the Yank's pitching staff, but it would take you several days to discover it. Even typing in just "New York Yankees" would give you a great deal of extraneous information on close to 1.5 million pages, most of which have no bearing on your article about

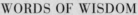

WORDS OF WISDOM

In their book *So You Want to Write*, Marge Piercy and Ira Wood point out: "Searching a data base on a computer is fast, but it still takes time. However, it sure beats writing things in a notebook, where you have to go through everything to find anything. It beats ordinary file cards, because when each piece of information in a filing system depends on spatial location, either in a file drawer or a card box, you can only get at that particular goody by one path, one label."

pitching. So your request actually should be "New York Yankees Pitching." Because you are that specific, you will receive approximately 14,700 listings relating directly to the pitching staff. Experiment with the Internet, if you haven't already, and discover for yourself what a priceless resource it is.

ORGANIZING YOUR ATTACK

You are the one who must decide what it is you are looking for and how best to find it. Once you have a sense of what's available to you from your reference librarian and the Internet or from your own limited knowledge of the subject, plan your attack. Which sources should prove fruitful and which of those are most easily accessible? Will it require days on the Internet or in the library reference room taking notes? What other books have been written on the subject with which you should familiarize yourself? Are there periodicals that deal with the material or at least carry occasional articles on the subject? With whom should you try to book interviews? Does researching this properly require a firsthand visit? The answers to these questions will be determined by the topic, and will form the basis of your approach.

THE INTERVIEW...NO REASON TO BE AFRAID

The majority of beginners cringe when they find it necessary to interview an expert, although this may well be old hat for you after years of interviewing as part of your job. If it is, that's great, because for most nonfiction books and articles you must interview and quote several authorities on the subject you select. Where can you find them? That, of course, depends on the topic. In most cases the academic world can provide a highly creditable source. Many colleges and universities now publish guides to their experts. Others ask you to contact their public relations office for referral to the faculty member best suited to help. In every case, they are happy to help for it gives the school additional recognition. Perhaps you want to select someone more directly involved—more hands-on—than an academician.

Try the *Encyclopedia of Associations*, produced by Thomson Gale Research. It lists 135,000 associations from international to state and local. You can choose one related to the subject you are writing about and find an expert among its members to interview and quote. The directory is available at most libraries. If you need assistance locating a proper source, try *Fast Facts*. It offers a huge directory of informational sources on a highly diverse list of subjects. Reach it on the Internet at *www.refdesk.com/fastfacts.html*. Another resource for experts on 7,673 topics is the Yearbook of Experts, produced every year by Broadcast Interview Source, Inc of Washington, DC (*www.expertclick.com*).

I prefer to conduct interviews in person with the experts I select. These one-on-one sessions, allow me to see the individual, study his/her body language and manner of dress and penetrate what otherwise might be a misleading façade to get a far better sense of the person. It also allows me to include any outstanding characteristics or quirks—physical or otherwise—that I would never have discovered if we hadn't spent time together.

> ### WORDS OF WISDOM
>
> Glen Martin, a California writer states in Writer's Digest Books' *Handbook of Magazine Writing*: "I've often felt I am in over my head. But I've learned you don't have to be an expert to cover a topic. You simply have to consult experts. The greatest talent a writer can develop is learning whom to talk to, or better yet, learning how to find out whom to talk to."

Although I don't like telephone interviewing, it often is necessary because of geographical distance or the schedule of the interviewee. But whichever your preference, quotations are essential in your book or article. They add the authority of an expert to your words, and make the reader even more willing to accept your thoughts.

Inexperienced writers, who are particularly skittish about conducting personal interviews, soon discover that with just a little practice, the process becomes a lot easier, even fun. The key is to be well prepared. Even if you are somewhat intimidated at first, don't show it. Experts are people, and people respond to confidence, warmth and respect. Your job is to relax your expert by transforming the question and answer process into a two-way conversation, not simply a staccato give and take. When you prepare for your visit, do a bit of advance research. Try to learn something about the person that you can comfortably open with and chat about. You will find most interviewees will respond warmly. You stroke their egos when they realize that you considered them important enough to merit some preparatory study. Of course, if you find a very tight, brusque person, all business with no smiles, then get right down to the matter at hand and fire away with the hardball questions.

CONTROLLING THE INTERVIEW

It is essential that you always remain in control of the conversation. If the interviewee begins to wander too far from the question, gently rein him/her in. You are allotted only a certain amount of time in most interviews, and you don't want to waste it on irrelevant chatter. But whatever you do, do NOT cut the person short if the conversation is germane to the question you asked. Something you never anticipated may come out of his/her musings, and present you with a completely new, exciting angle that you never thought of for the story.

Just a few more suggestions. I never go into an interview without a typed sheet of questions listed in the order I prefer to ask them. (Often the order will change as a result of the responses you receive.) In addition to ensuring you won't forget to ask something pertinent, seeing that you have the list reassures the person on the other side of the table that you have given the subject a good deal of thought and that this interview will remain on track and not meander throughout the afternoon.

ASSURING ACCURACY

Scribbling notes while interviewing can be very distracting to you. You want to concentrate on the answers you are hearing, so that you can respond with additional questions that you had not originally considered. I urge you to invest in a tape recorder. If you explain to your subject that you are using the device to be certain you quote him/her exactly without any errors, he/she almost always will agree to being recorded.

Having that tape protects you from any charge that you misquoted or slanted your interviewee's remarks. It also allows you to concentrate completely on the conversation without worrying about catching up as you rush to write your notes. Even with my self-designed shorthand developed over years of interviewing before these recorders reached the market, I find it difficult to follow every detail of a conversation while I am concentrating on note-taking. For phone interviewing I advise purchasing a very inexpensive little suction device that attaches to your telephone hand piece with a wire that plugs into your recorder. They are available at Radio Shack and other electronic stores. But if you use one, remember the law requires you to inform your subject that the interview is being recorded.

One last suggestion. If the interview goes well and the person is well respected in the field, possibly even a former acquaintance when you were actively working, at the end of the session ask whether he/she would be willing to review an advance copy of the book and possibly consider writing a blurb for the back cover.

WORDS OF WISDOM

In the book *So You Want to Write*, co-authored with Ira Wood, Marge Piercy states: "Interviewing is an undervalued art. As someone who has a lot of experience with being interviewed, I can tell you it is something usually done poorly. It requires empathy and direction, tact and a sense of tactics, patience and flattery."

CREATE A WORKING STORY FILE

Way back in Chapter 2, we talked at some length about the importance of filing clips of potential story ideas that interested you. Now that you have decided on your subject and are ready to actively research your book or article, shift the appropriate clip file to a *Working Story* file. As you continue to learn more and more from your investigations, it may be wise to refine the master file into sub files. Keep all of your research for the piece together in this single file—clippings, notes, research reports and tape recordings—so they are readily available when you need them. It is wise to take the time to transcribe an interview while it is still fresh in your mind. If a word or phrase is muddled on the tape, you will probably be able to recall what was said. Place the transcript in the working story file, and be sure to save the tape for protection.

MARKET RESEARCH

A writer's research program is two-fold. It is not limited only to digging out facts and information to improve content. Knowing and understanding your market is essential for success. Whether you've written a book or an article, there probably is a home waiting for it…somewhere. It's your job to locate the proper "somewhere"…to target the periodical, agent, publisher or editor who will respond to your magnum opus. If you speak with almost any magazine editor, he/she will bemoan the high percentage of submissions received that are totally irrelevant to the publication. Or if they are relevant, they conflict with the magazine's philosophy or style. The same holds true for literary agents and even publishers, for they too tend to specialize in certain subjects or genres. The age of specialization has impacted the world of publishing as it has so many other disciplines, so it is incumbent upon you to study the market and set your sights carefully before you "shoot."

TESTING THE MARKET

Selecting the right outlet for your work from among the endless possibilities the periodical world offers can be confusing. Chapters 9 and 10 dealt with choosing an agent and/or a book publisher. Here we take a look at the world of magazines and journals and the editors that run them. These publications are not only specialized by subject, they differ from one another in how they handle those subjects. Some want opinion and personal viewpoints built into your copy; others demand total objectivity. Some insist upon heavy use of quotations and lots of sources in a nonfiction piece. Others prefer a scholarly approach, at the extreme even requiring footnotes and possibly bibliographies. If you want to see your articles in print, it is essential that you take the time to analyze the specific needs and desires of each editor you plan to approach. That may sound a bit overwhelming, but there are many tools to help you make these decisions.

Directories of periodicals are readily available, as we discussed in Chapter 14. The information they offer will lead you to the right outlet. The annual editions of *Writer's Market*, *Poet's Market* and *Children's Writer's & Illustrator's Market* are highly respected bibles in each of these specialties, and list numerous periodicals. More specialized directories are available as well. For example, Dustbooks publishes the *International Directory of Little Magazines & Small Presses*. In the travel field, *Travel Writers.com* offers a directory of travel magazines and newspaper sections. There are similar directories for computer, medical and other publications. Your reference librarian will have recommendations for each category.

WORDS OF WISDOM

The 2006 edition of *Writer's Market* from Writer's Digest Books, recommends in its introductory notes: "A careful reading of listings will reveal that many editors are very specific about their needs. Your chances of success increase if you follow directions to the letter....The more research you do upfront, the better your chances of acceptance, publication and payment."

In addition to reading about editorial preferences in the directories, you can obtain a free, more detailed copy of writer's guidelines from most publications by sending a request accompanied by a SASE (self addressed stamped envelope). Many include guidelines on their web sites. If the publication doesn't offer them on its site, a quick check of the masthead or a telephone call will provide the address to which you can send your request. But reviewing published guidelines is never enough. As discussed in Chapter 14, it is essential to study several editions of the magazine. But remember, to gain any real value you must read like a writer. As explained in that earlier chapter, that means carefully analyzing each key section of the publication. Magazines will send you sample copies upon request, but they will usually charge for them.

HITTING THE BULL'S-EYE

Hundreds of manuscripts are submitted to magazines each month. The very first ones to be discarded are those that are not relevant or have not conformed to submission requirements. Editors regularly report that the vast majority of rejections writers receive stem from the fact that the writer has not studied a publication and tailored his/her work to its requirements.

It isn't enough just to write. What you turn out must be saleable. That's what this business is all about. It is understanding your target's preferences. It is recognizing the point of view of a publication. Only by spending the time on Marketing Research can you choose the most suitable periodical for your piece, or if you haven't begun to write it yet, determine the type of article to turn out. Whether it should be perky and fast-paced or more reflective and thoughtful; minimalist or flowery with lots of literary allusions, metaphors and similes. Perhaps it should be more academic in tone. Should you use anecdotes to tell the story, and to what degree? But whatever you choose, be sure the style is something you are comfortable with. Your writing must be natural. It must come from you and it must flow.

As we continue with the Three **R**'s, in the next chapter, we'll look at another critical aspect of preparing your article or book for publication—Revision. While a number of writers, especially novices, find this **R** somewhat difficult, it must be a carefully honed and polished component of every writer's chest of essential tools.

CHAPTER 23

FINAL TOUCHES

A precious stone demands cleaning and polishing to achieve the luster that transforms it into a gem of great beauty. And so it is with writing. Your first draft was an exercise in creativity. You were urged just to write, to overlook concerns that might interfere with flow and spontaneity, to let the words pour onto the paper. But when you now return to the first draft to review and edit it, you change roles and become a craftsman polishing your jewels until their brilliance becomes irresistible to anyone who reads them. Although not quite as creative and free flowing as composing your initial draft, revision and editing can be challenging and a great deal of fun.

REVISION/EDITING

This is when you make certain all the t's are crossed and all the i's dotted, the words spelled properly and the grammar correct. But there is far more to it than that. It's when you take a dispassionate look at what you've written, evaluating every word, sentence and paragraph to ensure they express precisely what you are trying to say. Your goal is to eliminate any possible ambiguity. To tighten up your copy and make it crisp. There is always a tendency to use more words—and even more sentences—than are needed to express your thoughts. Good rewriting tosses out extraneous material, carefully preserving only enough text to clarify the information you are passing on. You may decide to reshuffle the sequence of paragraphs or even chapters to make the piece flow more smoothly. Sentences are tightened up to deliver your message precisely and succinctly. Words that now seem extraneous are eliminated. These are all functions of the third "R"

(Revision), essential tools to polish your stellar prose (or poetry) until it becomes as perfect as you feel you can make it.

While this process is more mechanical than when you first placed your words on paper, you will still experience moments of exhilaration when you suddenly realize that a change in a word or a phrase precisely captures the thought that had eluded you in the original draft. That's the real fun and the reward of this phase of your work. But revision is work, exacting work, essential work.

WORDS OF WISDOM

Ernest Hemingway: "I take great pains with my work, pruning and revising with a tireless hand. I have the welfare of my creations very much at heart. I cut them with infinite care, and burnish them until they become brilliants. What many another writer would be content to leave in massive proportions, I polish into a tiny gem."

How fortunate we writers are to be able to review and revise our words! It is a distinct advantage that only authors enjoy. We have the opportunity to go back over sentences time and time again, and hopefully hone them to perfection. When you speak extemporaneously, you have only one chance to get it right, to phrase it exactly. Perhaps the reason some people find that public speaking is a lot easier than writing is because impromptu speakers are seldom as precise as writers in choosing their words.

GETTING STARTED

Take your favorite dictionary down from the bookshelf and place it on your desk alongside a thesaurus and a book on basic grammar. You are now ready to begin. Opinions vary widely over the best source to use; I offer my choices as non-binding suggestions. A paperback *Webster's New World Dictionary* is always handy on my desk. Although easy and quick to use because of its size, its content is limited for the same reason. When I occasionally must search for a missing word or a proper noun not found in the little Webster's, I look in my *American Heritage Dictionary* which has never yet failed me. For a thesaurus, I find it is convenient and faster to use one that is alphabetized and formatted like a dictionary, for example *Roget A to Z* from Harper Perennial. I back that up with a copy of the traditional *Roget* and a *Dictionary of Synonyms* from Merriam Webster.

There are many options for a reference book on grammar. Strunk and White's *The Elements of Style* has been a favorite of English teachers for generations. *Grammatically Correct* is a guide for writers by Anne Stilman. You might also want to have handy a style book like the *Manual of Style and Usage* developed for the *New York Times*.

There is one more component that I find essential to my ready reference tools, a list of the handful of words that constantly trap me. For example, I frequently forget whether "nonfiction" is one word, two words or a compound word split by a hyphen. I always have the same trouble with "part-time," and both of these recur frequently in this book. I place the troublesome words on a list along with stylistic rules to be followed in laying out my copy. As an example, spacing between section heads and body text or the layout of the WORDS OF WISDOM text boxes. You will find jotting these down and keeping the list in a handy place will save you substantial amounts of time as you write your initial draft and, of course, when you go back and edit your work.

WORDS OF WISDOM

Truman Capote: "I believe more in scissors than I do in the pencil."

DIFFERENT WRITERS, DIFFERENT TRICKS

Techniques of revision vary. Some authors are more comfortable editing a hard copy and then transferring those changes to the computer. Others prefer to work right on the computer and take advantage of the remarkable flexibility it offers. They can experiment with words and sentences, even paragraphs, moving or changing them with ease. The upside of computer editing is the ability to view the revision clearly and evaluate it. If need be, to change it again. The downside is that once the original is revised, it is impossible to return to it for any reason unless you have stored a copy on a disk, filed a copy under another name on your hard drive or printed a hard copy for reference. Once printed in hard copy, a document remains available for review until you discard it.

To enjoy the advantages of both, other writers use these two approaches simultaneously when editing. As they move along through the hard copy and spot a change that should be made, they turn to the computer and enter it at once. I often do this myself, and keep the original hard copy for reference, if needed, when I do another read-through. There is no right way or even best way. Your choice depends upon the level of comfort you find as you work.

You may have your own preferred technique if your former job required you to edit manuals, speeches, advertising copy or other documents. Whatever approach you select, it is best not to read and edit your draft immediately after you write it. With the original still fresh in your mind, you tend to gloss over constructions that will cry out for change when you re-read them after a delay. Only by taking a break—and that should be at least a day, preferably a week or even a month—can you regain the objectivity that allows you to view your precious words the way a careful reader or a critic would. No matter how long you wait between original draft and revision, be certain that you never lose continuity. Don't begin revising, and let a lengthy period of time and distractions pass before you continue the process. Try to do it all at once: several hours for an article; consecutive days for a book. Just as you did in the initial writing, you must maintain a consistency in your editing.

One last tip: When you edit, remove words or add some, sloppy mistakes frequently occur. As you complete your changes, reread them…check them again carefully.

Even after your book is accepted by an agent or a publisher, or if an editor says "yes" to your article, revision doesn't end. In fact, it is almost a certainty that you will be asked to go at it again, but this time with a set of specific directions based on the agent's or editor's reactions and suggestions. Be grateful! The manuscript can't help but be improved by a close collaboration between you and a literary expert. So take the fullest advantage of his/her advice.

WHAT SHOULD YOU LOOK FOR?

The obvious answer is anything that interrupts the flow of the text or distracts the reader. These can be incorrect facts, clumsy constructions or the basic errors of grammar and spelling that we've talked about. A careful author is constantly on the watch for those and for much more. Six additional concerns are always near the top of my list:

STYLE: Consistency of style is extremely important. Your writing is and should be a direct reflection of you, the author, and of your unique method of expression. But moods vary from day to day, creating the danger that any time you return to the computer to continue the previous day's work, the style of your writing can change to match your state of mind. You know the problem. Perhaps too much to drink or eat the night before. Possibly awakening with a headache. Or just a case of not enough sleep.

Since your writing style is generally a reflection of the way you think and speak, one of the best ways to test for consistency is to read the manuscript aloud. You will quickly note any deviations as you hear the words. Reading aloud allows you to feel the pace and the rhythm of the writing, and quickly flags any words that seem out of context. It will also help you detect overly long sentences that should be broken up for clarity. Be wary of a tendency to mimic the style of another author whose work you have just read and admired.

If you are confused by the many definitions of style, listen to the advice the revered British poet and thinker Matthew Arnold offered more than a century ago. It is still relevant today, "Have something to say, and say it as clearly as you can. This is the only secret of style."

DESCRIPTION: No instruction is more universal than "Show, don't tell." It is stressed in every book on writing and in every course. You have encountered it time and again in the preceding chapters of this book. But it is worth one last reminder Very simply, it means minimizing your use of adjectives to reduce "telling." Instead, it describes ("shows") your characters through their actions, mode of speech, attire and other distinguishing factors that give the reader insight into the person. It makes places become real by painting a picture. It uses metaphors, similes, analogies when describing scenes or events, even people. Mark Twain, one of American literature's greatest stylists, loathed adjectives. He counseled young writers, "If you catch an adjective, destroy it." That may be a bit harsh, but we do visualize a picture best when the text shows, not tells, "She walked swiftly, her body tilted forward like a runner reaching for the finish line." Compare that to the dull statement, "She was a fast walker." Or "This leaf season was beautiful" comes alive when you draw the picture, "White turbans capped the vivid red and orange of the mountains as their peaks pierced the clouds."

SPECIFICITY: Always try to be specific. Specificity makes your writing more compelling. It gives your reader the opportunity to visualize more exactingly the object or the idea that you are projecting. Your character's pet isn't simply a dog. It's a Maltese. Your protagonist isn't just "driving his motorcycle fast along the road." He's "racing his Harley on State Highway 77." As you can see from this last example, verbs are words that describe action. Used with care, they need no extra modifier (and that would please Mark Twain). Because your character was driving fast in the example above, you would have had to use the word "fast" to describe his speed. "Racing" expressed it vividly with just one word. Don't be afraid to exercise your computer's delete key. Rid your text of every useless modifier you find that is either redundant or adds nothing to the verb or noun it describes. Even better, in the case of a verb, find one that connotes action. Here are just a few examples of nouns and verbs that are frequently found with superfluous modifiers: Racing *fast*, yelling *loudly*, *humiliating* insult, *stupid* blunder, *final* conclusion, *wearing* apparel.

VOICE: It is an accepted fact that wherever possible a sentence should be written in the active voice. Avoid the passive if you can because it is a weaker statement and has a tendency to retard flow. Compare "John and his brother painted the room" with "The room was painted by John and his brother."

(Now go back and edit the first sentence of the preceding paragraph as a demonstration of some of things I have talked about. Did you catch the unneeded modifier "accepted" in the first five words? In fact, the first eight words should be

tossed. How about the passive statement "should be written?" Try it this way, "Wherever possible, write every sentence in the active voice." That's to the point and eight words shorter.)

FLOW: Your writing must have a sense of unity to bring the reader comfortably from page one to the end. The rhythm and pace of the piece must remain steady. Obviously, the subject matter must be consistent, as well as the tone and the style of your writing. The point of view with which you open the book must remain the same throughout, as discussed in earlier chapters. The tense of the book as well as the spelling of names and proper nouns—indeed of all words—must always be the same.

> ### WORDS OF WISDOM
>
> Educator and author Theodore A. Rees Cheney writes in his helpful book *Getting the Words Right:* "Unity and coherence are closely allied, but we must keep them distinct, at least for the purpose of discussion. Unity is a matter of keeping all elements of a piece of writing, whether a paragraph or a book, centered on the primary topic. Coherence has to do with the order in which the various elements are presented and the devices used to make clear the relationships between those elements."

SIMPLICITY: You probably have heard the admonition (Gosh, should I have better used *warning, advice* or *caution?*) never to use a large, complex word when a simple one will do. Reading your text out loud will help you catch these unwanted monsters. For example, is your character inebriated? Or drunk? Is she pulchritudinous? Or pretty? Was it a nugatory comment? Or was it worthless? Using a word that is unfamiliar to your reader can break the spell of the most exciting story, and in the extreme, lose your reader entirely. However, don't interpret this to mean that every word must be monosyllabic. There are multiple (Oops, wouldn't *many* have done just as well here?) times when it is necessary to choose a longer or less common word to capture the exact meaning you intend.

BRIDGE WORDS: While you are tidying and tightening up your copy, don't be afraid to use your delete key to rid your sentences of what I call *bridge words*. These begin the new sentence with "and" or "but" or "in other words" or "what that really means is." Introducing a sentence this way might seem necessary as you zip through your initial draft, but upon re-reading, most often you'll find the bridge word is unneeded and in most cases slows the pace.

If keeping alert for all of these possible problems intimidates or even just confuses you, try focusing on one or two of the elements when reading through your manuscript. Although time consuming, gear each consecutive reading to ferreting out one or two other specific problems until you've covered them all. There is a corollary benefit to this process. Each time you read, you have the chance to spot and revise other aspects of the text that don't fully satisfy you.

CONSISTENCY IS CRITICAL

Let's go back a moment and expand on the importance of accuracy that we talked about much earlier. Providing information that is relevant and factual is the essence of nonfiction, but those facts must remain consistent throughout. In fiction, time, place, elements of character can easily become distorted in the course of writing thousands upon thousands of words. To maintain consistency, chart the first entry of any fact that will be referred to again in the book.

WORDS OF WISDOM

In their strongly recommended *Write It Right*, Dawn Josephson and Lauren Hidden point out: "If an editor has a choice of two writers—one who turns in an 'almost perfect' piece and another who turns in a very rough first draft—whom do you think the editor will call when the next assignment comes up? An editor's job is to polish your work to ensure your message comes across clearly. But an editor needs an 'almost finished' product to work with; he or she is not supposed to rewrite your work."

Include a description of each character and place. Continually check the chart as you edit the book. If Jane J. Jones lives at 30 Harrison Street when introduced in chapter 2, she must have the same middle initial and live at the identical address by the final chapter, unless you have orchestrated a move or change of name for her. Similarly, you must be very careful to ensure that any characteristics you ascribe to a place or person in later chapters never conflict with the way you described them initially.

RECHECK YOUR OPENING

When you are satisfied with the finished manuscript, take one more look at your opening paragraphs, whether you have written an article or a book. Do they grab the reader and impel him/her into the piece? Think back. How many times have you begun an article with some anticipation, only to close the page after reading the first one or two paragraphs? Unless the early graphs are gripping or entertaining, the reader of fiction will bid you an early farewell. When beginning a nonfiction piece, especially how-to, the reader must immediately feel confident that he/she will gain a real benefit by continuing to read the entire book or article. You are now reading Chapter 23 of *The Writer Within You* because from the first page on, you apparently believed this book would help you fulfill your long-held desire to write. If at any point you felt it would not, you would have brought it back to the bookstore for a refund or tossed it away. As you spend more and more time at revision, you will come to value the result of being both precise and concise in your own prose, and to respect that in the output of other writers as well.

WHEN IS ENOUGH ENOUGH?

The question always arises: Have I edited sufficiently? Should I give it one more go-around? The answer is totally subjective. It depends upon your level of satisfaction. You saw above how demanding the great Hemingway was of himself and his prose. When you begin your final read, make certain that it is a catch-all: spelling and grammar corrected, meaningless clichés and words eliminated, facts checked for accuracy and flow made natural and comfortable.

It makes a great deal of sense to try and find a friend or relative whom you trust and respect to read your manuscript. Caution that person that it isn't praise you want. It is hard nosed, objective evaluation. Anything short of that is of no value. Indeed, it is harmful, for it will leave you with an unjustified sense of accomplishment. Receiving unbiased critical comment is of particular benefit if you are a beginning writer. The euphoria of completing an article or a book frequently skews the judgment of a beginner. An honest evaluation by second person you can trust to be truthful can be extremely helpful. The one you pick should be a strong reader with a keen eye for grammatical errors, misspellings and typos. If you are really fortunate he/she has done extensive reading, and is able to sense shortcomings in pace, characterization, believability, lack of clarity and possibly even errors of fact. Discuss the piece in depth with your reader. Ask probing questions about content, pace, clarity of specific characterizations and whether the piece held your reader's interest or lagged in spots.

Although we have come to the end of our chapters related directly to writing skills and publishing techniques, there are two more essential matters that must be discussed now that you are ready to become a functioning author. Under the chapter heading **Setting Up**, you'll discover many tips on how to organize your work environment in an inexpensive, functional way. Following that, **Money Matters and More**, a topic certainly of interest to most of you, will deal with efficient ways to maintain control of your submissions, billings, payments and receivables. It will also give you information on what expenses the IRS allows you to deduct. Be sure to read both of these. They will help you organize yourself and your work space, and will guide you on financial matters so that at no time will you be in jeopardy with the Internal Revenue Service as your new business hopefully grows and grows.

CHAPTER 24

SETTING UP

Housekeeping. Nowhere near as glamorous as conducting a book signing nor as exciting as writing your final chapter. Indeed, it probably sounds terribly boring. Far too simplistic even for starting authors. Certainly a come-down from the old days when you could call on secretaries and assistants to service your every need. Nevertheless, every beginner must understand the housekeeping needs of an author or he/she will never have a book to sign. Years of interfacing with wanna-be word slingers in my writing classes have made me aware of how important it is to include some guidance on equipment and supplies. Far too many newcomers insist upon throwing obstacles in their paths to stardom by not having the basic tools of their newly adopted craft.

Maybe you are willing to struggle with just a yellow pad and a pencil…to head to your kitchen table, searching for peace and quiet in the wee hours when mom, dad, siblings, spouse and children are tucked away in bed. It's certainly possible to write, even publish, under those trying circumstances. But frankly, it's tough enough to turn out saleable text under the most ideal situations. Why burden yourself with unneeded hurdles?

THE DIGITAL DEVIL

If you never learned to use a computer during your years of work, it is time to overcome your fear. They aren't the awesome gizmos that in the past caused so many to be phobic over their use. In this day and age, most of us, even old timers, own one of these incredible machines and have a basic familiarity with it…at least enough for word processing. That's all you need to be able to write, to edit your work and to shift and alter your words and sentences, even paragraphs and pages, to capture precisely what it is you want to say. Of course, we also learned earlier how valuable the Web is as a tool for research and how easy it is to use to ferret out the facts you need before putting words on paper.

Despite the myth that only younger generations are computer literate, studies have shown that of the 76 million Americans 50 years or older, 36 million—almost half—own computers.

PASS UP THE BELLS & WHISTLES

Today, almost anyone can afford a computer. You don't need the latest hi-tech Pentium model costing thousands. It may be fun to impress your friends with all the bells and whistles, but you're paying for luxuries you'll undoubtedly never use. Computers grow outdated by the week. Their selling prices drop just as quickly. Many of us work well on quality machines that seem like anachronisms to devotees of state-of-the-art technology. But we require no more than what we have, and they fit our budgets. These miraculous machines provide us with the ability to process words with an ease that paper and pencil or even the most advanced typewriter never offered. In today's competitive market, computer manufacturers are offering deals and discounts that allow you to purchase a highly efficient machine with more than adequate memory and speed, the two most valued components of a computer, at prices well within most budgets.

Many years ago, while still a timid author cranking out copy on an electric typewriter, I was given a demonstration of the benefits of switching to a computer while visiting a dear friend who specialized in writing books for teenagers. Fearful that attention to the technology would distract me from my creativity, I wasted three or four more years of wrestling with carbon paper and white-out and all of the other frustrations of my antiquated methodology. But once I got up the courage to take the necessary leap, I discovered within the first week that I had found "writer's nirvana." This digital wonder not only made writing so much easier; it offered me unanticipated opportunities for research, communication and the other needs of a writer. I include this anecdote because I urge you to follow my lead.

> ### WORDS OF WISDOM
>
> In her highly informative book *Writing.Com*, Moira Anderson Allen points out: "If you're serious about writing and getting published, being online isn't just a good idea. It has become a necessity...It has become the arena in which writing business is conducted."

When you type your words into a computer, you format them *digitally*. That means you have transformed the letters into *bits* and *bytes*, in simplest terms into an electronic, numeric format. There are several programs available to do this; the most widely used in our industry is *Microsoft Word*. To safely store those words and make them readily accessible, you create a *file* (your text) that can be saved on the computer's *hard drive* (the memory center of the machine), or on a disk or flash memory device or stored on all three. Because this digital language is universal and can be read by computers throughout the world, the file can be sent to them regardless of their location.

MAKING LIFE EASY

By writing digitally, much of the pain and drudgery of editing and rewriting is automatically avoided. If you were lucky enough to take a typewriting course in high school, dredge up that skill to make the process of inputting text on your computer keyboard easier. Unlike the old typewriter, shifting words, sentences or even paragraphs to new locations is effortless. You have ready access to tools like underlining, changing the size or boldness of your type or even writing in italics. If after all these years, your grammar and spelling are a little rusty, *spell checks* and *grammar checks* are built into many computers sold today. When you venture beyond just word processing, you'll find these remarkable machines are superb tools for other functions too. The Internet outstrips encyclopedias and even reference libraries as a research tool, offering this service free in the convenience of your own home or office. Once you are comfortable with your computer, you will also find it quite useful for much of your financial or other record keeping.

Try not to go on a computer shopping spree alone. If one of your friends is a knowledgeable techie, ask—if necessary, beg—him/her to come along. If no one is available, ask your friends and neighbors about helpful dealers in the area. Visit the local stores of some of the best known national computer retailers. Explain to the sales person exactly what your needs are. You want a sturdy computer, with as much word processing speed as your pocketbook will allow. A machine that will also permit you to access the Internet quickly and effectively.

WORDS OF WISDOM

Author Bill Jordan writes in *Tools of the Writer's Trade*, an excellent book produced by the American Society of Journalists and Authors (ASJA): "I approached computerization most reluctantly, with a bad case of high-tech paranoia. Now I am fully overcome with admiration for the mystical powers of the box in front of me. It was the user-friendliness of my computer that made the transition possible, even easy."

You also require adequate memory to store the text of the book or books you plan to write and a machine that is simple to operate. At the time of this writing, you should be able to find a brand new computer to meet all of those needs for between $300 and $400. Second hand machines are also available, and will cost even less. In both cases, ask about the *software* that comes with your purchase. (You undoubtedly remember from previous chapters that "software" is the term used for the electronic programs that operate within the computer to allow you to type, erase, move and perform endless other functions.) You will also hear the word *hardware* as you shop. This term refers to the physical elements like the computer itself, printers, scanners, as well as a variety of other utilities that you really don't need to get started.

Let me give you one suggestion for making the transition to a computer smoother and faster. From the first day my son helped me set up my desktop I have always maintained a file labeled "Computer Instructions." Each time I discover or am shown another secret about this magical machine, I immediately jot down step-by-step the procedure to follow, and file it away for future reference. There are many procedures that you may use infrequently, and as a beginner, it is very easy to forget them. Janice Hopkins Tanne, a board member of ASJA and prolific article writer, uses a notebook to "write down how to do things with the computer once you figure them out," a system she calls "invaluable." Ms. Tanne adds that "referring to your notebook is faster than wading through the manual, and your how-to-do-it description is probably a great deal clearer."

OUTFITTING YOUR OFFICE

Try and find a relatively untrafficked corner of your home with decent lighting where you can set up a desk or at least a flat table to work on. If your budget and space allow, you may want to place a metal or wood filing cabinet on your purchase list. If not, use cardboard boxes rescued from your liquor store's trash bin. The size used by most liquor manufacturers is ideal. Stationery stores offer inexpensive plastic or cardboard filing tubs. But if you can afford it and want something more permanent and easier to access, head to a second-hand office furniture outlet. Most of these reconditioned cabinets are far superior to the cheap construction found in the "bargains" offered by discount stationers. Check the suspension system of the drawer. The drawers on many inexpensive cabinets don't open completely, robbing you of valuable file space.

To fill those drawers in an organized manner, you need nothing more than some inexpensive file folders. A few pens and pencils, several reams of modest grade white copy paper and personalized stationery will get you on your way. If budgets are too tight, you can skip the printed stationery, although that does give your correspondence and queries a more professional look.

Perhaps you can stretch the dollars just a bit, and include a tape recorder. It's not an absolute necessity to start, but it is a tool you will find extremely helpful for many tasks. When interviewing in person or even on the telephone it allows you to concentrate on what your subject is saying. Unburdened by the need to scribble at breakneck speed, your mind can frame new questions and new responses to what you hear. Sure, many of us

> ### WORDS OF WISDOM
>
> In his classic, The *Magazine Article,* journalism professor and columnist Peter Jacobi recommends: "Use a tape recorder… Most sources feel reassured by the presence of a recorder. They know at least you're more likely to get things right. Take notes as well, in case the recorder didn't operate properly."

have interviewed hundreds of times with just pencil and paper, and done it successfully. But these marvelous little machines make life a lot easier, and usually produce better interviews and an exacting back-up if your subject later takes umbrage at something you have quoted.

A HANDY AND HELPFUL COMPANION

In addition, your tape recorder should be your constant companion. Whenever I am alone in the car, it sits immediately available on the passenger seat, ready to capture those momentary flights of inspiration that disappear too quickly if not locked in at once. (Unfortunately, too many of us find our memories start to wilt as our hair begins to gray.) Perhaps it will be a new idea for the book or an unorthodox, but very effective, approach to a new article. Maybe you'll suddenly discover the resolution to a troublesome plot problem or experience a burst of creativity that better portrays the essence of one of your characters. A tape recorder, whether mini cassette or standard, is one of the best investments a serious writer can make. But don't scrimp. Be sure your device has a quality microphone that can pick up a voice at a fair distance. Nothing is worse than taping a lecture, a panel discussion or even a one-on-one interview and discovering the sound is so dim you can't transcribe it

You'll need nothing more in equipment or furniture to get started. Just add an up-to-date dictionary that includes current slang, a thesaurus to find the perfect word and a book on basic grammar, as discussed in the previous chapter. Now that these essential, albeit mundane, physical needs have been satisfied, we add one more basic in the next chapter—how to maintain the records that are so essential to running your new writing business.

CHAPTER 25

MONEY MATTERS AND MORE

Writing becomes a business once you sell to others what you have created. Unfortunately far too many beginners overlook that fact. So in this final chapter, I ask you to set aside the glamour, the exhilaration of becoming a published author, and bring your head down from the creative clouds to take a hard look at the "nuts and bolts."

When you sell your first article, story, poem or book, you become an entrepreneur operating your own small business. You are no longer an amateur writing just for fun. Because you have earned income you must comply with the regulations of the Internal Revenue Service. But that's no reason to be frightened. At this level, it's just a simple matter of reporting the income your writing generates each time you file your return when April 15th rolls around.

Unless you were self-employed, your status as an independent author is quite different from what it was when you worked. You now must maintain your own records because you are working for yourself, not for a company, and will not receive a W2 form from an employer. Your book publisher, literary agent or magazine to which you submitted articles will send you a Form 1099 that shows the amount of money you made during the tax year with no deductions taken. However, if you don't receive a 1099 and sometimes you don't, you still must report your income, and that makes maintaining accurate and complete records all the more important.

KEEPING THE IRS HAPPY

Record keeping should begin when you send out your first query. It makes little difference whether you store a copy in a query file or log it into a query ledger by date. But there should be a record of every query or submission you send and the response to each. This control is essential for many reasons. It allows you to keep track of your queries and submissions, particularly important when more than one is circulating at the same time. It also serves as a reminder of when either to follow up or disregard and query another publication, agent or publisher. The log also proves to the IRS that, although your income is minimal as a result of the rejections you received as a start-up writer, you have continually tried to place your work. It is proof that you are a serious writer, not just a dilettante. That allows you to deduct expenses when you calculate your taxes.

PROFESSIONAL VS. HOBBYIST

Maintain a ledger of your expenses as they occur. These can be deducted when you file your annual income tax forms. Postings should include supplies, equipment, travel, professional dues, business subscriptions, business lunches and dinners and legitimate office costs. But they must all relate directly to the operation of your business. The IRS understands that, like the operator of any other start-up, you cannot be expected to post a large profit at the outset. In fact, it is highly likely that you will show a loss because expenses of the start-up outstrip the minimal income you are generating. Maintaining complete records will demonstrate that you are actively trying to bring your fledgling business to a profitable level.

You will recognize the importance of all of this when you understand that the IRS makes a distinction between professionals and hobbyists, as Kelly James-Enger explained in the WORDS OF WISDOM on the opposite page. If you are a hobbyist, you can justify expenses only to the amount of your writing income, and cannot claim a loss. You will be considered a professional running a business if you post a net profit in three out of five years. If you experience more than two years of red ink during the preceding five years, you will probably fall into the hobbyist category, unless you can convince the IRS otherwise by showing that you have spent a significant amount of time and effort at your writing and have made a profit in the past. This seems to be only a momentary slump.

With professional status, there are many deductions available that can reduce your income tax burden. In addition to those listed earlier, your home office, utilities for the office, insurance, even a portion of cleaning and landscape maintenance can be deducted under exacting regulations. But if and when you arrive at that point in your writing income, I recommend you consult with a qualified accountant.

KEEP IT SIMPLE

You have the option of maintaining these records manually or on your computer. If you prefer to do it manually, purchase a simple ledger at any stationer. Create individual pages for your expenses and income. My expense ledger usually separates **Office Expenses** (phones, supplies, postage, etc), **Dues and Subscriptions** (professional memberships, newspapers, journals, magazines and books purchased as tools of the trade),

Travel and Entertainment (expenses like tolls and parking incurred on an assignment, plus allowable, deductible business meals) and **Car Expenses** (gas, repairs, insurance, etc).

Most of you will be using the same car or truck for both business and pleasure. If so, record both the starting and ending total mileage for the vehicle each year. Whenever you have to travel for work, post the date, mileage and purpose. (I use a separate, inexpensive appointment book that I leave in my car.) At the end of the year, calculate your total mileage, as well as the amount you used exclusively for work purposes. Divide the total mileage by the miles driven for work to calculate the percentage of the year's mileage devoted to your freelance efforts. Multiply the annual cost of operating your car by that percentage to determine the portion of your total car expenses that can be deducted. The alternative is to total your assignment mileage and apply the standard IRS allowance per mile. If you choose this method, be certain to check the figure because it changes from year to year.

FILLING THE COFFERS

When you submit your work to a periodical as hard copy or on a disk, enclose an invoice in the package. If you transmit it electronically, a hard copy invoice should immediately follow by snail mail. Place a duplicate copy in an *Open Invoices* file. When payment checks begin to roll in, it is important to maintain a clear record of the date and source, as well as the portion of payment that is base compensation and the amount, if any, paid as reimbursement for expenses. (Remember, you pay taxes only on compensation, not on expense reimbursement.) After making those notations on your invoice, staple the check stub to the invoice and move it from the open to a *Paid Invoices* file. I know all of this sounds very simple and perhaps "overkill," but I assure you that when income tax day rolls around, you will be pleased that you took the time to maintain these records.

To keep tight control, I urge you to create a simple, standard billing form (invoice or statement) on your computer. This is particularly important for the article writer who may have several articles in process at the same time. Store the basic form on your computer. When you bill a client, fill in the specifics for that transaction, print and mail it. You may prefer to print out copies of the basic form in advance and fill in the information by hand. Use a sequential numbering system, (never start with 1; that's a sure sign you are a beginner) so that you can refer back to that invoice if any problem develops with the magazine.

Some publications are notoriously late payers, and require periodic reminders that they owe you money. Check your Paid Invoice file on a regular schedule, and diary ticklers to follow up when necessary. Use common sense in determining if and when a reminder is in order. Obviously, you do not want to antagonize the editor, but you certainly are entitled to be paid... and on time as promised. I suggest you not telephone the editor until you have contacted him/her by e-mail or snail mail three or four times. A sample invoice follows on the next page.

As I mentioned earlier, most of this billing information applies to those of you who choose to write articles. Billings for book authors are minimal, but it is important to record all expenses incurred for research and writing before your book is finished. Once your book is completed and accepted by an agent, he/she will handle all financial records for you, but even so, it is wise to catalogue both income and expenses for future reference.

WORDS OF WISDOM

Writer's Digest Books' *2005 Guide to Literary Agents*: Because the agent only receives payment when the publisher pays the writer, it is in the agent's best interests to make sure the writer is paid on schedule.... Having an agent distances you from any conflict over payment and allows you to spend your time writing instead of making phone calls."

Your Letterhead

Invoice No _____

Soc Security _____

Date_____

To   _____

      _____

      _____

INVOICE

Story Working Title..…...…$000.00

(If publication has agreed to pay expenses, list them here by category)

Mileage (date and destination) 000 miles @ 00 cents...................$00.00

Tolls (per attached receipts)....................................…......00.00

Telephone (per attached receipts).....................................00.00

Total Invoice $000.00

(If phone bill has not yet arrived, note here): Telephone expenses to follow when bill arrives

Thank you,

John Jones

WHAT TO CHARGE

This is always a difficult decision for beginning writers, even for pros who venture into new arenas for the first time. If you are a book author, your agent is at your side helping you with all financial negotiations. But as an article writer without an agent, you are on your own. Magazines and newspapers vary widely in their payment schedules. *Writer's Market* includes pay scales for almost every magazine it lists. You have every right to ask the assigning editor where on that scale you fall and to negotiate if you believe you deserve better. The vast majority of editors are highly ethical professionals who care about their writers, but they are saddled with tight budgets, and try hard to keep costs down. Nonetheless, there are times when editors will increase their offers if they sense potential in your query or submission and if you are reasonable and make a sound argument for a higher fee. The process is no different from the way you negotiated when still active in business. Refer back to Chapter 16 for more details on negotiating the price.

Deciding what to charge is somewhat more difficult for those of you who want to harness your writing skills to continued involvement in your former line of work or to the business world in general. You will find that fees vary widely when trying to establish rates for business and professional clients, corporate PR departments or advertising agencies. They depend on the type of business, competition from other freelancers, your experience and even geography. If you are friendly with business writers in the area, try and establish what they charge.

WORDS OF WISDOM

www.freelancewriteabout.com: "If you're just starting out in the field, you're not going to be able to pull as much for a project as someone with 10 years of experience. You can set your rates competitively with other freelancers in your area and your experience level. If you're charging as much or close to someone with a large amount of experience, a client is going to tend to hire the freelancer with more experience for the money."

Rates paid by similar industries within a given geographical area are pretty standard for tasks like speech writing, turning out advertising copy, writing press releases, preparing public relations stories or creating brochures. Refer to a current edition of *Writer's Market* to see an up-to-date listing of standard fees for various commercial writing tasks. While these vary from area to area, they will give you some guidance and a basis for comparison.

Use basic logic when calculating a flat rate. Estimate how long the assignment will take. Multiply that by the hourly compensation you feel you're entitled to. If you do negotiate a flat rate, it is important that both you and your client understand exactly what it is you are expected to do to avoid conflict arising later. When you set the price, be generous enough with yourself to allow for unexpected delays. You and the client also have the option of agreeing upon an hourly rate instead of contracting on a per job basis.

ROYALTIES

A *royalty*, as you know by now, is the term used for the payments from the publisher to the author for the right to publish his/her book. Royalties are based upon a percentage of the revenue generated by each sale of the book. However, I can't help but re-emphasize the most important concern for any author is to clarify whether this percentage is based on the retail price of the book or on the net price the publisher receives after distributor discounts are deducted. Because this bears so heavily on the financial return you can anticipate, let's take an example to clarify this in your mind. If a book sells for $19.95 and the royalty negotiated in the contract is 10%, the royalty based on list price would be $2. If it were based on net price, the $19.95 price would be cut in half by a distributor's 50% discount, leaving the author a royalty of $1. Obviously, the goal of every author is to receive royalties on the full retail price. If the publisher is a small house that actually offers its catalogue of books directly to the consumer this too should be factored in when the level of royalty payments is negotiated.

Royalties almost never rise above the 15 % level. Many contracts are based upon a step-up scale. That means you will reach the 15% level only after a certain number of books have been sold. For example, royalties may be paid at 10% for the first 5,000 sales and 12.5% for the next 5,000, capping at 15% for sales above 10,000 copies. Although rare, some agreements have been known to start as low as 5%. Royalties on foreign sales are usually lower than domestic, principally because of the added costs involved in overseas publishing and marketing.

ADVANCES

Your adrenalin rushes whenever you hear of million dollar advances against royalties. Stop salivating. They just don't happen unless you are a top celebrity—a movie star, a high level politician or a writer who has proved his/her worth over and over again on the book market. A beginning writer can expect anywhere from $5,000 to hopefully $50,000. There certainly have been cases of higher advances, but they are few and far between for start-up authors.

It is important for you to understand the nature of the advance payment. It is designed to help support the author while finishing the book and waiting for the publication date when the book will begin to generate revenue. But the advance payment is just that: an advance. It is a down payment against the royalties you hope to earn. You won't start receiving those royalties until enough books have been sold to allow the

WORDS OF WISDOM

The very informative web site *www.fonerbooks.com* states: "Since so many writers live a hand-to-mouth existence, the promise of an extra few thousand dollars up-front may lure them into signing a contract with a lower royalty rate or longer escalation schedule. It's always a gamble, and many trade authors never see any ongoing royalties because their books never sell enough copies to pay back the advance."

publisher to recapture the amount of money that was advanced to you. Some publishers will pay the advance in a lump sum, but many will stagger payments throughout the publishing process. Staggered payments can be a problem for the author if for some reason publication is excessively delayed or cancelled. In far too many cases, authors never see a penny in royalties because their books have not sold enough copies to cover the initial advance. In the worst scenario, the publisher may go "belly up," leaving you with a substantial balance unpaid on your advance.

So much for money matters. There are books listed in the Appendix to give you more detailed information, and as stated earlier, I urge you to speak with your accountant once you reach the stage of receiving compensation for your work.

AFTERTHOUGHTS

Just as every author reaches that point in his/her writing and editing when enough is enough, so I feel it is time to end this book. If I have done my job, you now have a basic familiarity with writing as a craft and publishing as an industry. Certainly enough to face your computer with total confidence.

After reading this book carefully, you should now be liberated from the daunting mystique that surrounds our industry. No longer will it keep you from tackling your long-held dream of seeing your thoughts in print, your name on the cover of a full-length book or eBook or your byline atop a magazine or newspaper article.

I urge you not to end the learning process here. You will find a number of outstanding books, web sites and newsletters that will help refine what space has forced me to touch on lightly as I tried to give you a very broad, inclusive overview of both the craft and the industry. Books I felt were valuable enough to highlight in the WORDS OF WISDOM are identified in the Appendix with their ISBN to make it easier for you to locate them.

My web site (*www.retirement-writing.com*) and blog (*www.retirement-writing.com/blog*) continually post new articles that I and other experts in the writing and publishing arenas have written. If you are not already a subscriber (it is free), sign up now and view these sites regularly to supplement the knowledge you have gained from this book.

Keep learning, but as you do, start writing. You will learn as you write, so there is no reason to wait another day. Carpe diem!

Farewell and good luck!

APPENDIX

ADVANCE REVIEW COPIES
PRE-PUBLICATION REVIEWERS
www.publishersweekly.com
www.kirkusreviews.com
www.bookpage.com
www.libraryjournal.com
www.ala.org/booklist
www.forewordmagazine.com
www.booklist.com

SHORT RUN PRINTERS
www.longdash.com
www.bookmasters.com
www.craneduplicating.com
www.sterlingpierce.com
www.countrypress.com
www.pubgraphics.com
www.bookmobile.com

ARTICLE DIRECTORIES (DIGITAL)
www.ezinearticles.com
www.freesticky.com
www.ideamarketers.com
www.contentdesk.com
www.goarticles.com

ARTICLE WRITING
The Magazine Article by Peter Jacobi, ISBN 0-89879-450-1

Handbook of Magazine Article Writing published by Writer's Digest Books, ISBN 0-89879-328-9

The 30 Minute Writer by Connie Emerson, ISBN 978-0-5950930-0-7

How to Sell What You Write by Jane Adams, ISBN 0-399-12982-0

A Complete Guide to Marketing Magazine Articles by Duane Newcomb, ISBN 0-91165-432-1

Making Money With Words by Clement David Hellyer, ISBN 0-13547-406-X

Handbook of Magazine Article Writing published by Writers Digest Books, ISBN 0-89879-328-9

A Writer's Guide to Magazine Articles by Patricia Fry, ISBN 0-9612642-6-8

BLOGOSPHERE

www.blogger.com
www.livejournal.com
www.blogsome.com
www.blogads.com
www.swarmtraffic.com

BOOK COACHES

www.bookcoaching.com
www.longdash.com
http://parapub.com
www.writers-editors.com
www.janicephelps.com
www.wellfedwriter.com
www.bookshep.com
www.haraldanderson.com

BOOK DISTRIBUTORS

www.atlasbooks.com
www.midpointtrade.com
www.ipgbook.com

www.pmaonline.org
(Relationship with Ingram, plus own heavy promotion program)

www.bookmarket.com/distributors.html
(Directory of distributors)

www.uniquebooksinc.com
(Specializes in libraries with books from small presses)

www.quality-books.com
(Specializes in libraries with books from small presses)

BOOK WHOLESALERS

www.btol.com
(Baker & Taylor) (Major wholesaler to libraries, also retailers)

www.ingrambook.com
(Major wholesaler to retailers, also libraries)

BOOK MARKETING & PROMOTION

www.resmarketingalliance.com
www.amarketingexpert.com
www.contactanycelebrity.com
www.absolutewrite.com
www.yudkin.com
www.prpr.net
www.freepublicity.com
www.ksbpromotions.com
www.freeradioairtime.com
www.bookmarketingworks.com
www.writing world.com
www.angelahoy.com

Book Marketing from A-Z by Francine Silverman,
ISBN 0-7414-2431-2

Handbook for Public Relations Writing by Thomas Bivins,
ISBN 0-84423-436-2

1001 Ways to Market Your Books by John Kremer,
ISBN: 0-91241-149-X

BOOK REVIEWERS

(Lists of reviewers can be found on the web sites of Angela Hoy and
Midwest Book Review. For pre-publication reviewers, see Advance
Review Copies in this Appendix)

www.angelahoy.com/writing/archives/001219.html
www.midwestbookreview.com/links/othr_rev.htm
www.bookpleasures.com
www.bookreview.com
www.nybooks.com (New York Review of Books)
www.myshelf.com
www.heartlandreviews.com

BOOKS FOR WRITERS

Dan Poynter's Self-Publishing Manual, ISBN 978-15-6860-134-2

The Well-Fed Self-Publisher by Peter Bowerman,
ISBN 978-09-6705-986-0

The Right Way to Write, Publish and Sell Your Book by Patricia L.
Fry ISBN: 0-9773576-0-0

So You Want to Write co-authored by Ira Wood & Marge Piercy,
ISBN 0-97289- 845-X

The American Directory of Writer's Guidelines published by Quill
Driver Books, ISBN 18-84956-40-8

The 29 Most Common Writing Mistakes and How to Avoid Them by
Judy Delton ISBN 0-89879-453-6

Show, Don't Tell by William Noble, ISBN 0-83977-767-1

Word Painting by Rebecca McClanahan, ISBN 1-58297-025-4

Description by Monica Wood, ISBN 0-89879-908-2

Dialogue by Lewis Turco, ISBN 0-89879-947-3

The Street-Smart Writer by Jenna Glatzer and Daniel Steven,
ISBN: 0-97493- 444-5

How to Sell What You Write by Jane Adams,
ISBN 0-399-12982-0

Give 'Em What They Want by Blythe Camenson and Marshall J.
Cook, ISBN 1-58297-330-X

Making Money with Words by Clement David Hellyer,
ISBN 0-13547-406-X

BROADCAST CONSULTANTS & PUBLICATIONS

www.freepublicity.com
www.freeradioairtime.com
www.plannedtvarts.com
http://booktalkradio.blogspot.com
Bradley's Guide to the Top National TV Talk & Interview Shows
Radio-TV Interview Report (RTIR)
Talk Radio for Authors by Francine Silverman,
ISBN 978-0741437877

CHAT GROUPS

Click on Chat Groups on your search engine for lists, addresses and information

www.yahoogroups.com

COVER DESIGNERS

(Information on cover design, plus designers)

www.brennerbooks.com/coverdesigners.html
http://www.publishingcentral.com/subject.html?sid=109&si=1
www.bookcoverdesigner.com
www.brennerbooks.com/coverdesigners.html
www.bookdesignonline.com
www.fonerbooks.com/print.htm

Front Cover: Great Book Jacket and Cover Design by Alan Powers,
ISBN 1-84000-421-5

By Its Cover: Modern American Book Cover Design by Ned Drew
and Paul Sternberger, ISBN 1-56898-497-9

COPYRIGHTS

U.S. Copyright Office
www.copyright.gov/

CREATIVE NONFICTION

www.creativenonfiction.org
www.pitt.edu/~bdobler/readingnf.html

www.goucher.edu/x9141.xml (Mid-Atlantic Creative Nonfiction Conference)

Writing Creative Nonfiction, published by Story Press, ISBN 1-88491-050-5 Creative Nonfiction Magazine

EBOOKS

CONSULTANTS

www.bookcoaching.com
www.theebookcoach.com

ONLINE PUBLISHERS

www.booklocker.com
www.ebookomatic.com
www.ebookcrossroads.com/epublishers.html
www.author-network.com/epublishers.html
www.ereads.com

BOOKS

www.ultimateebookpublishing.com

How to Get Your eBook Published by Richard Curtis and W.T. Quick, ISBN 978-15-8297-095-0

EQUIPMENT

Tools of the Writer's Trade, published by The American Society of Journalists and Authors, ISBN 0-06-016363-1

EZINES (WEBZINES)

www.ezinehub.com
www.websuccesscentral.com
www.merlesworld.com/ezines.htm
www.ezineuniversity.com
http://ezinearticles.com

www.zinester.com
www.mailloop7.com
www.everyone.net
www.constantcontact.com

FICTION

Writing the Novel by Lawrence Block, ISBN 0-89879-208-8

Writing the Novel from Plot to Print by Lawrence Block, ISBN 0-89879-208-8

Writing the Breakout Novel by Donald Maass, ISBN 0-89879-995-3

How to Write & Sell Your First Novel by Oscar Collier and Frances Spatz Leighton, ISBN 0-89879-770-5

The 29 Most Common Writing Mistakes and How to Avoid Them, Judy Delton, ISBN 0-89879-453-6

Scene and Structure by Jack Bickham, and Frances Spatz Leighton ISBN 0-89879-906-6

13 Ways of Looking at the Novel by Jane Smiley, ISBN: 1-40003-318-7

Show, Don't Tell by William Noble, ISBN 0-83977-766-3

Description by Monica Wood, ISBN 0-89879-908-2

Building Believable Characters compiled by Marc McCutcheon, ISBN 1-58297-027-0

Word Painting by Rebecca McClanahan, ISBN 1-58297-025-4

Dialogue by Lewis Turco, ISBN 0-89879-947-3

Writer's Digest Sourcebook for Building Believable Characters compiled by Mark McCutcheon, ISBN 0-89879-683-0

So You Want to Write co-authored by Ira Wood and Marge Piercy, ISBN 0-97289-845-X

FORMATTING A BOOK

Suzanne Guelli sguelli@verizon.net
www.budgetbookdesign.com
www.self-pub.net/layout/
www.dotdesign.net
www.aulicinodesign.com

Book Design and Production by Pete Masterson,
ISBN 0-96698-190-1

Formatting and Submitting Your Manuscript by Cynthia Laufenberg,
ISBN 1-58297-290-7

HELPFUL WEBSITES FOR FREELANCERS

www.absolutewrite.com
www.fonerbooks.com
www.writingcorner.com
www.freelancewriteabout.com
www.yudkin.com
www.matilijapress.com
www.amarketingexpert.com

HELPFUL BOOKS FOR FREELANCERS

The American Directory of Writers Guidelines, published by Quill
Driver Books ISBN 1-88495-640-8

Profitable Freelancing by Clair Rees, ISBN 0-89879-012-3

1,000 Tested Money-Making Markets for Writers by Walter G.
Oleksy, ISBN 0-06463-411-6

The Silver Pen by Alan Canton, ISBN 1-88342-211-6

FULFILLMENT

(Many larger printers also offer fulfillment services for their
print customers)

www.bookmasters.com
www.fulfillco.com
www.pathwaybook.com
www.psifulfillment.com

INDEXING

www.asindexing.org American Society of Indexers
www.stcsig.org/idx/ Helpful for self-indexers
lesleypeters@earthlink.net
Janet Ware jwware@aol.com
http://www.stcsig.org/idx/

ISBN NUMBERS

(US ISBN Agency) R.R. Bowker is exclusive distributor
www.isbn.org

LIBRARY OF CONGRESS CONTROL NUMBERS

www.loc.gov
www.dgiinc.com The Donohue Group

LINKS

www.linkpartners.com
www.webcredible.co.uk
www.theallineed.com

LITERARY AGENTS

www.aar-online.org (Official web site of the Association of
Authors' Representatives)

www.agentresearch.com Talking Agents, a newsletter published
by Agent Research and Evaluation

www.sfwa.org (Reports unscrupulous agents)

Writer's Market FAQs by Peter Rubie, ISBN 1-58297-071-8

Literary Agents: A Writer's Introduction edited by John F. Baker,
ISBN 978-00-2861-740-4

Guide to Literary Agents Writer's Digest Book (revised annually)

Writer's Guide to Book Editors, Publishers and Literary Agents by Jeff
Herman, ISBN 0-871162-016

My Book Proposal, The Complete Software Program for Aspiring Authors Poets. (This CD can be purchased through the website www.markshawbooks.com.)

How to Write a Book Proposal by Michael Larsen, ISBN 1-58297-251-6

Give 'Em What They Want by Blythe Camenson and Marshall Cook, ISBN 1-58297-330-X

LITERARY ATTORNEYS
Bomser & Studnicky, abomser@pipeline.com
Alan Kaufman http://kaufmanpublaw.com
Robert Dannay (Specializes in copyright law)
http://www.rxd@cll.com
Frank R. Curtis e-mail: fcurtis@remcur.com

LITERARY PUBLICISTS
www.resmarketingalliance.com
www.amarketingexpert.com
www.yourownbookseller.com
www.prpr.net
www.imageshaper.biz
www.smithpublicity.com
www.anniejenningspr.com

MAGAZINE & NEWSPAPER DIRECTORIES
www.writersmarket.com
www.woodenhorse.com
www.burellesluce.com
www.editorandpublisher.com/yearbook.

Travel Publications Update found on www.travelwriters.com

Writer's Market (Print) Writer's Digest Books (Updated annually)

Editor & Publisher International Yearbook (Print)

International Directory of Little Magazines & Small Presses, Dustbooks, ISBN 0-91321-800-6

Novel & Short Story Writer's Market, Writer's Digest Books
(Updated annually)

Poet's Market, Writer's Digest Books (Updated annually)

Children's Writer's & Illustrator's Market, Writer's Digest Books
(Updated annually)

MAGAZINES FOR WRITERS

www.writersdigest.com Writer's Digest,
Poets & Writers, 72 Spring St, New York, NY 10012
www.cjr.com *columbia Journalism Review*
www.writermag.com The Writer,

MEMOIRS

www.familyhistories.com
www.turningmemories.com

Writing About Your Life: A Journey into the Past by William Zinsser,
ISBN 1-56924-379-4

Writing the Family Narrative by Lawrence P. Gouldrup PhD,
ISBN 0-91648-927-2

Writing the Memoir: Truth to Art by Judith Barrington,
ISBN 0-93337-750-9

You Can Write a Memoir by Susan Carol Hauser,
ISBN 0-89879-998-8

Living to Tell the Tale: a Guide to Writing Memoir by Jane Taylor
McDonnell andVivian Gornick, ISBN 0-14026-530-9

So You Want to Write co-authored by Ira Wood and Marge Piercy,
ISBN 0-97289-845-X

NEWSLETTERS FOR WRITERS

www.yudkin.com
www.bookpromotionnewsletter.com
www.writing-world.com
www.absolutewrite.com
www.amarketingexpert.com

www.parapub.com
www.writers-editors.com
www.publishinggame.com
www.prpr.net
www.angelahoy.com
www.matilijapress.com/publishingblog

NONFICTION

The Complete Guide to Writing Nonfiction, published by The American Society

Journalists & Authors, ISBN 0-06097-135-5

Write by Jane Adams, ISBN 0-399-12982-0

The 29 Most Common Writing Mistakes and How to Avoid Them, Judy Delton, ISBN 0-89879-453-6

Show, Don't Tell by William Noble, ISBN 0-83977-766-3

Word Painting by Rebecca McClanahan, ISBN 1-58297-025-4

The Writer's Idea Book by Jack Heffron, ISBN 1-58297-179-X
The Successful Writer's Handbook by Patricia Fry,
ISBN 978-0961264277

ONLINE WRITING

www.haraldanderson.com
www.bookcoaching.com
http://www.web-source.net/syndicator_submit.htm
http://www.authorconnection.com/
http://www.ideamarketers.com/
http://www.ezinearticles.com/
http://www.marketing-seek.com/

How to Get Your EBook Published by Richard Curtis & William Thomas Quick ISBN 1-58297-095-5

How to Publish & Promote Online by M.J. Rose & Angela Hoy, ISBN 978-03-1227-191-6

Writing.com by Moira Anderson Allen, ISBN 1-58115-029-6

PITCHING AGENTS AND EDITORS

www.writing-world.com/publish/pitch.shtml
www.customline.com/wordware/individual/getting/pitching.html
www.agentquery.com/symposium_pitcheditors.aspx

Give 'Em What They Want by Blythe Camenson & Marshall Cook, ISBN 1-58297-330-X
Kirsch's Guide to the Book Contract by Jonathan Kirsch, ISBN 0-91822-635-X

Guide to Literary Agents published annually by Writer's Digest Books

Writer's Market FAQs by Peter Rubie ISBN 1-58297-071-8

POETRY

Poet's Market, published by Writer's Digest Books, ISBN 978-15-8297-275-6

Poets & Writers Magazine, 72 Spring St New York, NY 10012

PRINTERS, DIGITAL

www.bookmasters.com
www.opm.com (Berryville Graphics & Offset Paperback Manufacturers)

http://booksjustbooks.com
www.gorhamprinting.com
www.longdash.com
www.morganprinting.org
www.tristatelitho.com
www.lightningsource.com

PRINTERS OFFSET

www.bookmasters.com
www.bangprinting.com
www.bookprinters.com (McNaughton & Gunn)
www.deltaprintingsolutions.com
www.booksjustbooks.com

PROMOTIONAL RESOURCES

www.resmarketingalliance.com
www.contactanycelebrity.com
www.bigfishmarketing.com
www.publiclibraries.com
www.bookmarketingworks.com
www.marketingtips.com

Handbook for Public Relations Writing by Thomas Bivins, ISBN 0-84420-350-5

Associations Unlimited from Gale Research

Directory of Associations by Marketing Resource

PUBLICATIONS DIRECTORIES

www.newspaper.com
www.newspaperlinks.com
www.onlinenewspapers.com
www.ap.org/pages/contact/contact.html (list of bureaus)
www.burrellesluce.com
www.editorandpublisher.com (International Yearbook)
Writer's Market (Updated annually by Writer's Digest Books)
International Directory of Little Magazines & Small Presses by Len Fulton, ISBN 0-91321-838-3

PUBLISHERS (POD)

www.longdash.com (very short press runs)
www.authorhouse.com
www.xlibris.com
www.iuniverse.com
www.trafford.com (Canadian)
www.infinitypublishing
www.beaverspondpress.com
www.outskirtspress.com

PUBLISHING CONTRACTS

www.authorsguild.org (Click on Contracts)

www.nwu.org National Writers Union

www.nationalwriters.com National Writers Association

Writer's Market FAQs by Peter Rubie, ISBN 1-58297-071-8

Kirsch's Guide to the Book Contract by Jonathan Kirsch, ISBN 091822635X

PUBLISHING TRADE JOURNALS

www.publishersweekly.com

www.kirkusreviews.com

www.bookpage.com

www.libraryjournal.com

www.ala.org/booklist

www.forewordmagazine.com

QUERY LETTERS
(See Pitching Agents and Editors)

SELF-PUBLISHING

BOOKS

Self –Publishing Manual by Dan Poynter, ISBN 978-15-6860-134-2

The Well Fed Self-Publisher by Peter Bowerman, ISBN 13: 978-09-6705-986-0

The Fine Art of Self-Publishing by Mark Levine, ISBN 1-93353-856-2

Book Design and Production by Pete Masterson, ISBN 0-96698-190-1

The Right Way to Write, Publish and Sell Your Book by Patricia Fry, ISBN 0-97735-760-0

WEB SITES

www.go-publish-yourself.com

www.writing-world.com/selfpub/index.shtml

www.matilijapress.com

CONSULTANTS

Christopher Watson (www.selfpublishingservices.com),
Dan Poynter (http://parapub.com)
Peter Bowerman (www.wellfedsp.com)
Linda Radke (www.fivestarpublications.com)
Ron Pramschufer www.selfpublishing.com
Ellen Reid (www.bookshep.com)

SPEAKING ENGAGEMENTS, RESOURCES FOR

Encyclopedia of Associations published by Gale Research
Directory of Associations from Marketing Resources

TAX (IRS) & LEGAL ISSUES

Writer's Legal Guide: An Authors Guild Desk Reference,
ISBN 1-58115-230-2

Fair Use, Free Use and Use by Permission, ISBN 1-58115432-1

TRAVEL WRITERS RESOURCES

BOOKS AND WEB SITES

www.adventuretravelwriting.com
www.travelwriters.com
www.tia.org (Travel Industry Association of America)

Complete Guide to Writing Non-Fiction (Check list on pg 702)

The Travel Writer's Guide by Gordon Burgett, ISBN 0-97086-211-3

ASSOCIATIONS

www.natja.org/ (North American Travel Writers Association)
www.satw.org (Society of American Travel Writers)

TOLL FREE PHONE SERVICE

www.everdial.net
www.tollfreelive.com
www.kall8.com

THE WEB & WEB SITES

WEB SITE DESIGN & DEVELOPMENT

www.icca.org (The Independent Computer Consultants
Association offers listings of qualified specialists in all phases of
web site creation and maintenance.)
www.sky-bolt.com
www.web-source.net
www.thesitewizard.com
http://webdesign.about.com
http://officelive.microsoft.com
www.web.com
www.premissdesign.com
www.g-dev.org

DOMAIN NAMES

www.icdsoft.com
www.icann.org/registrars/accredited-list.html
www.whois.net
www.godaddy.com
www.melbourneit.com.au

WEB SITE HOSTING

www.icdsoft.com
www.thehostreport.com
www.hostindex.com
www.webhostinginspector.com
www.thehostingchart.com
www.sky-bolt.com
www.americanauthor.com
www.web.com
www.websource.com

ADVERTISING ON THE WEB

www.clickz.com
www.google.com/adsense
www.commercialreality.co.uk
www.ad-to-the-web.com

PAY SYSTEMS

www.paypal.com
www.goemerchant.com
http://clickbank.com
www.storesonline.com
www.prostores.com

SEARCH ENGINE OPTIMIZING (SEO) & OPTIMIZERS

www.haraldanderson.com
www.webworkshop.net/search-engine-optimization-basics.html
www.bruceclay.com
www.seolid.com
www.searchenginewatch.com
www.submitexpress.com
www.technorati.com
www.wordtracker.com
www.haraldanderson.com

SEARCH ENGINE OPTIMIZING SOFTWARE

www.axandra.com
www.scamfreezone.com/spider/
www.keywordelite.com

WEB SITES FOR WRITERS

www.writing-world.com
www.fonerbooks.com
www.absolutewrite.com
www.yudkin.com
www.amarketingexpert.com
www.sfwa.org (Science Fiction & Fantasy Writers of America)
www.writersweekly.com
www.bookcoaching.com
www.matilijapress.com

WRITERS ASSOCIATIONS

www.authorsguild.org
www.spj.org (Society of Professional Journalists)
www.nationalwriters.com (National Writers Association)
www.publishers.org (Asociation of American Publishers)
www.spammet.org (Small Publishers Association of North America)
www.ala.org (American Library Association)
www.pma-online.org (Publishers Marketing Association)
www.spannet.org (Small Publishers Association of North America)
www.SPAWN.org (Small Publishers, Artists and Writers Network)

HIGHLY RECOMMENDED

I can recommend these excellent resources from personal experience. All
have played a key role in the development of this book and my web site
and blog.

Cover & Book Design	JoDee Winger
	zacol@verizon.net
Text Design & Formatting	Suzanne Guelli
	sguelli@verizon.net
Indexing	Lesley Peters
	lesleypeters@earthlink.net
Printing (ARC and Book)	Bookmasters, Inc
	Regina Hamner
	rhamner@bookmasters.com
Distribution & Fulfillment	Atlas Books
	Meghan McVicker
	mmcvicker@atlasbooks.com
Web site Design	Premiss Design
	Allison Lefebvre
	allielefebvre@yahoo.com
Web Programming & Multi-Media Development	Michael Gartner
	info@g-dev.org
Marketing & Promotion,	RES Marketing Alliance
	Reina Santana
	rsantana@resmarketingalliance.com

QUERY LETTER SAMPLE

John Jones
J.J. Literary Agency
000 Jones Street
Jonesville, JJ 00000

Dear Mr. Jones:

In its nationwide coverage of Bill Brown's trial for the brutal double murder of a 79-year-old farmer and his wife, potential readers of my new book
Justice in the Boondocks were introduced to the story of a self-serving legal
system in Tennessee's backwoods. To a sheriff whose political ambition
overrode his sense of duty and to a district attorney whose determination
to become a judge undermined his obligation to safeguard due process. It is
a disturbing local example of the ills that now have begun to plague our
national judicial system.

To further their personal goals, these two men disregarded the continuous
opposition of their case investigators, who protested that the evidence was
insufficient to convict. Their self-serving vanity caused 22-year-old Brown
to spend 52 months in prison and 34 under house arrest as the region's
approach to "justice" creaked along. Three trials and two suicide attempts
later, Billy Brown was found not guilty of a vicious double murder.

The author's fascination with the Brown saga has grown as key elements
of his ordeal—due process, the death penalty and DNA testing—have
become prime components of the current national debate over ethical and
judicial issues. *Justice in the Boondocks* personalizes these national issues by
transposing them to a local setting with which readers can readily identify,
giving the book particular relevance today. The author's knowledge of
these subjects, coupled with his years as an award-winning journalist who

has covered both courts and police beats, makes him the ideal person to write this book.

The author will reach out to the many contacts in the journalistic world that he has made as an editor and a publisher on both coasts to help publicize the book and write cover blurbs. As an active travel writer, he will promote the book during his frequent trips around the nation. Competent literary public relations support will be retained.

The market for this book, of course, includes devotees of true crime, detective stories and mysteries, readers of books by authors like John Grisham, Ann Rule and Scott Turow. More important, it will attract a broad spectrum of readers intrigued by the "hot button" issues of the day: judicial corruption and infringement upon civil liberties. I hope you agree that *Justice in the Boondocks* meets the criteria you have set for books you agree to represent. Thirteen chapters are complete and the research on the balance is well advanced. I look forward to your response.

Sincerely,

INDEX

INDEX

KEEP IN TOUCH

Add to the knowledge you've gained
from reading this book

Click onto
www.retirement-writing.com
A web site designed to inspire you to write

Read new articles posted regularly on all aspects of
WRITING, PUBLISHING & PROMOTING YOUR BOOK
As a new visitor you'll receive
A FREE EBOOK
Free reports and articles by Email
The opportunity to ask any questions
you'd like and receive an expert's answer
within 24 hours at no cost

www.retirement-writing.com/blog
Read a new "Charlie's Choice" column every week
with updated information and resources to help you
write, publish and promote your book or articles

The blog also contains pertinent info on happenings in
the publishing industry and in the Senior world
Interactive write-to-writer segment. When you hit a snag
you can ask for help from an expert
Most responses will arrive within 24 hours

CONTACT INFORMATION
carosbooks@gmail.com or
charles@retirement-writing.com